Volume 1

DOLLS

MAKERS AND MARKS
INCLUDING ADDENDA
by

Elizabeth A. Coleman

IN COLLABORATION WITH DOROTHY AND EVELYN COLEMAN

WASHINGTON, D.C.

1966

FOREWORD

A tremendous interest in the collecting of antique dolls has developed during the past score of years. To assist the serious collector and attract the beginner new doll museums all over the country are being opened, and more and more is being written on the subject of dolls. A few authors have pioneered with scholarly research on dolls, but a tremendous amount of painstaking work in primary sources is still needed in this field. We three Colemans with our experience in historical research and aided by the unique facilities offered here in the Nation's Capital have compiled a documented history of the principal doll makers recorded from 1600 through 1879 and their marks. Someday we hope to cover all known doll makers and extend the period to the end of the nineteenth century and into the twentieth century.

Eva Haddaway Jones, who became a member of the Doll Collectors of America in 1939, before two of the authors of this book were even born, inspired our first love of antique dolls. Her dolls can now be seen in the Historical Society Museum at Westminster, Maryland. When Mrs. Jones generously gave us her library of doll books we became fascinated not only with dolls but also in learning about their makers and marks. Now we hope through writing our own book to share with others some of the knowledge we have gained.

Clara Fawcett has been a constant guide and inspiration in the preparation of this material and we are deeply indebted to her for all her assistance. This volume would not have been possible without the tremendous help generously given to us by many other doll lovers. Genevieve Angione provided not only some of her excellent photographs but also considerable data on marks. We are similarly indebted to Kitty Smith for lovely pictures and many unusual marks. Dorothy Annunziato, E. J. Carter, Eleanor Childs, Flora Gill Jacobs, Florence McCarter, Jessica Norman and Mary Roberson have all contributed valuable data on doll marks. Many other members of the Washington Dollology Club have kindly shown us their fascinating doll collections and each one has contributed to our knowledge. Eleanor Childs, a native German and past President of the Washington Dollology Club gave us needed help with the translation of German trade Journals. Mrs. Edgar Dawson spent many hours in the New York City Public Library obtaining data from early Directories not in the Library of Congress. Mr. H. Clinton Smith has contributed his technical talents to the preparation of this volume and Alma Cramer has patiently proofread the manuscript. To each and everyone of these people we owe our appreciation and gratitude.

E. A. Coleman
4315 Van Ness Street
Washington, 16, D. C.

i

Wooden French Doll, 34 inches tall, ca. 1840
Courtesy Musée des Arts Décoratifs, Louvre, Paris

Head of painted wood, wooden hands, mounted on a wooden stand,
painted eyes and hair. Dressed in blue silk costume ornamented with
bouquets of roses in green velvet. The bonnet is of ecru silk trimmed with a yellow plume. A long gold metal chain hangs around the
neck.

INSTRUCTIONS TO THE READER.

The reader is urged to study carefully the following information in order to facilitate the best use, comprehension and enjoyment of the material contained in this book.

The doll makers included in this first volume are only those for which some records have been found prior to 1850 plus those from 1850 to 1880 which have one or more of the following qualifications: (1) having an exhibit in a national or international exhibition; (2) having an identifiable mark; (3) being an American doll maker; or (4) making dolls of earlier type materials such as wax, wood, etc. The histories of the approximately 400 doll-making families plus their successors and associates recorded in this volume have been carried into the beginning of the twentieth century whenever possible.

Records of doll makers prior to 1840 are rather meagre. During the 1840's classified directories, exhibition reports, and patent applications all begin to supply data on doll makers. After 1850 primary sources are sufficiently plentiful that it was deemed advisable to qualify the selection. Generally the finest doll makers were represented by displays in the exhibitions. The Official Reports including catalogs and Jury Reports contain accounts made by trained experts and presumably give a contemporary evaluation of the finest and newest products of the most important doll makers in each country. In some cases the opinions expressed in these Official Reports differ considerably from modern appraisals of corresponding dolls. The importance of Austrian and English doll makers as well as French and German are indicated by the awards at the international exhibitions. Very few other records of Austrian doll makers have been found and this is an area in which further research is needed. Available German records are not abundant for the period covered and many more German firms, no doubt, would come into our classification if more records could be located, for example, Simon & Halbig for whom no records prior to 1890 have yet been found. The exhibition awards help collectors to date their dolls, for example, a Jumeau doll marked "Médaille d'Or" must have been made after Jumeau won his first gold medal in 1873 at Vienna but it must be remembered that the doll could have been made many years thereafter. Of great importance to doll collectors is the authentic evidence of the types of dolls exhibited at the various periods, for example, Jumeau dolls at the 1873 Vienna Exhibition are described as having "enameled porcelain" heads.

Doll marks are usually the key to the identification of the doll maker. A doll becomes much more interesting when the symbols on its head, shoulders or torso can tell the collector who made the doll and sometimes, approximately when it was made. Doll marks are often difficult to decipher and in some cases need the study and experience of an expert, as for example in identifying the Meissen crossed swords which were frequently imitated. A single doll maker often used several different marks or the same mark made in slightly different forms. An inscribed maker's mark frequently varied slightly from one master mould to another. The student of doll marks must study as many samples as possible and learn the characteristics which are often the clue to identification. For example the Kestner way of writing "Germany" can sometimes distinguish these dolls even when the "J. D. K." is not present. However, care must be taken not to jump to conclusions which are unwarranted. The word "breveté", meaning patented, has been found on dolls also marked"Bru" but that does not necessarily mean that all dolls marked "breveté" are Brus. A doll collector seeking to identify the marks on a doll should first look in the index under the name, initials or symbol found as a mark in order to locate possible doll makers and then study carefully the marks of those doll makers. Sometimes the marks of more than one maker are found on a doll's head, for example,- "Jutta", the Cuno and Otto Dressel mark and "S & H" for Simon & Halbig. There are many clues to be studied in identifying dolls and the more marks that can be definitely identified the greater are the chances of solving some of the riddles of dolldom. Some of the numbers on dolls were used for trade identification, see the "975 line" advertized by Louis Wolf. There were relatively few American doll makers prior to 1880, therefore it seemed advisable to include all recorded ones that were found. Many American doll collectors are interested in facts about native doll makers; although some of the material has previously been covered the doll student will find many new facts in this book. For example the paragraphs on the doll makers in Springfield, Vermont, under Ellis, Martin and Mason contain considerable new information.

From 1850 to 1880 the majority of dolls were papier-mâché, including wax over papier-mâché, or porcelain which includes both china and bisque. The earlier wooden dolls and wax dolls were beginning to disappear. Since doll makers were often in existence long before the dates found in the records the information on makers of dolls in these older materials was included when found. Also included are doll makers with special contributions such as patenting rolled metal doll heads. The terminal date of 1879 was chosen partly for expediency and partly because that was the beginning of a new era in dolls. The bisque head, ball jointed composition doll known to the trade as"indestructible jointed bébé", was just beginning to appear commercially in 1879 and the old wood or wax type doll had nearly disappeared. However, the collector of bisque head, ball jointed composition dolls will find considerable information in this volume because a great many doll makers of the earlier period changed to the new type and records are reported on these doll makers into the twentieth century. In fact the majority of the marks were taken from this type of doll. The first recorded date which is given after the surname in the text may not always represent the beginning of the firm's doll making activities due to the lack of precise records and the fact that some firms made other products before making dolls. The producers of doll heads or doll bodies as well as makers of complete dolls are included. Firms that assembled dolls are generally classified as doll makers.

The Official Reports of national and international exhibitions have already been mentioned as an important source of data. Other sources include patent applications, classified directories and trade journals. Many of the American and French patents and registered trade marks have already been compiled and published by Luella Hart and others, but due to the inadequacies of the official indexes additional ones have been found and some of these are very important to the history of doll makers, for example the 1861 patent by Calixte Huret for a swivel neck to be used on doll heads. Heretofore Jumeau has been credited with this invention. The German and English patent data help to complete the patent material. No patent data for the German States prior to 1870 have been found by the authors. Further research may discover more doll patents in all countries. The classified commercial directories contain contemporary advertizements generally written by the doll maker himself describing his products at a particular date and sometimes giving his mark. This is factual primary evidence but the opinions expressed in these advertizements such as "the finest quality doll" must be considered as commercialism. The French and English classified directories found in the Library of Congress and the New York Public Library up to 1900 have been examined. The files of classified directories in these libraries start in the 1840's but do not contain all issues, especially during certain early periods. For this reason the date of a firm or individual doll maker could be some years earlier than that noted because gaps of a few years exist in the records. The publishers of KELLY'S WORLD COM-

CERCE DIRECTORY in London and the LONDON POST OFFICE DIRECTORY publishers have very kindly made available data from their early directories which have not been found in this Country. The London data goes back to 1803. Many local directories of places in the United States and local and national directories of Germany have also been consulted. The principal toy trade journals of America and Germany, notably PLAYTHINGS, DEUTSCHE SPIELWAREN ZEITUNG, etc., are not available prior to 1900 but a careful searching of the later issues of these periodicals has revealed many articles giving the history of doll makers, especially as obituaries. Often the twentieth century advertizements of a doll company give the date of its founding and its marks. The above sources are in several different languages and an exact translation is not always possible or practical. In some cases the original meaning of the term is not precisely known as for example "mignonette". In these cases the original word is used without attempting to make a translation which might be misleading.

For a different reason the family relationship terms such as Gebrüder (German for brother), Frère (French for brother) etc., have been kept in the original language because the initials often are the best identification and a translation might destroy this valuable clue. In seeking to identify initials on a doll the collector should remember that the initials can represent not only family relationship but also the town where the factory was located, such as "G.F.N." which stands for Gebrüder Fleischmann of Nürnberg.

In records that are a century or more old spelling variations sometimes occur. The spelling should correspond phonetically but in different languages the pronunciation varies so that it is sometimes difficult to identify names. There are also basic differences in given names, for example, John is Jean in French and Johann in German. The spelling in the country where the doll maker resided has been used wherever possible.

Doll collectors are most grateful for information provided by descendants and successors of early doll makers. However, if the descendants or successors were small children or not even born when the events described took place, caution must be used in the acceptance of this hearsay evidence. When such evidence is referred to in this volume it is generally verified or refuted by contemporary records.

It is not practical to define all terms used but the principal ones that might cause confusion are as follows:

AÎNÉ, French term meaning Senior or the elder.
ARTICULATED, jointed, with one or more moving or movable parts.
AUTOMATONS, mechanical dolls.
BATHERS, dolls that can be placed in water without harm. Appears
　　to refer to porcelain dolls.
BÉBÉ, French term for child dolls. The French distinguish between
　　poupées (lady dolls) and bébés (child or baby dolls).
BISQUE, unglazed porcelain.
BONNET DOLLS, dolls with molded bonnets or hats, usually made of
　　stone bisque or wax.
BREVETÉ, French term meaning patented or patentee.
CA., Latin abbreviation for circa, meaning around or about.
CAOUTCHOUC, soft rubber or India rubber as opposed to hard rubber.
CHARACTER DOLLS, dolls made to resemble real people. They can be a
　　composite as well as individual portraiture.
CHINA, glazed porcelain.
COIFFURES, French term for dolls whose hairdo showed the current
　　fashion.
COMPOSITION, a mixture of ingredients usually with a paper, sawdust
　　or flour base that is held to-gether with glue or paste. Papier-
　　mâché is one type of composition.
CRÈCHE FIGURE, dolls made for Christmas nativity dioramas. Lay and
　　religious figures usually made of wood, terra cotta, wax or
　　composition.
DÉPOSÉ, registered (abbreviated form is "dep.")
DOLLS, the French differentiate between poupées (dolls) and bébés.
　　For French firms dolls usually refer to lady type dolls.

FILS, French term meaning son or sons.

FRÈRES, French term for brothers.

FROZEN CHARLOTTE, all-china or all-bisque dolls without joints.

GEBRÜDER, German term for brothers

GESSO, a plaster covering on wooden doll heads to facilitate painting and give greater detail.

GUTTA PERCHA, a natural material that is white or reddish in color, not porous to water like rubber nor will it float. Oxidizes in air and has form of a hard resin. Chief use besides dolls is for the covering of golf balls.

INCASSABLE, indestructible or unbreakable. The French term for jointed composition body dolls is "bébés incassables".

INDESTRUCTIBLE, trade term for the jointed composition type doll body.

JEUNE, French term for Junior or the younger, the abbreviated form is Jne.

JNE, French abbreviation for Jeune meaning Junior.

JOINTED, any type doll joint, such as: peg joint, gusset joint, ball joint, swing joint, spring joint, wire joint, etc.

JOUETS, French term for toys.

KÖNIGLICHE, German term meaning royal.

MAISON, French term for house or business firm. It is generally applied to an establishment after being taken over by successors.

MIGNONETTES, French term which appears to mean the little all-bisque jointed dolls, but the exact meaning has not been discovered.

MILLINER'S MODEL, special type doll with papier-mâché head, kid body and wooden limbs. The hairdos on these dolls showed the current fashion.

MOUNTING, the manner in which parts of a doll are put together.

NANKEEN, a buff colored cotton fabric made to imitate the fabrics of Nanking, China.

PANTINS, articulated wooden or cardboard dolls which move when a strand of wire, leather or string is pulled.

PAPIER-MÂCHÉ, a type of molded composition made with a paper base that is held together with glue or paste and sometimes other ingredients.

PARIAN, very fine white bisque.

PORCELAIN, fine translucent pottery, when glazed it is called china, when unglazed it is called bisque.

PORTRAIT DOLLS, dolls made to resemble a particular person.

POUPARDS, a baby in swaddling clothes, a doll without legs. (see opposite page)

POUPÉE, French term for doll. Refers to the lady type doll rather than the bébé.

PUPPEN, German term for dolls.

RAG DOLLS, dolls made of fabric or cloth, includes dolls of cotton, wool, linen, etc.

S.F.B.J., French abbreviation for Société Française de Fabrication de Bébés et Jouets.

SCHUTZ-MARKE, German term meaning trade mark.

SOCIÉTÉ, French term for company or partnership.

STE., French abbreviation for Société meaning partnership or company.

SWIMMERS, dolls that can be placed in water and will float.

TÄUFLING, German term for baby, Dolls can be called Täufling when representing a child several years old.

TOYMAKERS, many toymakers made dolls. Among the ones that were included as doll makers were porcelain toymakers and makers of mechanical figures that performed human functions such as dancing.

VVE., French abbreviation for veuve meaning widow.

WAX, poured wax dolls were made of beeswax as well as paraffin base wax or a mixture of the two. In the early nineteenth century plaster was combined with wax. Papier-mâché doll heads were dipped in the paraffin type wax.

The reader is urged to make full use of the comprehensive index. The original doll makers are listed alphabetically and not included in the index but their associates and successors must be located through the index. The marks are indexed according to identifying words or letters; lacking these, there is a group of miscellaneous marks listed under the word "marks" with brief descriptions of the symbols. The index also includes types of dolls, materials of which the dolls are made, places where the dolls were made, trade names of dolls etc.

This book is designed especially for those doll collectors who want to learn more about their own dolls, for students of dolls, students of doll makers and for all those who love antique dolls.

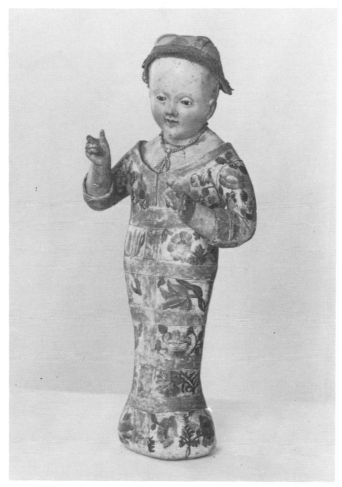

17th Century Italian Baby Doll, 21 inches tall
Courtesy Musée des Arts Décoratifs, Louvre, Paris

Papier-mâché "Bambino" painted with large flowers. A cloth bonnet is on the head and beads around the neck. Eyes appear to be made of glass. Very little is known about Italian doll makers but some very early dolls were made in the Italian States. The Neapolitans made crèche figures with terra cotta heads, glass eyes and wooden limbs. Many of the nineteenth century London wax doll makers have Italian names.

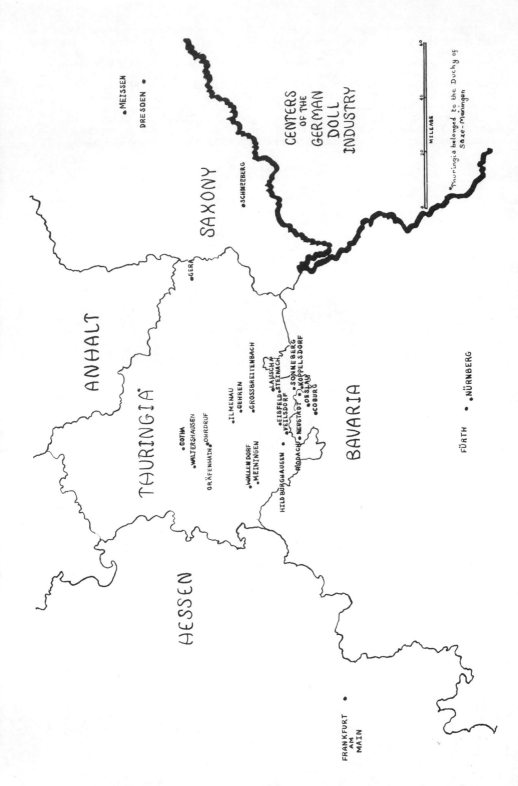

CENTERS OF THE GERMAN DOLL INDUSTRY

ANHALT

SAXONY

•MEISSEN

DRESDEN •

•SCHNEEBERG

•GERA

THURINGIA

•GOTHA
•WALTERSHAUSEN
GRÄFENHAIN •OHRDRUF

•ILMENAU
•GEHREN
•GROSSBREITENBACH

•WALLENDORF
•MEININGEN

HILDBURGHAUSEN

•LAUSCHA
•STEINACH
•SONNEBERG
•EISFELD •KOPPELSDORF
•VEILSDORF •OESLAU
•RODACH •NEUSTADT •COBURG

BAVARIA

FÜRTH •NÜRNBERG

HESSEN

FRANKFURT AM MAIN •

MILEAGE

•Thuringia belonged to the Duchy of Saxe-Meiningen

viii

MAKERS AND MARKS.

A

ADAMS, 1878   Samuel Adams of Boston, Massachusetts was issued a U.S. patent in 1878 for a perambulating toy or mechanical doll.

ALBERT, 1851   J. V. Albert, Jr. of Frankfurt-am-Main, Hessen exhibited dolls at the London Exhibition of 1851. His London agent at this time was A. Pritchard.

ALDIS, 1878-   Frederic Aldis of London was a doll importer and a doll maker. As such he is found in the London Directories between 1878 and 1901. A doll body marked "F. Aldis" has been located with a head marked "Pierotti". (see TOY TRADER Nov. 1961, p. 18.)

Aldis Mark

ALIX, 1851-   A. J. L. Alix of Paris was awarded a prize medal at the London Exhibition of 1851 for his hairdresser's wax figures which had hair eyebrows and eyelashes inserted singly in the wax. The exhibition report stated that the manufacture closely resembled doll making. Later under the doll and toy classification at the Paris Exposition of 1855 Alix had a display of colored wax busts.

ALLEN, 1870   Arthur M. Allen of New York was granted a U.S. patent in 1870 for a tricycle on which a doll was to ride. Probably this was one of the mechanical dolls made by Ives. (see Ives)

ALTHOF, BERGMANN & CO., 1860-   Althof, Bergmann & Co. of New York City were listed as toy importers in 1860. They displayed mechanical dolls in the Philadelphia Exhibition of 1876. Their products were commended for imitating very naturally the motions of the human body, for their originality and cheapness.

AMBERG, 1872-   Louis Amberg is first found in the Cincinnati Directory of 1872 but he does not appear to have entered the doll and toy business until 1878. In 1881 he was associated with J. K. Fechheimer and in 1894 with Henry Brill. Louis Amberg moved to New York City in 1899. Haun seems to have joined Amberg in 1910 but the firm was known as Louis Amberg & Son from 1906 on. Joshua Amberg succeeded his father as head of the firm when Louis Amberg died in 1915. It was one of the large American doll firms in the first

Amberg's "New-Born Babe" Dolls

2

decades of the 20th century. Details on the many copyrighted dolls which they produced are given in ANTIQUES JOURNAL, April and May 1962. Their most famous doll was "New-Born Babe" copyrighted in 1914. The "Bye-Lo Baby", copyrighted in 1923, was very similar.

© L.A.& S. 1914
#G45520
Germany #4

Mark on Amberg's
"New-Born Babe"

AMERICAN MECHANICAL TOY CO., 1876   The American Mechanical Toy Co. of New York exhibited dancing and revolving figures at the Philadelphia Exhibition of 1876. Their products were commended as being of "pleasing design".

ANGIOLINI, 1867   Angiolini & Co. of Paris was listed in the Paris Directory for 1867. The firm made Infant Jesuses in wax, mechanical wax dolls and products for export.

ANNERS, 1822   Thomas S. Anners of Philadelphia, Pennsylvania advertized in the 1822 issue of POULSON'S AMERICAN DAILY ADVERTISER. He sold "leather dolls with composition heads", the so-called Milliner Model type dolls.

APEL, 1844-   Rudolph Apel of Oberlind, Germany began making crèche figures in 1844. The firm was still in operation after World War I. They had an agent in Hamburg in 1926.

ARNAUD, 1852-   Jean Louis Hubert Arnaud of Paris headed the Arnaud doll making firm between 1852 and 1873. In 1855 at the Paris Exhibition Arnaud showed dolls. Monsieur Arnaud obtained four French patents, 1852, 1855, 1857 and 1864, for jointed kid body dolls with rubber joints or wooden bodies covered with vulcanised rubber. The Widow Arnaud was listed as head of the firm in 1879.

ARNOLD PRINT WORKS, 1876-   The Arnold Print Works of North Adams, Massachusetts was founded in 1876. The firm manufactured fabrics for making dolls. The dolls were sold by the yard or half yard. Costing twenty cents a yard a purchaser would get between two and eight dolls per yard depending on the size of the dolls. The dolls, printed in color, were to be cut out and sewn together. They were to be stuffed with cotton or bran and pasteboard was to be inserted in the bottom to make the dolls stand up. Design

Arnold
Mark

patents obtained by Palmer Cox and Celia M. Smith of Ithaca, New York in 1892 and 1893 were used by the Arnold firm. Charity Smith of Ithaca, New York also obtained patents in 1893 in England and the U.S. for a jointed rag doll that was manufactured by Arnold. Selchow and Righter of New York, toy manufacturers and jobbers, were Arnold's agents. The Arnold firm was still operating in the 1940's.

ARTOLA, 1878   The Artola Brothers of Cobija, Bolivia exhibited dolls in Indian costumes at the 1878 Paris Exposition.

ASCHARD, 1842-   Aschard of Paris was listed in the 1842 and 1843 Paris Directories as a doll maker.

ATWOOD, 1877   Kimball C. Atwood of New York secured a U.S. patent in 1877 for a metal doll.

B

BAHN, 1851   A. E. Bahn (Bohne) of Berlin showed various types of dolls at the 1851 London Exhibition.

BALLARD, 1840-   E. Ballard of Clinton, Massachusetts produced dolls
between 1840 and the 1890's according to TOYS IN AMERICA, by
McClintock, p. 450.

BANIGAN, 1875   Joseph Banigan of New York City was assigned a U.S.
patent for manufacturing a rubber doll with a flexible framework
which had been granted to Wesley Miller of New York City in 1875.

BARROIS, 1860-   E. Barrois of Paris
specialized in materials for making
dolls of all kinds. Between 1860 and
1864 he advertized that he carried
bébés and doll heads in composition
and porcelain from France and Germany.
Barrois was listed in the Paris Directories from 1860 until 1873. The
Widow Barrois was found in the directory for 1879 as a merchant selling
doll heads in bisque and porcelain.

BARTH, 1857   Pierre Joseph Barth of
Paris was an engraver who took out a
French patent for making molded dolls
in 1857. The patent application stated that heretofore France, England,
Russia and America had all depended
on Germany for all kinds of toys and
doll heads in particular.

BARTON, 1875   Elijah C. Barton of
East Hampton, Connecticut was issued
a U.S. patent in 1875 for a toy dancer or mechanical doll.

BARTON, 1847-   John Barton of London was listed as a wax doll maker
between 1847 and 1856 in the London
Directories.

A porcelain doll's head
similar to those which
might have been sold by
Barrois.
Photo by G. Angione

BAWO & DOTTER, 1873-   Bawo & Dotter of Limoges, France appear in
French Directories from 1873 on as a porcelain workshop that exported white and decorated porcelain ware. This company in the 20th
century was listed as a porcelain manufacturer. In 1893 Bawo &
Dotter exhibited decorated porcelain ware at the Chicago World's
Fair. At the beginning of the 20th century there was a doll and
chinaware importing firm in New York City named Bawo & Dotter. It
seems probable that the New York firm with the same name and business line must have been a branch of the Limoges company or had some
connection with it. The New York Bawo & Dotter handled "Best quality goods with A 1 heads: Simon & Halbig make". Simon & Halbig (see
Simon) was a German porcelain manufacturer located in Gräfenhain,
Thuringia who made doll heads and dinnerware. Besides china and
bisque doll heads Bawo & Dotter of New York imported celluloid,
metal, rag, wood, etc. dolls. Another possible connection with Bawo
& Dotter of Limoges is Charles T. Dotter of Brooklyn who obtained a
U.S. patent in 1880 for a cloth-body doll with a corset drawn on the
body. The unusual thing about Dotter is that
most of the china heads on his patented bodies bore the inscription "Pat. Dec. 7/80" on
the back of the shoulders. Inscribed marks
are very rare on china heads and if Charles
Dotter was related to the porcelain makers
named Bawo & Dotter in Limoges it would explain this unusual marking. The McClintocks
in TOYS IN AMERICA definitely state without
giving a source that Charles Dotter of Brooklyn later became Bawo & Dotter of New York.

Pat. Dec. 7/80

Inscribed
Dotter Mark

Bawo & Dotter of East Orange, New Jersey registered the trademarks "Barclay" and "Baby Belle" in 1910, in the United States

BAZZONI, 1843- Anthony Bazzoni of London was listed in the London Directories between 1843 and 1878. He made wax dolls, composition dolls and "speaking" dolls.

BELTON, 1843-   Belton and Jumeau (see Jumeau) of Paris advertized dressed dolls in 1843. At the Paris Exposition of 1844 Belton and Jumeau had a display for which they were cited with an Honorable Mention. In 1847 Belton was listed in the directory as making dressed and undressed dolls. By 1855 Widow Belton was listed; she made dressed and undressed dolls and dolls of the world for export.

BENDA, 1855-   Gabriel L. Benda & Co. of Coburg, Bavaria first appears in the London Directory of 1855 as a foreign goods importer. There is also a similar listing for George Benda at another address in 1855. In 1857 and 1858 Gabriel Benda & Co. was listed at both addresses with no mention of George. Anton Benda, also an importer of London, was probably related to Gabriel Benda. In 1858 Anton Benda acted as an agent for a foreigner in obtaining an English patent for joining doll limbs, head and body with elastic cord. G. Benda & Co. exhibited dolls in 1862 at the London Exhibition. By 1863 a C. Benda was listed in Paris Directories as selling German toys but this may be an error for G. Benda, because in 1872 Gabriel Benda, a trader of Paris, is again listed. Benda was listed with Marc Wemschenk Sons in 1867 and with P. Guénot in 1873. Gabriel Benda obtained first an English patent in 1871 and then a French and a U.S. patent in 1872 all for a doll, the front of whose face could be detached from the neck and back of the head so that faces with various expressions could be substituted. Benda & Hipauf, doll manufacturers and importers, of London were found in the 1909-1912 directories and may have been related to the earlier Bendas. It is possible that the mark "G.B." found on doll heads, which is sometimes combined with "S & H" for Simon & Halbig or "A.M." for Armand Marseille, indicates Gabriel Benda.

Germany
G. 329. B
A. 1. M
D.R.G.M. 267/.

Germany
G B

Possible G. Benda Marks

BEREUX, 1867-   Madamoiselle J. L. Bereux of Paris exhibited dolls in both the 1867 and 1878 Paris Expositions.

BERRY, 1867   Long Berry of Providence, Rhode Island was listed in the NEW ENGLAND BUSINESS DIRECTORY for 1867 as a doll manufacturer.

BETTS, 1879-   Thomas Betts of London was listed in classified directories as a wax doll maker between 1879 and 1905. In 1881 Miss H. Spratt, a doll maker, was listed in the London Directory at the same address as Betts. In 1907 Mrs. Marion Betts was head of the establishment.

BIANCHI, 1855   P. Bianchi was listed in the 1855 London Directory as a wax doll maker.

BIERER, 1851-   L. Bierer of Sonneberg, Thuringia founded a toy and doll firm in 1851. By the 1890's Bierer had a branch in Furth, Bavaria and in 1908 Strauss, Haas & Co. were their American partners in New York. Emil Bierer was head of the firm in 1931.

BISCHOFF, 1863-   Christian Bischoff & Co. of Sonneberg, Thuringia
made doll heads as early as 1863 when they were listed in a directory. Charles Bischoff and Emil Bischoff, both Sonneberg doll head
makers, were also listed in the directories from 1863 through 1874.
All three Bischoffs had Gottschalk & Co. as their Paris agent.
Christian Bischoff and Emil Bischoff both exhibited at the 1873
Vienna Exhibition. Christian Bischoff & Co. or Bischoff & Co. continued to be listed until after the beginning of the 20th century.
L. M. Bischoff, a doll maker from 1896 to 1898, and Peter Bischoff,
a doll maker between 1909 and 1915, both of Sonneberg, were probably
relatives.

BLAMPOIX, 1842-   Blampoix Senior was
first listed in the Paris Directory for
1842 as a doll merchant. In 1855 Blampoix,
Sr. took out a French patent for the application of glass or enamel eyes to porcelain
dolls. This is probably the beginning of
glass-eyed porcelain headed dolls in
France. Though listed until 1867 Blampoix,
Sr. worked at a different address from his
son. The advertizement submitted by Blampoix, Jr. for 1860-1864 states that he
made dolls in rose kid; specialized in
porcelain dolls; porcelain bébés; all porcelain dolls and German articles. For
1863 through 1867 the advertizement of
Blampoix, Sr. announced that he made kid
dolls but specialized in applying enamel
eyes to porcelain heads. This was done at
a large factory where the porcelain heads
were made and dolls were dressed in the
latest and most elegant style. Note the
similarity in types of dolls in the above
two advertizements. In 1873 the Blampoix,
Sr. establishment was taken over by Dalloz.

Doll with porcelain
head and rose kid
body such as those
made by Blampoix.

Dalloz's advertizement for that year pro-
claimed that the Blampoix firm specialized
in jointed dolls, heads in porcelain and
were a large maker of unglazed and enameled heads as well as talking dolls. At the
same time Blampoix, Jr. was merely listed
as a doll maker. Between 1876 and 1878 the Widow Blampoix was also
listed in the directories as a doll maker. It was she who exhibited
dressed and undressed dolls in the Paris Exposition of 1878; where
she was awarded a bronze medal. Again in 1879 Dalloz had a larger
advertizement than Blampoix, Jr. who was listed as making jointed
dolls and bébés. At this time Dalloz was making swivel neck porcelain doll heads and talking bisque dolls. The last notice found for
Blampoix, Jr. was in 1881 when his advertizement read that he made
jointed bébés and dolls which came dressed in the latest fashion
trousseaux or undressed. He also sold "swimmers", doll heads and
"coiffures". The final Dalloz notice came in 1885 when bébés with
kid bodies, indestructible bébés and doll heads were advertized.

BLONDEL, 1829-   Blondel Fils of Paris advertized in the Paris Directory between 1842 and 1847 that they made shoulder heads for dolls.
Blondel Fils worked at a second address during 1842 and 1843 where
they also made dolls. Their father made products of tin at still
another address.

BLUETT, 1856   Thomas Bluett of London was making wax and composition dolls in 1856 according to the London Directory.

BONAFÉ, 1879-   Only one descriptive advertizement has been found

under P. Bonafé of Paris. In 1879 he was making rose cloth and kid
body dolls of all kinds. By 1885 he had been succeeded by J. Cros
who advertized between 1885 and 1890 that he made kid or cloth body
dolls, enamel eyes, heads of bisque, porcelain, composition, rubber
and wood. His products were for domestic or export purposes. In
1892 Cros was offering kid body dolls, rigid and jointed, "turning"
heads, rose and white cloth bodies, "Parisienne" heads, glazed
china heads and wigs. He also performed repairs. The 1895 advertizement of Cros stated that he sold rose or white cloth body dolls,
as well as kid body dolls; bébés with composition and bisque heads
and enamel eyes.

BONTEMPS, 1867-   B. Bontemps of Paris exhibited automatic figures
at the Paris Exhibition of 1867. At the 1873 Vienna Exhibition
Bontemps displayed automatons for which he was awarded a Medal of
Merit. Bontemps is possibly a spelling variant of Bontems.

BONTEMS, 1878-   Charles Bontems, a
London toy maker, was awarded a silver
medal at the Paris Exposition of 1878.
In 1880 he was awarded a bronze medal
for his mechanical toys displayed at
the Melbourne Exhibition. Then in 1889
at the Paris Exposition Bontems again
won a silver medal. By 1890 he was making singing birds. In 1898 he obtained
an English patent for a Jack-in-the-Box.

Bontems Mark

BORREAU, 1878-   The Borreaus of Paris first appear in the records
of the 1878 Paris Exposition when they were cited with an Honorable
Mention for their dolls. It may be assumed that the firm at this
time was under I. Borreau who can be identified with the firm between 1879 and 1881. In 1881-1882 J. Borreau was head and by 1885
G. Borreau appeared as manager of the firm. The advertizements of
the Borreau's from 1879 through 1885 state that the firm sold jointed "bather" dolls, as well as dressed indestructible bébés. They
also specialized in doll clothes for domestic consumption and export.
By 1890 the Widow Borreau was in charge but in 1895 the firm passed
to Bijard who sold dolls and dressed "mignonettes". The second
successor, Paillard, assumed control in 1898. He sold dolls and
"mignonettes". Paillard headed the old Borreau firm until 1920 when
G. Velter succeeded him.

BOUCHET, 1851   A. Bouchet of London was an exhibitor at the 1851
Crystal Palace Exhibition in London. He was awarded an Honorable
Mention for "Her Majesty's representation of the Great Exhibition
with moving figures and various dolls".

BOULOCH & LAPORTE, 1842-   Bouloch (Madame) & LaPorte are listed in
the Paris Directory as early as 1842. In 1843 they were called doll
makers and in 1847 Madame Bouloch and the Widow LaPorte advertized
"Dolls made with rose kid bodies and either French or German heads.
Assorted doll heads and French or German dressed dolls." By 1873
Deltour had become the successor of Widow LaPorte and in 1881 he
advertized that the firm still made fine kid body dolls and dressed
dolls. A. Cassanet & Co. werethe successors in 1882 when they advertized "dolls and bébés dressed in the costumes of provincial
peasants". Cassanet continued the business into the 1890's. In
1898 Raymond LaPorte of Limoges, France was making doll heads in
bisque and china.

BOUTARD, 1869   Boutard of Paris secured a French patent in 1869 for
a "Flying Doll" to be known as "Inhabitant of the Moon". The doll
was to have a composition body, head of papier-mâché, wood, gutta
percha, wax or paste and wings of paper or gauze.

BRAITLING, 1869-   Charles F. Braitling began to manufacture doll bodies and doll shoes in Bridgeport, Connecticut in 1869. Earlier he had operated a toy store in Bridgeport and New Haven. His business grew to be one of the largest of its kind in the world. The doll bodies were made of kid or muslin, stuffed with genuine Sea Island cotton which, according to Braitling's advertizements, was the cleanest cotton obtainable. It had long fibers so the body retained its shape. The muslin bodies were made of Dwight Anchor brand muslin. The doll bodies were made in various sizes and the doll shoes were made in 22 different sizes from less than half an inch to nearly five inches in length. In 1900 Charles F. Braitling retired and was succeeded by his son Frederick K. Braitling. As the demand for kid and cloth body dolls diminished Braitling started to make other doll accessories besides shoes. The firm made stockings to match the shoes and in 1909 they began to make real hair wigs in blond, brown, tosca and auburn. Charles Braitling died in 1912 but the Braitling firm continued far into the twentieth century.

BRANDENSTEIN, 1867   Benjamin Brandenstein of New York City was listed as a doll maker in 1867 in McClintock's TOYS IN AMERICA, p. 451.

BRASSEUR & VIDELIER, 1865-   Brasseur & Videlier were listed in the 1865 Paris Directory. In 1867 the firm was selling dressed and undressed bébés; ordinary, fine and jointed dolls. Then in 1868 Chevallier & Brasseur obtained a French patent for a composition-bodied doll made of sawdust and glue as an imitation of wood. The body was to be painted or varnished or covered with linen and the legs and arms were to be made of the above composition or bisque or porcelain. From 1879 to 1882 Brasseur & Videlier specialized in fine jointed dolls and dolls of carved wood.

BRIENS, 1860-   Briens of Paris in 1860 was credited with a French patent for a rubber doll head with enamel eyes and invisible joints. The arms were joined to the papier-mâché body with wooden rings. Two years earlier Monsieur Hammond had also obtained a patent for invisible joints. Then in 1862 a second French patent was issued to Briens which was for a doll's head that rolled on a semisphere inside the neck so that the head could move in all directions. The heads were to be made of varnished or enameled metal with enamel eyes. Mademoiselle Huret had patented a swivel neck for porcelain dolls the preceeding year. However, no patent record has been found for Jumeau on this subject as stated by Singleton and later authors.

BRIX, 1878   Mademoiselle Brix of Copenhagen, Denmark exhibited dolls in national costume at the 1878 Paris Exposition.

BROCK, 1874   William E. Brock of New York secured a U.S. patent in 1874 for the manufacture of hollow doll heads. The heads were to be made by pressing leather into molds.

BROGDEN, 1843-   James Brogden of London was listed in that city's directories as a maker of composition dolls between 1843 and 1848.

BROUILLET & CACHELEUX, 1842-   In 1811 Cacheleux was listed as a toy merchant in Paris. By 1842 the firm was known as Brouillet & Cacheleux, a wholesale house of French and German goods, specializing in rubber goods. In 1844 Brouillet exhibited dolls at the Paris Exposition. He was awarded an Honorable Mention for these dolls. The report of the exposition records that Brouillet made dolls so well constructed that they could stand upright without the support of sticks; these dolls could easily be dressed and undressed and therefore little girls could learn to cut out and sew doll's clothes for them. Brouillet advertized this type of doll in 1847. Brouillet made many dolls and their little clothes. In 1856 a French patent was secured for making papier-mâché dolls. The papier-mâché was to be mixed with resins or oils to form a plastic and resistant substance for making dolls.

BROWER, 1873   H. L. Brower of New York City obtained a U.S. patent
for a dancing doll in 1873. C. H. Brower of New York City sold
toys in New York in 1875.

BROWN, 1857-   George W. Brown & Co. of Connecticut began making tin
toys in 1857. The business grew and in 1868 Brown and J. E. Stevens,
who made iron toys, formed the American Toy Company as a sales outlet.
This new company had its headquarters in New York City. Philip
Goldsmith of Cincinnati later used the name American Toy Co. but no
connection has been found. In 1868 William Farr Goodwin patented
both in England and the United States a clockwork mechanism for a
walking doll pushing a wheeled toy chair, perambulator, wheeled carriage, etc. Brown produced mechanical dolls based on this Goodwin
patent but he did not have exclusive use of it. He also made other
mechanical dolls such as ones riding a velocipede, dolls rolling a
hoop and waltzing dolls. The American Toy Co. was listed in the New
York Directories through 1872. The McClintocks in TOYS IN AMERICA,
pp. 223-224 state that George Brown continued in the toy business
until the 1880's.

BRU, 1867-   The Bru doll making family of Paris was possibly related to the Monsieur Bru, a partner in the firm of Bru & Cazelles
of Marssac, Tarn and Garonne (Southwest France) which in 1855 obtained a French patent for a method of molding architectural ornaments, statues, etc. In the Paris Directory for this year no Brus
were listed. (Also see Pierotti and Montanari who also had ances-
tors or relatives who were modelers of architectural ornaments.)
During the years 1867 to 1869 several French patents were obtained

by Leon Casimir Bru. Included
among these were the following
two doll patents, one for a
crying doll and the other for
a double-faced "Surprize Doll".
The crying doll contained a
rubber ball fitted with a reed
which when placed in the doll's
body produced a crying sound.
The "Surprize Doll" worked on
a rod mechanism imbedded in
the chest which allowed the
head to turn without disarrang-
ing the doll's hair. In 1869
Leon Casimir patented a doll's
body which he claimed was more
durable. Made of papier-mâché,
the body had ball joints, including joints at the wrists,
ankles and waist. Madame Bru,
Leon Casimir's wife, was also
associated with doll patents.
In 1872 she obtained a patent
for a "Surprize Doll"; this one
having a body of wood, metal or
any other substance which would
allow the torso to contain a
multi-disc music box.

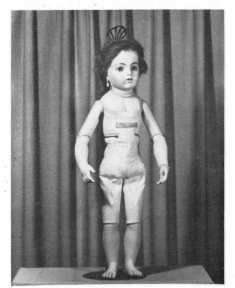

Bébé Bru
Courtesy of Kitty Smith

Casimir Bru Jeune, founder of
the doll firm, Bru Jne. & Co. (1873 or earlier), continued the
family's experiments in creating doll innovations. From 1873 to
1882 Bru Jne. took out several patents among which were a French
patent, 1878, for a jointed rubber bébé, a bébé of India rubber with
the rubber built over a wire frame as a skin, and both a French and
German patent, 1879, for a nursing bébé which was called "Bébé
Teteur". Equipped with a feeding bottle this doll's head held a
container for milk, the feeding process worked by gravity. The

body was a regular ball jointed papier-mâché one. Also in 1879 Bru
obtained a patent for a doll with a kid body. The 1882 doll patent
was for the improved making of dolls. This was to simulate the natural action of the eyelids, the arms, legs, hands, and fingers so
that they would take any desired position and hold it naturally.
The eyelids were to be fixed so that they would move while the eyeballs remained stationary. Also in 1882 Bru and Jumeau took out a
patent for a mechanical boat.

The following are abstracts of Bru advertizements in the Paris
Directories:- 1873 Bru Jeune & Co., Doll maker. The Bru firm,
located at St. Denis, 374, was a large maker of dressed and undressed dolls of all kinds. They specialized in dolls of the latest
models and inventions which were entirely new and exclusive: dolls
with music (called magic); dolls in carved wood, compared to other
known articulations these possessed a shape, hands and feet which
gave them the most perfect grace; dolls in ordinary wood with simple joints; dolls entirely of rubber costumed as a boy or girl bather; dolls in kid of a new form with arms and hands in jointed wood;
double-faced dolls, one face asleep, one awake; and kid body dolls
with rubber heads. All these different models were patented or
trademarked (déposé). The firm also carried bisque doll heads,
stationary or swivel; rubber doll heads, stationary or swivel, on
dolls that could be dressed and undressed. The doll clothes were
of luxurious materials and in the latest fashion. These dolls were
marketed in France and exported. 1879 New items appearing in the
Bru advertizements were: Patented bébés entirely jointed in hard
India rubber, the only ones guaranteed absolutely unbreakable; dolls
and bébés in carved wood, completely jointed; and mechanical talking
dolls and bébés. 1881 Bru Jne. & Co. was located at Boulevard de
Strasbourg, 1 & 3, and St. Denis 14. By this time 21 inventions had
been patented by Bru according to their advertizement.[*] The Bru line
for 1881 included bébés in kid, an unbreakable doll of greatest perfection, this bébé was supple, light, firm and offered at a very
low price. The advertizement stated that by all reports it was the
most complete doll. Again mentioned was the patented bébé in hard
India rubber, guaranteed absolutely unbreakable; the completely
jointed carved wood bébé and the bébé with music. The sucking
"Bébé Teteur" was included and was described as a new and ravishing
bébé of kid, except for the head. Patented both abroad and in
France, the Bru firm claimed that its simple mechanism functioned
most successfully and that it was the finest toy for little girls
that had ever appeared. The delightful "Bébé Gourmand", a patented
doll with the surprizing ability to eat and digest food by itself,
also appeared. The advertizement goes on to state that the Bru
firm manufactured bisque heads and made rubber dolls for French and
export consumption and that always the latest novelties were being
made.

Bru like other leading doll makers of his day showed his handi-
crafts in international exhibits. While he was head of the firm
dolls, rather than bébés, were exhibited at Paris in 1878. The
dolls were awarded a silver medal. In 1880 Bru dolls and bébés
were displayed at Melbourne, again meriting a silver medal. At
this exhibition Bru also received a certificate for mechanical toys.
The Bru agent in Melbourne in 1880 was Arles, Dufour & Co.

By 1883 the firm of Bru Jeune & Co. had passed to H. Chevrot, but
the Bru name remained. (An 1883 French patent for organic substance
appears to be the last record of Bru's activities.) It is possible
that Chevrot was related to the Chevrot of Limoges, France who was
succeeded by Lebon & Co. before 1863. In 1874 Lebon & Co. made
porcelain articles and toys for export. From 1880 to 1883 Chevrot
was listed as a Paris toy maker. Chevrot took out one patent for a
doll. On November 23, 1883 a patent was obtained for a jointed kid
body doll in which the system of joints were manipulated from the

[*]The Bru family obtained many patents but a considerable number did
not pertain to dolls. Bru patented toy boats and in 1882 even a
machine for chopping raisins and vegetables.

interior of the doll.

The 1885 Bru advertizement under Chevrot reads:- Bru factory at Montreuil-sous-Bois; 25 patent inventions. The bébés Bru, with new patented joints were declared the newest, prettiest, the best built, the best jointed, and the most luxurious of all Parisian dolls. The words "Bébé Bru" could be examined on each bébé. The darling patented bébé, "Le Teteur", that sucks all by herself is still being shown, as is "Bébé Gourmand" (see 1881 advertizement). The new bébé is "Le Dormeur". A patented bébé, this one opens and closes its eyes naturally by means of its eyelids. The bisque heads were manufactured at the factory at Montreuil-sous-Bois.

All the gold medals won by the Bru firm at exhibitions were received under Chevrot's management. The exhibitions and awards were: Paris 1885, gold medal; Liverpool 1886, gold medal; Paris 1886, gold medal; LeHavre 1887, gold medal; Toulouse 1887, gold medal; Barcelona 1888, gold medal; Melbourne 1888, gold medal; Paris 1888, gold medal; and Paris 1889, silver medal. At Melbourne Chevrot had an exhibit in his own name as well as the Bru Jne. exhibit.

Chevrot's successor as head of the Bru Jeune & Co. was Paul Eugene Girard. Taking over the firm in 1889 he managed it until 1899. In 1899 the Bru company became part of the Société Française de Fabrication de Bébés et Jouets (S.F.B.J.). While Girard was head of the company he took out at least five French patents on dolls. In 1891 a patent was obtained for the combined movement of eyes and eyelids of dolls and another for a walking and talking bébé with a key winding mechanism known as "Baby's Little Steps". The patent for eye movement was also secured in Germany in 1891. 1892 was the year in which the Mama-Papa doll with an expanding chest was patented. In 1895 and 1897 varieties of kissing dolls were patented. The 1897 patent was taken out by Eugene Frederick Girard. The first one threw kisses when a string was pulled, but the second one performed by leg movement and this one also walked and talked.

The 1890 and 1892 Bru advertizements announced new and unbreakable bébés with hollowed wooden bodies, which were more solid and lighter than those in composition. Also mentioned were composition heads, the latest novelty, which Girard claimed to be as pretty and as well molded and decorated as the bisque heads. The advertizement also stated that the bébés Bru were the only bébés having natural eye lashes. They were distinguishable by the fineness of their hands and feet as well as by the beauty and good taste of their attire. As late as 1892 the Bru firm was still advertizing "Bébé Teteur" and India rubber bébés.

Girard showed his products in one exhibition, Chicago, 1893, where his display won a silver medal. In 1898 the Bru factory was still at Montreuil-sous-Bois, but the shop address was at Boulevard St. Denis 9.

After 1899 see notes on S.F.B.J. under Jumeau.

B
R
U

BÉBÉ BRU

BÉBÉ BRU

BRU·Jⁿᵉ   BRU Jⁿᵉ

Bru Marks   Trademarks

BRUNSWICK, 1853   Hyman Brunswick of New York City exhibited wax dolls at the New York Exhibition of 1853 and was cited with an Honorable Mention.

BUCKLAND, 1843   Edmund Buckland of London was listed in the London Directory for 1843 as a doll maker.

BURLEY, 1862   George Burley of Southwark, London had an exhibit of dolls of a novel description in the 1862 London Exhibition.

BUTLER, 1843   Charles Butler of London was listed as a doll maker in the directories for the years 1843 to 1848.

C

CALOTS, 1855   Calots of Paris advertized in the 1855 Paris Directory that he specialized in making fashion doll heads.

CAPO DI MONTE, 1736-   Capo di Monte porcelain factory near Naples was founded by Charles III of Spain in 1736. It came under Ferdinand IV of Naples in 1759. Dolls have been found with marks that resemble those of this porcelain factory but identification should be authenticated by experts as this factory, like Meissen, has been imitated and copied.

Madrid	Naples	Naples Mark
Marks	Mark	found on
		faience only

Capo di Monte

CARON, 1855-   J. Caron was listed in the Paris Directory from 1855 to 1860 as a doll maker. At the Paris Expositions of 1867 and 1868 Caron displayed his mechanical dolls for which he was awarded a silver medal in 1868. In the 1878 Paris Exposition there was a listing for A. J. Caron and he too showed mechanical dolls as well as clowns and other dressed toys. In 1882 J. Caron, toy maker, was listed as using the mark "J. C.". From 1885 to 1900 A. Caron was listed in the directories as a doll maker.

CHALTÉ & LEBORGNE, 1863-   Chalté & Leborgne of Paris was listed in Paris Directories from 1863 to 1867 and advertized in 1867 that they specialized in little dolls; undressable and pliant bisque dolls, dressed and undressed; clothes for bébés; and a patented doll that walked alone.

CHAMBRE SYNDICALE DES FABRICANTS DE JOUETS FRANCAIS,   By 1890 there were at least 31 doll and toy companies that belonged to the Chambre Syndicale des Fabricants de Jouets Français. Péan Frères (Brothers) was No.1 (see Péan), Henry Alexandre was No. 13 (see Steiner) and Falck & Roussel was No. 31. Falck & Roussel made "Bébé Mignon". Dehais used the mark of this organization but his number is not known (see Dehais).

Mark of the		
Chambre		Falck & Roussel
Syndicale	Chambre Syndicale-	Mark
	Falck & Roussel Mark	

CHAUVIÈRE, 1861-   Mademoiselle E. Chauvière of Paris acquired a
French patent in 1861 for improvements in making a jointed stuffed
kid body doll. Then in 1870 she took out a French patent for an
automatic talking bébé made in a lighter and more resistant composition with better articulation in the arms and legs. It also had a
better talking and crying mechanism. The bébés (bodies) were to be
covered with cloth or kid which was glued or stiched on. Though not
appearing in 1881 Mademoiselle Chauviere again was found from 1890
to 1895 at the shop called "Au Nain Bleu". Her speciality was
jointed bébés. Several dolls have been found with the body marked
"Au Nain Bleu, E. Chauvière". One has a kid body, bisque head,
molded breasts and a closed mouth. (see Johl, MORE ABOUT DOLLS,
p. 248) Another has a cloth body, bisque head, open mouth with
seven teeth on each jaw and a key winding mechanism. (see DOLL
COLLECTORS OF AMERICA, 1946, p.43)

CHECKENI, 1866-   D. Checkeni of Marion, Connecticut and Brooklyn,
New York secured a U. S. patent in 1866 for a doll with a wax face
which revolved, displaying four different expressions. In 1867
Checkeni patented a toy rope dancing doll.

CHÉRET & MOREAU, 1879-   From 1879 to 1885 E. Chéret & Moreau of
Paris were agents of doll makers. They were a wholesale house for
nankeen (cotton) bodied dolls and in 1881 handled "bathers", "swimmers" and jointed dolls with hair, as well as German bébés and
patented walking bébés. By 1890 the firm had come under the sole
control of E. Chéret. He acted as an agent for doll makers of
Saxony, Bavaria and Austria; and in 1892 his advertizement read
the same as in 1881.

CHINNOCK, 1875-   George Chinnock of Brooklyn, New York was issued
a U.S. patent in 1875 for an articulated toy figure. Charles
Chinnock obtained a U.S. patent in 1878 for a baby doll that was
put into motion by a spring.

CHIQUET, 1873-   F. Chiquet of Paris was listed in the Paris Directory for 1873 as a maker of talking bébés and mechanical toys. By
1879 he was making talking bébés and indestructible bébés.

CHURCHILL, 1847-   James Churchill of London was making composition
dolls from about 1847 to 1858 according to the London Directories.

CLARKE,1871   George P. Clarke of New York secured a U.S. patent in
1871 for a creeping doll. (see Clay)

CLARKSON, 1849-   Thomas Charles Clarkson of Surrey, England was
working on patents as early as 1849. He obtained two English doll
patents, one in 1867 for a rubber and cork doll and the other in
1876 for a cork and wood doll.

CLAY, 1868-   Robert J. Clay of New York City obtained his first of
several U.S. patents for mechanical toys in 1868. Around 1870 his
business became known as the Automatic Toy Works. In 1871 Clay's
patent was for a creeping doll and in 1872 for a toy producing a
crying sound. In 1873 he obtained another U.S. patent for a toy
automaton. Robert Clay became one of the largest producers of
clockwork operated mechanical toys in America. His dolls often
performed a series of amazingly complicated actions in a true to
life manner. For example, his lady at a sewing machine not only
pushed the foot treadle and moved the sewing forward but from time
to time lifted up her sewing and appeared to examine it. In the
early 1880's Ives (see Ives) bought and took over this company.
For further details see McClintock, TOYS IN AMERICA, pp. 215, 288.

COCHET, 1811-   Cochet was listed in the Paris Directory of 1811 as
a sculptor in wood and Cochet & Dehenne as makers of masks. Then
in 1842 A. Cochet, Jne. was listed as the successor of his father.

The former was classified as a maker of dolls. In 1843 he was making undressed dolls in papier-mâché and heads with coiffures. At the same time Cochet & Verdey were making dolls in papier-mâché and "empeausees" (?kid bodies?) as well as heads for milliners and hair dressers. A. Cochet advertized in 1874 that he made undressed dolls which he packed in boxes and doll heads with all types of hair-dos.

Doll with papier-mâché head, kid body, and wooden limbs such a those made by Cochet.

COHEN, 1862   D. S. Cohen of New York city was one of the manufacturers of the "autoperipatikos" doll patented in England and in the U.S. in 1862 by Enoch Rice Morrison of New York City. (see Lyon) The Cohen name appears on an original box pictured in THE DOLLS OF YESTERDAY. by Eleanor St. George, opposite p. 92. This walking doll with a clockwork mechanism came with a papier-mâché, china, or parian bisque head.

COIFFE, 1873-   Coiffe of Limoges, France was mentioned in the 1873 directory. By 1882 L. Coiffe had joined with Touron & Simon and they were listed as porcelain manufacturers. G. Taraud was their Paris agent. Then in 1898 there was a listing for Coiffe, Jne. who made special articles for France, England and the United States. His Paris agent was Guindon. The 1904 directory lists Coiffe as a porcelain manufacturer. Coiffe, Couty & Co. was one of the three firms

Doll heads made at Sèvres in 1917
Courtesy of Musée des Arts Décoratifs
Louvre, Paris

who benefitted from the experiments on doll heads conducted at the the laboratories of Sèvres in 1915-1916. The 1920 advertizement notes that Couty, Magne & Co. had become the successors of H. Coiffe & Leon Couty, manufacturers of porcelain doll heads.

Coiffe Mark

FRANCE

COLOMBO, 1843-   John Columbo of London was listed in the London Directories from 1843 through 1848 as a doll maker. From 1856 to 1868 William Colombo was listed in the directories as a doll maker.

COPENHAGEN, 1772-   The Royal Copenhagen Manufactory, Denmark
was founded in 1772. Sylvia Brockman in DOLL NEWS, Nov. 1961,
p.17 quotes a letter from Estrid Faurholt of Denmark stating that
Mr. Grandjean, President of Royal Copenhagen, had said that doll
heads, arms and legs were made at the Royal Copenhagen Manufactory
from 1843 until about 1880. All these doll heads were marked and
were made in six sizes. The marks with vertical lines appear on
dolls owned by Mrs. Faurholt.

Copenhagen Marks

COUSIN, 1873   E. Cousin of Paris in 1873 was operating a shop
known as Aux Amis de l'Enfance, where jointed dolls were made.

COUTERIER, 1869-   Alice Couterier of Paris operated a shop in
1873 known as Aux Enfants de France. Here she made jointed dolls
and other small dolls as well as doll clothes and she also performed
repairs on dolls. In 1891 Charles Couterier, also of Paris,
secured a French patent for a flying doll to be made of papier-
mâché, rubber or wood. Gustav Couturier exhibited doll toilettes
at the Chicago Exhibition of 1893.

CRANDALL, 1876   Charles M. Crandall & Co. of Montrose, Pennsylvania secured a U.S. patent for doll joints in 1876.

CREMER, 1862-   Cremer & Son of London exhibited toys in the 1862
London Exhibition. William Henry Cremer, Jr. displayed his pro-
ducts at the Paris Exposition of 1867 and at Vienna in 1873.
Some of his dolls had wax heads made by Pierotti.

CROMWELL, 1865   J. M. Cromwell of New York obtained a U.S. patent
for a dancing doll in 1865.

CROW, 1864   Thomas Noe Crow and James Noe Crow of Motthaven, New
York were granted an English patent in 1864 for a dancing doll
which worked on a vibrating board.

CRYER & NAYLOR, 1803   Cryer and Naylor of London were making dolls
as early as 1803.

D

DANJARD, 1860   In 1860 Danjard of Paris was granted a French
patent for the decoration of doll heads with bonnets.

DARROW, 1866-   Franklin Elijah Darrow of
Bristol, Connecticut obtained two U.S. patents
for dolls of rawhide leather in 1866. One of
these patents was taken out with Deon E. Peck.
Darrow and his partner, John A. Way, had already been making leather products for some
eight or nine years. The patented leather
heads were pressed into shape and hand painted.
The Darrow Manufacturing Co. was listed in the
Connecticut Business Directories until 1877
when the firm went bankrupt. Their advertizements indicate that they made both doll heads
and doll bodies.

Darrow Mark
label is black on
green background

DARTHENY, 1855   J. Dartheny of Paris exhibited shoulder heads
molded in wax at the 1855 Paris Exposition.

DEFOREST, 1875   Benjamin DeForest of Mount Vernon, New York
obtained a U. S. patent for a dancing doll in 1875.

DEHAIS, 1836-   Dehais of Paris in
1843 made fancy paper goods. By
1847 Dehais and Laforest had become
partners. This firm was to continue until about 1855. During this
period they made mechanical dolls
that beat drums and all types of
poupards. By 1860 Dehais had become associated with Verger. They
continued to make mechanical dolls,
poupards and pantins. In 1873
Verger took control of the firm of
Maison Dehais. By 1890 the firm
had passed on to L. M. Renou who
managed it until 1914. Renou won
a bronze medal for his doll display
at the 1900 Paris Exposition. In
1884 a French patent was obtained
by a Jean Charles Dehays, a clock
mechanic, for dolls that danced on
compressed air; but no relationship
has been established.

DEHORS, 1860-   Madame Dehors and
her husband, A. Dehors, of Paris
made toys of porcelain, faience and
English metal. In 1860 they were
advertizing bébés, dolls and doll
dresses. In 1866 Monsieur Dehors
obtained a French patent for the
perfection of joints for dolls and
doll heads. In 1867 A. Dehors
exhibited in the Paris Exposition
porcelain and metal toys. Then in
1878 both Monsieur and Madame Dehors
exhibited in the Paris Exposition.
He showed children's toys and she
showed dressed dolls and bébés.
Madame Dehors disappeared from the
records around 1879 but A. Dehors
was still advertizing in 1890.

Advertizement in the
1890's of L. Renou,
nephew and successor of
Maison Dehais founded in
1836. Note printer's
error in spelling of the
name "Renou".

DENAMUR, 1857-   E. Denamur of Paris began business in 1857. By
1890 the firm was known as the "House of Bambin" where jointed
bébés were sold. The "Bambin" advertizement for 1892 reads that
their dolls had the highest notches on the legs, and the best
articulation and the most perfect to the present day. Yet at the
same time they were less expensive than other dolls of the same
type. Denamur's advertizement in 1898 mentions a large model
factory for indestructible bébés as well as "Le Bambin" (the Babe).

DEROLLAND, 1878-   Basile Derolland of Paris showed India rubber
dolls and won a silver medal at the International Exposition of
Paris in 1878. The Paris Directory for 1881 lists B. Derolland,
successor of J. Callaz & B. Derolland, rubber manufacturer, who
made dolls and bébés, dressed and undressed as well as doll heads.
The Derolland steam operated factory was located at Asnières-sur-
Oise. Derolland won a gold medal for his exhibit
at Antwerp in 1885. At the 1889 Paris Exposition
Derolland was a Member of the Jury. The U.S. report
on the 1889 Exposition states, "Mr. Derolland, the
great India rubber toy manufacturer, his interesting
exhibit contained a number of models well known in
the States. There was the greatest possible variety

Derolland
Mark

in the faces; there were the Punches, soldiers and little girls
hanging from a thread and squeaking when squeezed ... all taste-
fully colored on the dull gray India rubber, which have emigrated
by thousands to the banks of the Hudson or Mississippi carefully
packed in small cardboard boxes." In 1895 B. Derolland was still
listed in the Paris Directory but in 1900 Turburt was listed as
head of the Derolland firm. Ch. and H. Collet won a bronze medal
for Maison Derolland at the 1900 Paris Exposition. In 1914 B.
Derolland and B. Delacoste were making bébés in rubber.

DE SAINT DENIS, 1843 -   De Saint Denis of Paris was listed as a
    doll maker in the Paris Directories from 1843 through 1865. All
    types of dolls were made by this firm.

DESPORTES, 1879-   V. Desportes of Paris was listed in the director-
    ies from 1879 through 1885. He made doll heads, both swivel and
    stationary and bisque bébés that cried and talked.

DESROSIERS, 1867-   Th. Desrosiers of Paris was listed in 1867 as
    making patented mechanical tableaux, wax crèche figures and infant
    Jesuses. By 1881 he had joined with Assuerus, the firm becoming
    Assuerus & Desrosiers. They sold wax heads portraying little
    children and wax arms and legs.

DEVANAUX, 1878   Madame L. Devanaux of Paris exhibited dolls in the
    1878 Paris Exposition.

DIXON, 1807   John Dixon of London was making dolls in 1807
    according to the London Directory for that year.

DORST, 1839-   Julius Dorst of Sonneberg
    founded in 1839 one of the most important
    wooden doll making firms in Thuringia,
    Germany. He displayed his dolls at the
    Vienna Exhibition in 1873; at the Mel-
    bourne Exhibition of 1880; and at Paris
    in 1900 where he was one of the Sonneberg
    group which took the grand prix. Dorst
    also exhibited at St. Louis in 1904. By
    1927 George F. Dorst, born 1877, was head
    of the firm which was still specializing
    in wooden toys.

DOUGLAS & HAMER, 1843-   Douglas & Hamer
    of London were making dolls between 1843
    and 1847. In 1848 William Hamer became
    head of the establishment. Working at
    the same address, he made wax and composition dolls between 1848
    and 1865.

Dorst Mark

DRESSEL, 1700-   Cuno and Otto Dressel of Sonneberg, Thuringia
    is the oldest doll firm for
    which records have been dis-
    covered. It was founded in
    1700 but nothing is known of
    the company for the first 150
    years of its existence except
    that they specialized in wood
    and papier-mâché toys. Ernst
    Friedrich Dressel appears to
    have been head of the firm in
    the second half of the 19th
    century and when the company
    obtained its well-known "Holz-
    Masse" trademark in 1875. The
    initals " ꓱ" are found on it.
    Other Sonneberg doll makers,

Sonneberg wooden dolls ca. 1735

probably related, were Otto Dressel, Sr, and Jr.,
Charles Dressel, Friedrich Dressel and his two
sons Wilhelm and Hugo Dressel. A Dressel succeeded Gotthelf Greiner as head of the Porzellan
Fabrik Limbach near Sonneberg. (see Greiner for
details about this factory which produced bisque
doll heads.) The Cuno and Otto Dressel company
had displays in the following exhibitions: Vienna,
1873; Philadelphia, 1876; Melbourne, 1880; Melbourne, 1888; Chicago, 1893; Paris, 1900; and
St. Louis, 1904 but no record has been found of
their winning any medal except at Paris in 1900
when they were one of the grand prix winners.
In 1876 at Philadelphia they displayed doll ladies and heads and were "commended for great variety, solid material and cheapness, especially
heads with good-looking features." At Melbourne
in 1888 they displayed dolls of every description. Their mark has been found on dolls having
heads of papier-mâché, wax, composition, and
bisque. In 1891 they advertized "täuflinge"

Abb. 10a
„Täufling" mit beweglichem
Mund.

Wax over compos-
ition "täufling"
ca. 1870 with
voice box and
moving mouth

(babies) and dressed dolls. They had a London branch in 1894.
There were three Cuno & Otto Dressel establishments, the one at
Sonneberg made dolls, the one at Nürnberg, made metal toys and the
one at Grünhainichen made wooden toys. They not only made dolls
but also had a branch making movable and nonmovable advertizing
figures. It has not been determined whether Dressel & Koch who
made bisque doll heads in nearby Köppelsdorf in 1898 were related.
Cuno & Otto Dressel were still advertizing dolls in 1929.

Trademark, 1875

1469.

C. & O Dressel

Germany

1926
Advertizement

Jutta

Trademark
used in 1926

Cuno & Otto Dressel Marks

DRESSEL, 1873-   Dressel, Kister & Co. of Passau, Bavaria exhibited
porcelain doll heads in Vienna in 1873 and at Chicago in 1893.
F. Kister and C. Hoffmann were head of the firm in 1873. This was
a porcelain factory that produced other
articles besides doll heads. In 1914
they had a Paris agent named A. Derombies
according to directories.

1349

Dressel

20th century Dressel
mark on bisque doll
heads. (Could belong
to Dressel & Koch)

DUCLOS, 1855-   Between 1855 and 1863 Duclos of Paris was listed in
the Paris Directories as a maker of patented gutta percha doll heads.
In 1900 Madame Victor Becq of Maison Andre Duclos exhibited dolls
at the Paris Exposition. Her display was awarded a bronze medal.

DUFFNER, 1867   Thérèse Duffner of Schoenwald, Baden exhibited
dolls dressed in national costumes at the Paris Exposition of 1867.

DUMONT, 1843-   E. Dumont (Domont) of Paris was listed in that
city's directory for 1843 as a maker of mechanical toys. Earlier
he had been cited at an Exposition with an Honorable Mention for
his inventions. At the 1844 Paris Exposition Dumont received
Honorable Mention for his doll display. The Dumont advertizement
in 1864 mentions that he was making kid body dolls, dressed and
undressed and dolls with porcelain heads. Dumont again showed
his dolls at the Paris Exposition of 1889. It is possible that
these records cover two generations of Dumonts.

E

EDISON, 1878-   Thomas Alva Edison of Menlo Park, New Jersey obtained an English patent in 1878 for a "Phonographic" doll which
would reproduce sound, having a "phonet" to move its lips. Later
the Edison Phonograph Toy Manufacturing Co. of Maine was established to manufacture phonograph dolls. They used French bisque heads
on jointed composition bodies with metal torso to hold the mechanism. These dolls were 22 inches tall. William White Jacques of
Newton, Mass. obtained English patents in 1888 and 1889 and an
American patent in 1888 for these phonograph dolls. He assigned
his patent rights to the Edison Phonograph Toy Manufacturing Co.
which made the dolls. These dolls were advertized in YOUTH'S
COMPANION, May 29, 1890 as costing $10.00.

EDWARDS, 1852-   Charles Edwards of London was a wax doll maker
between 1852 and 1865. He made
wax over composition dolls.
Listed in the London Directory
thirteen years later but at the
same address was Mrs. Henrietta
Edwards. She worked at making
dolls until 1891. Working con-
currently, 1856-1884, in London
but at a different address was
John Edwards, a model doll
maker.

ELLIS, 1856-   Joel Addison
Hartley Ellis, born 1830, came
to Springfield, Vermont in 1856
and became a partner in the
D. M. Smith & Co. firm along
with Henry Mason (see Mason),
A.H. Whitmore, David M. Smith
and Albert Brown. D. M. Smith
& Co. made patented spring
clothes pins and other items.
Ellis did not remain long with
D. M. Smith & Co. By 1857 Ellis
was developing children's carriages. In 1858 he formed a
company with Rodney G. Britton
and Ellis M. Eaton which made
children's toys, especially carriages invented by Joel Ellis,
sleds and pianos and later violin
and guitar cases. In 1864 Albert
Brown joined this partnership but
also remained a partner of H. H.
Mason.   After 1869 the Vermont
Novelty Works, specializing in

English doll with wax
over composition head
and voice box.
      Photo by G. Angione

children's carriages, succeeded the firm of Ellis, Britton & Eaton
with R. G. Britton as the Superintendent and Treasurer. The
upholsterer of the carriages made at the Vermont Novelty Works was

Hermann Dressel, born in Germany. Joel Ellis around 1872 appears to have concentrated on making dolls. The Co-operative Manufacturing Co. was formed to manu-facture the jointed wooden dolls for which Joel Ellis had obtained an American patent on May 20, 1873. Joel Ellis was the President, Alden Hamlin Whitmore was the Treasurer and Charles D. Brink was the Superintendent. Luke Taylor made the machinery for producing the dolls. The Co-operative Manufacturing Co. appears only in the 1873/74 Directory and according to Herbert Ellis, son of Joel Ellis, dolls were made only in 1873.

CO-OPERATIVE MANUFACTURING COMPANY;

MANUFACTURERS OF

PATENT MANIKIN

WOODEN DOLLS,

J. A. H. ELLIS, Pres. CHAS. D BRINK, Supt. A.H. WHITMORE, Treas.

SPRINGFIELD, VT.

These Dolls are superior to all other Dolls in the market in point of strength, durability and novelty of construction which permits them to assume and maintain the various postures of a living person, such as sitting, standing, kneeling, standing on their heads, etc., etc., and are offered to the public at prices that bring them within the reach of every family.

SEND FOR PRICE LIST AND ADDRESS AS ABOVE

1873 advertizement for Ellis's Cooperative Manufacturing Company

The Vermont Novelty Company had a display at the 1873 Vienna Exhibition but the British report described it as "some unnoticeable toys". The Joel Ellis dolls are believed to have been made on the premises of the Vermont Novelty Works because old doll parts are known to have come from the factory before it was finally torn down around 1940. This is substantiated by the fact that Ellis and Whitmore were officers of both the Cooperative Manu-facturing Co. and the Vermont Novelty Works. The so-called Joel Ellis dolls were 12", 15", and 18" tall and sold wholesale for $9.00, $10.50, and $13.50 respectively a dozen. A few of the dolls were painted black to represent negroes.

Joel Ellis left Springfield in 1878 and as soon as he left others began making jointed wooden dolls in the vicinity (see Martin and Mason). From 1881-1885 Joel Ellis was engaged in the manufacture of pottery in Beaver Falls, Pennsylvania. The only known pottery in the vicinity at that time was the Mayer Pottery Co. which em-ployed 100 men. They had two bisque kilns and made general pot-tery ware including glazed and bisque. No evidence has been found that dolls were made at this plant but it is difficult to explain Ellis's presence otherwise.

ELWICK, 1879   Mrs. Helena Elwick of London was making wax dolls in 1879 according to the London Directory for that year.

ENGLEHARDT, 1873-   Hermann Englehardt of Sonneberg, Thuringia exhibited dolls at the Vienna Exhibition of 1873. He appeared in various directories from 1882 through 1898 as a doll maker. At the 1900 Paris Exposition he was one of the grand prix winners.

ESCHER, 1863-   J. G. Escher of Sonneberg, Thuringia was listed in directories as a doll and doll head maker from 1863 on into the 20th century. For the first decade it was J. G. Escher, Sr. then it became J. G. Escher Sons. Probably either sons or relatives were Theodore Escher of Köppelsdorf near Sonneberg who exhibited doll heads in Vienna in 1873 and E. Escher, Jr. of Sonneberg who was granted a German patent in 1880 for an improved method of making papier-mâché doll heads. In 1891 E. Escher, Jr. advertized "täuflinge" (babies). J. G. Escher Sons displayed dolls at the Paris Exposition of 1900.

ESTIVALET, 1873-   Madame Estivalet of Paris was making dolls in 1873 according to the Paris Directory. At the Paris Exposition of 1878 Estivalet & Martin showed "porcelain families".

F

FAURIEZ, 1863-   Fauriez of Paris advertized in the Paris Directory for 1863 that he made doll heads in imitation of those made in Germany. Between 1867 and 1873 he was making doll parts. He also took commission orders.

FESSARD, 1855-   L. B. Fessard of Paris was a modeler in wax. In the 1855 Paris Exposition he was awarded a silver medal for his figures and busts in wax. An advertizement of his for 1867 states that he created infant Jesuses, saints, male and female with great grandeur and crèches of all kinds.

FIALONT, 1867-   The Widow Fialont of Paris exhibited dolls in the Paris Exposition of 1867.

FISCHER, NAUMANN & CO., 1852- Fischer, Naumann & Co. of Ilmenau, Thuringia was founded in 1852 by Gotthold Friedrich Fischer and Leberect Naumann. This factory made papier-mâché doll heads and figures. Their London agent in 1860 was Albert Frederick Haas. Fischer, Naumann & Co. were granted an English patent in 1860 for a doll's cloth body that was jointed so the doll could sit erect. They had displays at several secondary exhibitions

French crèche figure with a carved wooden head, ca. 1840.

and always won recognition. They won a prize at the Chile Exhibition of 1875. In 1879 at Sidney, Australia they were highly commended for original and well made products. They won a bronze medal for mechanical dolls at Melbourne, Australia in 1880. Later the factory was owned by Wilhelm Fischer and the Naumann family who had enlarged the scope of their products to include kid body dolls, Punch and Judy figures, baby dolls, celluloid dolls, wigs, doll parts, and supplies for doll hospitals. By 1927 new names had taken over and the owners were Mrs. F. W. Dollstadt, Moritz Rieth, Mrs. Margarethe Rieth, Hugo Henkel and Marie Henkel. In 1929 they were making dolls, baby dolls, and doll parts.

FLEISCHMANN, 1844-   Adolf Fleischmann of Sonneberg, Thuringia was one of the earliest of the many recorded members of this family whose name was associated with German and French dolls for nearly a century. At the 1844 Berlin Exhibition Adolf Fleischmann won a bronze medal for his mechanical dolls. His exhibit was described as follows:"Among the material sent in from Fleischmann was a wonderful tableau representing Gulliver's Travels. The little people surrounding Gulliver, as he lay tied up in Lilliput were most lifelike and amusing. They were made of a kind of plastic and papier-mâché. Many people were attracted to the scene." Fleischmann exhibited this same tableau at the 1851 London Great Exhibition where he won a prize medal and at the 1853 New York Exhibition where he received an Honorable Mention. "A Day in the New York Crystal

Palace" by the editor of the Official Catalog, 1853, described the
exhibit: "The greatest of all the toys in the Crystal Palace
'Gulliver among the Lilliputins'. This amusing work is made in
papier-mâché by Fleischmann whose toys ...(are)... best of the whole
collection." E. C. Spurin was the London representative of Fleischmann in 1851. A. Fleischmann & Co. of Sonneberg had a doll exhibit
at Vienna in 1873. Cramer appears to have joined the firm in 1881,
but A. Fleischmann & Cramer of Sonneberg and Nürnberg was described
as one of the oldest Sonneberg doll making firms. This company exhibited dolls at the 1893 Chicago World's Fair. In 1894 they had a
London branch and in 1904 they were succeeded by Cramer & Heron.
Other members of this Fleischmann family probably included J. P.
Fleischmann of Sonneberg who also exhibited at Vienna in 1873. J. P.
Fleischmann was represented by Gottschalk in Paris. This J. P.
Fleischmann no doubt was the Julius Fleischmann who with Paul
Fleischmann of Sonneberg obtained a U.S. patent in 1892 for a papier-
mâché doll's body. At the 1893 Chicago Exhibition, besides A.
Fleischmann and Cramer there were Ed. Fleischmann
& Son and Gebrüder (Brothers) Fleischmann all of
Sonneberg exhibiting dolls. Gebrüder Fleischmann
was also found in Nürnberg between the First and
Second World Wars. Gebruder Fleischmann also
exhibited at Melbourne in 1880 and in 1898 they advertized that they exported dressed and undressed
dolls. Both A. Fleischmann & Cramer and Gebrüder
Fleischmann had displays at the 1900 Paris Exposition where they were included in the Sonneberg
group which was awarded a grand prix. These two
companies also exhibited at St. Louis in 1904.
(also see Voit & Fleischmann)

Mark of
Gebrüder
Fleischmann
of
Nürnberg

FLEISCHMANN & BLOEDEL, 1873-   The firm of Fleischmann & Bloedel
was established in Furth, Bavaria in 1873. Fleischmann was possibly related to the earlier doll making Fleischmanns of Sonneberg.
This firm , who made the famous "Eden Bébé", had a branch in Paris
as early as 1890. Their advertizement in the Paris Directory of
1890 reads "office displaying samples in Paris, makes indestructible
bébés for France and for export. Models with stationary eyes, sleeping eyes and talking, all or partly jointed." The firm carried
samples of German articles and specialized in dressed and undressed
bébés. Fleischmann & Bloedel obtained many patents, among them were:
1890, three French patents for jointed dolls; 1892, a French patent
for unbreakable dolls; and also in 1892 English and German patents
for a walking doll that turned its head as it walked; 7 patents in
1894,- a French patent for moving eyelids, four French patents for
a walking doll, a French patent for a doll that threw kisses and
talked when a button was pressed and a German patent for a kiss-
throwing and talking doll; 1895, a German patent for a moving doll;
1897 a French patent for improvements on the kiss-throwing doll
that also walked. Fleischmann & Bloedel registered trademarks in
France in 1890 for "Eden Bébé" and in 1898 for "Bebe Triomphe".
The Paris Directory of 1898 advertized
that Fleischmann & Bloedel, creator of
the "Eden Bébé" had a steam factory and
made a speciality of toy soldiers.
Fleischmann & Bloedel were one of the
original members of the Société
Française de Fabrication de Bébés et
Jouets (S.F.B.J.) when it was formed in
1899. Fleischmann was head of the S.F.
B.J. when World War I broke out and
since he was an alien the property was
sequestered. The Directory of 1914
stated that J. Berlin, Sr., a porcelain
manufacturer, was the successor of
Fleischmann & Bloedel.

EDEN BÉBÉ

EDEN-BÉBÉ

BÉBÉ TRIOMPHE

French Trademarks
of
Fleischmann & Bloedel

FRANCK, 1867-   Carl Franck & Co. of Ohrdruf, Thuringia, was listed as a maker of doll heads from 1867 through 1873.

FRANÇOIS, 1811-   François, Sr. of Paris was listed in the 1811 Directory as a toy maker. Then when he appeared in the 1842 and 1843 Directories he was again making toys such as spring type mechanical dolls of large size and dolls that moved their heads. He displayed dolls at the 1844 Paris Exposition. Gwen White in DOLLS OF THE WORLD, p. 228 says a Madame Anna Cecile François made little dolls serving as actors in children's theatres. (puppets)

FRANK, 1867   L. Frank of Kloetz, Prussia exhibited materials for doll making at the Paris Exposition of 1867.

FRANKENTHAL, 1755-   Frankenthal Porcelain factory at Mannheim, Würtemberg was founded in 1755 and operated until 1799. After it was closed part of its moulds were taken to Nymphenburg. Porcelain doll heads if found with a Frankenthal mark would actually have been made at Nymphenburg in all probability. (see Nymphenburg)

Frankenthal
Mark

FROMANN, 1862-   Anton Fromann(Frommann) of Neustadt, Bavaria won a prize medal for his papier-mâché dolls at the London Exhibition of 1862. He was represented by Montréer in Paris and listed in the Paris Directories through 1873.

G

GAULTIER, 1860-   The Gaultier (Gautier) firm of Paris was founded in 1860. The name seems to appear in some records as Gaultier and in others as Gautier and Gauthier (see below) maybe another spelling variation except that both Gauthier and A. Gautier were listed as doll or toy makers in 1863. Luella Hart in SPINNING WHEEL, Aug. 1957 suggests that Gautier's given name was Fernand. In the 1878 International Paris Exposition F. Gaulthier was awarded a silver medal for doll heads. Between 1878 and 1885 when the Gaultier address as given in contemporary directories was St. Maurice, Charenton, Seine the firm made porcelain doll heads and specialized in doll parts. (see Jumeau for conflicting statement by Johl) Between 1880 and 1885 Gaultier and his sons exhibited in numerous exhibitions. In the 1880 Brussels Exhibition the entry for Gaultier and Fils (Sons) won a bronze medal, they also entered a display in the 1883 Amsterdam, 1884 Nice, and 1885 Antwerp Exhibitions. From 1885 to 1890 the firm of Gaultier & Fils were still making heads for dolls and bébés of porcelain. F. Gaultier again had an exhibit in the 1889 Paris Exposition for which he was awarded a silver medal. Then in 1890 the firm became Gaultier Frères (Brothers) and is so-called until 1892 or later. They won a bronze medal for their exhibit at the 1900 Paris Exposition. It seems likely that the French bisque doll heads marked "F. G." were made by Gaultier but it is also possible they were made for Gesland. (see Gesland) Bisque doll heads marked "F. G." have been found on dolls with stockinet bodies marked Gesland and also on Jumeau bodies.

Marks believed to be Gaultier but could be Gesland. (Greffier does not appear to be a possibility due to his early date.)

GAUTHIER, 1863-   Gauthier was listed in the Paris Directories from

1863 through 1867 as a doll maker. In 1856 Louis Jules Gauthier of Paris had been granted an English patent for the production of enamel and pottery ware. In 1872 Gauthier obtained a French patent for an improvedmethod of making doll heads.

GAY, 1843 Benjamin Gay of London was listed in the 1843 London Directory as a doll maker.

GESLAND, 1863-   Gesland was a wholesale toy dealer at Saintonge 45, Paris in 1863. By 1867 his address had changed to Notre Dame Naz-areth where he was listed as a doll maker. The name Gesland does not appear in the 1873 Directory but again was listed in 1879. From about 1879 on the Gesland address was Rue Béranger 5. This is the address that follows the name Gesland up into the 1920's. In 1898 an E. Gesland had the firm's listing in the Paris Directory. (A stockinet covered doll body has been found stamped "F. Gesland" with the Béranger Street address; it is difficult to judge whether this could be a misreading of E. Gesland.) A. Gesland was listed in 1900 and appears to be head of the Béranger Street doll making firm until 1919. In 1914 the firm was advertizing iron joints for bébés and was repairing bébés of all makes. But the Kelly's Dir-ectory for 1902 still lists the firm as E. Gesland. In 1919 J. Ortiz succeeded and took over the Béranger Street location. In 1919 he advertized the "Excelsior Bébé" and claimed he made dolls of all kinds. Dolls with Gesland marked bodies and "F. G." marked heads have been found but Gesland did not make porcelain and it is known that F. Gaultier did make porcelain doll heads.

GIBSON, 1854-   Mrs. Irene Wilkinson Gibson was listed in the Boston Directories at various addresses from 1854 through 1874 inclusive. In 1854 and 1855 she had a sewing room but was not a dressmaker. She was called a doll manufacturer from 1856 through 1862 and in the later directories no occupation was given. Mrs. Gibson prob-ably was a widow since Hosea B. Gibson and/or George H. Gibson were listed at the same address with her from 1861 on. Mrs. Gibson may have moved to Marlboro, New Hampshire around 1875. DOLL COLLECTORS OF AMERICA, 1942, p. 20 states that Mrs. Gibson of Marlboro, N. H. made "bodies for Cinderella Sitting Dolls some time before 1860". But the picture of the "Cinderella Sitting Doll" shows a doll whose hair-do, striped stockings and heeled boots all proclaim it to be at least in the 1870's. The head has the "Holz Masse" trademark registered by Cuno and Otto Dressel in 1875 so that if the head is original the body indicates it must have been made after Mrs. Gibson left Boston.

GIROUX, 1839-   Alphonse Giroux & Co. of Paris won a silver medal for dolls in 1839 at the Paris Exposition. Then between 1855 and 1864 they were listed in the directories as carrying French, German and English mechanical dolls. The 1867 Paris and the 1873 Vienna Exhibitions both contained displays of mechanical products made oy Maison Giroux. The Paris display was entered by F. Duvinage and A. Harinkouck who were successors. In 1873 Duvinage was listed as the successor of Maison Giroux and he won a medal of merit for his mechanical dolls. Estrid Faurholt of Denmark has a doll with a French kid body marked "Mon. Alph. Giroux" on the stomach. This doll is accompanied by a trunk of clothes and the lid of the trunk is marked "Maison Alphonse Giroux, successeurs Duvinage & Harinkouck". The bisque head of this doll is marked "B O S". Eleanor St. George in THE DOLLS OF YESTERDAY, p. 119 makes an undocumented statement that "B 2 S" is a Bru mark. The "B 2 S" head was found on a doll with a wooden body. Kitty Smith of Virginia has a "B 3 S" (a larger size) marked bisque head on a kid lady or fashion type body.

GOLDSMITH, 1870-   Philip Goldsmith, born 1844, was listed in the 1870 Cincinnati Directory as having a variety store which probably handled dolls. Goldsmith had a display at the 1875 Cincinnati Ex-hibition. At that time Wolf Flechter (Fletcher) was in business

with Goldsmith but they only remained together for a few years and
Flechter sold out in 1878 and went into business for himself. In
1877 Philip Goldsmith of Cincinnati advertized doll bodies and baseballs. By 1880 both Goldsmith and Flechter had moved across the
river to Covington, Kentucky. Wolf Flechter appeared in the Covington Directories as a doll maker from 1883 through 1895 and Samuel
Flechter was listed in the Cincinnati Directory as a doll maker in
1894. Goldsmith built a large factory in Covington at Russell and
Harvey Streets which he called the American Toy Co. No connection
has been found with the earlier American Toy Co. of New York. A
picture of the Goldsmith factory shows the words "Baseballs, Doll
Bodies & Doll Heads" written in large letters on the building which
shows that he made doll heads as well as doll bodies when the factory was built in 1880. His doll heads were composition made from
flour, glue and pulp. He used three part molds, one for the back of
the head and two for the face. The heads received two coats of
varnish. Later he tried to make imitation bisque heads by using
ether to give a dull finish instead of varnish. In 1885 Philip
Goldsmith was granted a U.S. patent for a doll body with a corset
embroidered on the body and outlined with an edging. These bodies
were usually of muslin with the lower part of the arms in leather.
They were stuffed with sawdust except at the joints where cattle
hair was used. About this time Cincinnati Potteries were experiment-
ing with the making of bisque doll heads probably at the instigation
of Philip Goldsmith but these efforts were unsuccessful and Goldsmith
had to continue importing his china and bisque doll heads. Misfor-
tune struck in 1890 when the Goldsmith factory was destroyed by fire
and they had to move into the building of the Hemingray Glass Co.
Goldsmith brought machines from Europe to make kid body dolls on the
new premises. He also brought workmen from Sonneberg to help produce model wax dolls. In 1890 he was one half assignee of a U.S.
patent for a wax doll head with imitation hair and glass eyes from
Julius Wolf. Philip Goldsmith drowned while vacationing in 1894.
After his death his sons Oscar and Alfred Goldsmith carried on the
business but only the sporting goods part, dolls were discontinued.

GOSSET, 1763   James Gosset of London was a wood carver of portraits.
And according to the London Directory for 1763 he was also a modeler
of wax portraits.

The Connoisseur

No. XI.—(1) LADY JEMIMA JOHNSON   (2) LADY ROCHETT   (3) LORD ROCHETT   (4) MRS. LEMON

Dolls from Ann Sharp's Doll's House
ca. 1700
Wooden or Wax Doll Heads

GOTTHELF, 1873-   The Gotthelf firm was founded in Remscheid, Germany in 1873. In 1915 and 1919 Johannes Gotthelf of Berlin obtained German patents for jointed dolls. Authur Gotthelf of Remscheid was head of the firm that made "Ulla" dolls and babies in the 1920's.

GOTTSCHALK, 1863-   Gottschalk & Co. was listed in directories from 1863 through 1867 as the Paris representative of the many Sonneberg, Thuringia toy makers as well as those of Saxony, Nürnberg, Tyrol, etc. By 1867 to 1873 they were announcing what a grand selection of dressed dolls they carried. From 1879 to 1890 their advertizements stated they were the agent of German doll makers. And as such they carried a grand choice of dressed dolls; nankeen dolls; or washable dolls, fine and jointed. Also in 1881 they were the agent of makers of infant Jesus in wax and paraffin. It is not known if Gottschalk was related to the later porcelain manufacturing firm of Alt, Beck & Gottschalck of Nauendorf, Thuringia which manufactured such well known bisque doll heads as the "Bye-Lo" and "Bonnie Babe".

Alt, Beck & Gottschalck Mark

GRAM, 1876   William Gram of Christina, Norway showed national costumes and figures in the 1876 Philadelphia Exhibition.

GRANDPERRET, 1878   L. L. Grandperret of New York displayed mechanical dolls in the Paris Exposition of 1878.

GREFFIER, 1844-   Francoise Alphonse Greffier of Nantes, Loire Inferier, France displayed dolls in the 1844 Paris Exposition and he displayed dolls and bébés in the 1855 Paris Exposition. Shortly afterwards Natalis Rondot wrote "Fr. Greffier showed some Japanese dolls called by the names of 'bébés', they were of good models, of excellent manufacture, and of low price." Greffier called his products " poupées genres" (natural dolls).

GREINER, 1760-   The Greiner family owned seven porcelain factories and managed an eighth one in eighteenth century Thuringia. Johann Andreas Greiner, the court painter for the Prince of Schwarzburg-Rudolstadt joined Georg Heinrich Macheleid in founding a porcelain factory under State patronage in 1760 at Volkstedt, Thuringia.

Volkstedt Marks

Georg Greiner, brother of Johann Andreas Greiner, became the manager of the Volkstedt factory. In 1764 Johann Andreas Greiner and Gotthelf Greiner with Hamman established a porcelain factory at Wallendorf, Thuringia.

Wallendorf Marks

Gotthelf left and started his own factory at Limbach near Sonneberg in 1772.

$$X \qquad \mathcal{X} \qquad L. \qquad E \qquad \%$$

Limbach Marks

Two members of the Greiner family assisted in establishing a porcelain factory at Gera, Thuringia in 1779, shortly thereafter it was combined with the older State protected Volkstedt factory but disputes arose and eventually Gera became an independent porcelain factory under the Greiners.

$$\mathcal{G} \qquad G \qquad C$$

Gera Marks*

In 1783 Gotthelf Greiner bought the porcelain factory at Grossbreitenbach, Thuringia which had been founded about 1778.

Grossbreitenbach Marks

Also in 1783 the Greiner Family founded a porcelain factory at Rauenstein, Thuringia.

$$R \atop * \qquad \overset{\times}{R-n} \qquad R-n$$

Rauenstein Marks*

Gotthelf Greiner took over the porcelain factory at Ilmenau, Thuringia in 1786. This factory had been founded about 1777.

$$i \qquad N \& R \qquad \&$$

Ilmenau Marks

*The marks of these and other fine porcelain factories are easily confused with those of other producers, some of which are shown to the right.

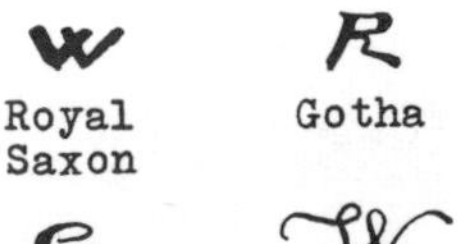

w Royal Saxon	**R** Gotha
G Gotha	**W** Worcester

The Closter (Kloster) Veilsdorf, Thuringia Porzellan Fabrik Co., founded about 1760, was managed by Wilhelm Heinrich Greiner in 1789 and sold to the sons of Gotthelf Greiner in 1797.

Closter Veilsdorf Marks

Thus towards the end of the eighteenth century Gotthelf Greiner or his relatives owned porcelain factories at Closter Veilsdorf, Gera, Grossbreitenbach, Ilmenau, Limbach, Rauenstein and Wallendorf, all in Thuringia.

The Greiner symbol of a trefoil or three leaf clover was used on the products of nearly all these factories. Dolls are definitely known to have been made at all seven factories except Gera, Ilmenau and Wallendorf. Marks similar to the Gera "G" and the Ilmenau "I" have been reported on dolls and we know that porcelain dolls were later made at a Wallendorf factory by the Heubach family. (see Heubach)

Another one of the Heubachs was directing the Closter Veilsdorf Porzellan Fabrik Co. by 1822. In 1880 Heubach obtained a German patent for jointed porcelain figures which appear to have been made at this factory. Luella Hart informs us in SPINNING WHEEL, Sept. 1954, pp. 14-18 that this Closter Veilsdorf factory made china doll heads including the china heads with a name on them. Hertwig & Co. also made this type of doll heads on which the following names have been found- "Agnes", "Bertha", "Daisy", "Dorothy", "Edith", "Ethel", "Florence", "Helen", "Mabel", "Marion", and "Pauline". The hair-do on these dolls suggest that they were made after 1880.

The Grossbreitenbach factory, owned by J. F. Greiner, was making porcelain doll heads in 1855 and exporting them. The Paris agent of J. F. Greiner & Son was Boullanger.

In the 1890's Fr. Chr. Greiner & Son made porcelain dolls for export at their steam and water powered factory at Rauenstein, according to directories.

fig. 1

Made in Germany
No X 70

E

Late Rauenstein Mark

At one time a Dressel directed the manufacture of bisque doll heads at Limbach but used the Greiner trefoil mark. Porzellan Fabrik Limbach exhibited dolls at the 1893 Chicago World's Fair. In 1897 the Porzellan Fabrik Limbach made porcelain dolls and "bathing children".

In 1898 at Neustadt, Bavaria

MADE IN GERMANY

fig. 2

Porzellan Fabrik
Limbach Marks

which is also near Sonneberg, Peter Greiner made small dolls and Reinhardt Greiner made dressed dolls but their relationship, if any, to the earlier Greiners is not known.

GREINER, 1840- Ludwig Greiner, born in 1804, emigrated to Philadelphia from Lauscha, Thuringia with his wife and two small sons in the early 1830's. No doubt he had received training in making doll heads before he left Germany. But he is not listed in Philadelphia Directories until 1840. Greiner is credited with the earliest known U.S. patent for a doll's head. This famous patent of 1858, later extended in 1872, listed the following proportions of ingredients: 1 lb. white paper, 1 lb. dry Spanish whiting, 1 lb. rye flour, 1 oz. glue, linen cloth to reinforce the doll's head. As is usual Ludwig's sons, Edward, William, Albert, Louis, and Henry all assisted in the business which was

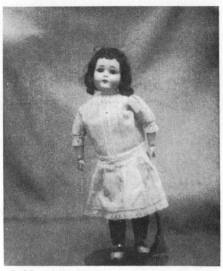

Doll with Limbach Bisque Head
Mark: see fig. 2
Courtesy of F. McCarter

known as Greiner Brothers after the death of Ludwig in 1874. Ludwig Greiner's will, dated 1872, was witnessed by Jacob Lacmann and Greiner doll heads have been found on labeled Lacmann doll bodies. The Greiners were listed as doll head makers until 1883. Francis P. Knell who was a brother-in-law of William Greiner, worked for the Greiner firm for a few years and later established his own doll making business. Knell appears in the Philadelphia Directories from 1890 until 1900 and made not only doll heads but also doll bodies. Further details on the Greiner dolls and Greiner family history are given in "Ludwig Greiner, Doll Head Maker" by Marion B. Wilson in the GERMAN-AMERICAN REVIEW, Dec. 1959-Jan. 1960, pp. 29-33.

Doll with Greiner Head
mark: see fig. 2
Photo by G. Angione

GREINER'S
IMPROVED
PATENT HEADS.
Pat. March 30th '58

fig. 1

GREINER'S
PATENT DOLLHEADS.
No 7.
Pat. Mar 30 '58. Ext. '72

fig. 2

Greiner Marks

GREINER, 1860- Greiner & Co. of Steinach, Thuringia was founded in 1860. They primarily made kid body dolls. In the 20th century they were succeeded by Kuhnert & Egli who made various kinds of dolls.

GROSS, 1854-   Carl Gross of Stuttgart, Württemberg made mechanical
dolls. He won the following awards for his products:- a prize medal
at Munich in 1854, a bronze medal at the Paris World Exposition of
1855 and a prize medal at the London World Exhibition in 1862. He
specialized in dancing figures ranging from a "varnished French
dancer" for 1 fl. 24 kr. (about 50 cents) to a "dancing saloon with
music" for 45 fl. (about $18). In 1862 he also showed "Mexican
dancers and colored dancers".

GROSSMANN, 1844   Madame Louise Grossmann of the free city of
Hamburg exhibited dolls in national costumes at the first commercial
exhibition in Berlin in 1844. These dolls were described as "out-
standingly beautiful".

GUICHARD, 1854   Edouard Auguste Desiré Guichard of Paris in 1854 was
granted an English patent for ornamenting dolls by a flock surface.
This was to be done by first applying solutions of varnish, caoutchouc or gutta percha and then covering the area with any powdered
material such as wood, metal, leather, cotton, etc.

GUILLARD, 1853-   Francois Guillard, a toy maker and dealer, located
at Rue Neuve des Petite Champs, Paris obtained in 1853 a French patent
for a talking doll made of wood which would take various natural
positions. Then in 1855 the Widow Guillard displayed mechanical
dolls in the Paris Exposition. Between 1863 and 1867 A. T. Guillard
of the above address was dealing in wholesale toys and was furnishing
toys to the Imperial Prince. Also in the 1867 Paris Directory Rémond
& Perreau of 156 Rue de Rivoli were listed as the largest store in
Paris specializing in children's toys. In this same year J. A.
Rémond showed dolls and doll accessories at the Paris Exposition. At
this event he was identified as being the successor of Maison Guillard.   And again at the 1873 Vienna Exhibition the Maison Guillard
display was entered by the successor, Ré-
mond. This display was cited with a medal
of merit. The 1873 address for Rémond's
Maison Guillard was the same as it had
been in the 1860's. However, at the same
time Perreau Fils (Sons) had retained the
156 Rue de Rivoli address where their shop
was known as "Au Paradise des Enfants".

Guillard Mark

In 1883 a Edme Louis Rémond was issued a
French patent for a puppet type dancing
doll. By 1890 Rémond was selling children's
toys at both the Petite Champs address and
188 Rue de Rivoli. But the establishment
of "Au Paradise des Enfants" had passed to
Ouachée who was selling patented and trademarked toys.

Rémond Mark

GUILLORY, 1878   G. Guillory, Jeune of Paris exhibited dolls and
pantins in the 1878 Paris Exposition.

GUIMMONEAU, 1879-   G. Guimmoneau, Henry & Co. of Paris was awarded
a bronze medal in the 1879 Paris Exposition for their display of
dolls with kid bodies and indestructible bébés. In 1882 they were
advertizing dolls with kid bodies, indestructible bébés and doll
dresses, luxurious and ordinary.

GUYOT, 1879-   Maison Guyot of Paris in 1879 was specializing in
indestructible bébés, dressed and undressed. They also carried fine
dolls and doll clothes and in addition they performed repair work.
Between 1885 and 1890 they were merely listed as a doll making firm.
In 1888 Maison Guyot was awarded a silver medal at the Paris Exposition. The Guyot mark for dolls in 1892 was "À La Tentation". This
mark was still in use after 1900.

H

HACHMEISTER, 1872-   Hermann Hachmeister of Sonneberg,
Thuringia began making dolls in 1872. Hachmeister &
Franz of Sonneberg had a display at Vienna in 1873.
Hermann Hachmeister was one of the grand prix winners
at the 1900 Paris Exposition. Hachmeister & Co. made
jointed dolls and babies in the 20th century. In
1921 they had a London branch.

Hachmeister
Mark

HAINHOFER, 1617-   Philipp Hainhofer of Augsburg,
Bavaria made mechanical dolls that moved in 1617 and
in 1632 he made mechanical dolls that danced according to Max Von Boehn.

HALLER, 1851   J. Haller's widow and son-in-law of Vienna, Austria
were awarded a prize medal at the 1851 London Exhibition. They exhibited dressed and undressed dolls and their group of toys was the
largest in the exhibition.

HAMMOND, 1858   Thomas Rundle Hammond of Paris, a trader, was granted
a French patent in 1858. His invention was for invisible joints on
dolls, heretofore they had been visible. The dolls were to be made
of flesh colored vulcanized rubber to prevent harm from paints.

HAN, 1862   C. Dorpat Han of Russia exhibited dolls in national
costumes at the London Exhibition of 1862

HANLON, 1861   Thomas, George, William, Alfred, Edward and Frederick
Hanlon of New York secured an English patent in 1861 for a walking
doll that operated by a clockwork mechanism.

HANSEN, 1878   Madame E. Hansen of Copenhagen, Denmark showed dolls
at the Paris Exposition of 1878.

HARMUS, 1873-   Carl Harmus, Jr. of Sonneberg,
Thuringia began making dolls in 1873. Later
he made doll heads, jointed dolls and baby
dolls for export, as well as "unbreakable"
dolls in 1898. Carl Harmus, Jr. was one of
the grand prix winners at the 1900 Paris
Exposition and had a display in the 1904 St.
Louis Exhibition. From 1903 to 1915 and in
the 1920's Harmus had a London agent. The
firm was operating at least until World War II.

Harmus Mark

HART, 1874   W. H. Hart, Jr. of Philadelphia, Pennsylvania was issued
a U.S. patent in 1874 for a doll.

HARTWIG, 1863-   C. Hartwig made doll heads in Sonneberg, Thuringia
from 1863 through 1874. Robert Hartwig of Sonneberg was one of the
grand prix winners at the 1900 Paris Exposition and had a display
in the 1904 St. Louis Exhibition. From 1900 until after World War I
Robert Hartwig and Albert Hartwig of Sonneberg were listed as doll
makers.

HARWOOD, 1877   William A. Harwood of Brooklyn, New York secured a
U. S. patent in 1877 for a crying and talking doll. This was allegedly the first American talking doll and it worked by blowing across
reeds.

HATCH, 1848-   Thomas Hatch of London was listed in the London Directories between 1848 and 1881 as a maker of wax and composition dolls.
From 1884 to 1891 Mrs. Sarah Hatch was listed as a London doll maker.

HAWKINS, 1868-   George H. Hawkins of New York City was an inventor as well as a doll manufacturer. In 1868 he obtained U.S., French and English patents, all for the improvement in the manufacture of papier-mâché doll heads reinforced with fabric similar to the 1858 Greiner patent. Hawkins used his doll heads on mechanical dolls based on the 1868 patent of William Farr Goodwin of Washington, D.C. for a walking doll. Other makers also used Goodwin's invention. Goodwin had previously patented a two or four legged automaton in 1867, as well as industrial machinery. Hawkins obtained a second U.S. patent in 1869 for further improvements in his papier-mâché doll heads. A doll with a Hawkins label attached to its shoulders rides a tricycle which is marked on the side "Pat. Feb.1, 1870; Jan. 25, 1870".

Hawkins Mark

HAWSKY, 1854-   Adalbert Hawsky of Leipzig, Saxony won an Honorable Mention for his doll display at the 1854 Munich Exhibition. He also won an Honorable Mention at the London Exhibition in 1862 for dolls and puppets. In 1862 he sold dolls in glass cases for fifteen shillings ($3.75) but puppets heads with natural hair cost from 16 shillings 10 pence ($4.15) for no. 7 to two pounds five shillings and seven pence ($11.35) for no. 14. Crying dolls ranged from no.3 at fourteen shillings ($3.50) to no. 15 but no. 12 was the most expensive at one pound seventeen shillings and six pence ($9.40). Dolls with porcelain heads were:

    No. 3/0 7 shillings, 6 pence ($1.90)
    No. 2/0 9 shillings, 7 pence ($2.40)
    No. 0   11 shillings, 6 pence ($2.90)
    No. 1   13 shillings, 6 pence ($3.40)
Fine dolls cost:
    3 inches 4 shillings ($1.00)
    4 inches 4 shillings 6 pence ($1.15)
    5 inches 5 shillings ($1.25)
    6 inches 6 shillings ($1.50)
Ordinary dolls cost:
    2 inches   1 shilling 10 pence (45¢)
    2½inches   2 shillings   (50¢)
    3 inches   2 shillings 3 pence (55¢)
    4 inches   2 shillings 6 pence (65¢)
    5 inches   3 shillings 3 pence (80¢)

HELM, 1854-   Ottilie Helm and George Wellhausen of Friedrichroda near Gotha, Thuringia won a prize medal for their doll display at the 1854 Munich Exhibition. In 1862 at London they were cited with an Honorable Mention. Killy, Traub & Co. was their London agent.

HERBILLON, 1858-   Herbillon of Paris was granted a French patent in 1858 for an improvement in doll making. (It probably pertained to the cork to which wigs were to be tacked.) The 1863 Paris Directory listed Herbillon as a toy maker.

HERISSEY, 1842   Madame Herissey of Paris was listed in the Paris Directory for 1842 as a doll maker.

HERTAULT, 1819   Hertault of Paris obtained a French patent in 1819 for a mechanical figure with a swinging head. The inventor stated that the figure could be made in stucco, bronze, plaster, wax, mastic or wood.

HERTWIG, 1864-   Hertwig & Co., founded in 1864 at Katzhütte, Thuringia, was a porcelain and fine stone goods factory. They are best known for their china doll heads with names on them such as: "Agnes", "Bertha", "Daisy", "Dorothy", "Edith", "Ethel", "Florence", "Helen", "Mabel", "Marion", and "Pauline". This type of doll was also made by the Closter Veilsdorf porcelain factory and it is not known which names were used by each factory. From 1881 through 1884 Hertwig & Co. was listed in the London Directory as a china doll maker. Up until the second World War they were making porcelain dolls and babies, including small dolls. In 1939 they advertized "Bisculoid" dolls which were made of colored sun-brown porcelain; their bodies were hard burnt ceramic. This description suggests that they made the "Story Book" or similar type doll.

HEUBACH, 1820-   Gebrüder (Brothers) Heubach founded a porcelain factory in 1820 in Lichte near Wallendorf, Thuringia. Janet Johl had an interview with a Margaret Heubach who was the granddaughter of Jean Paul Heubach, born 1808 in Thuringia, died 1874 in America. Jean Paul

A china-headed doll with the name "Ethel" raised in the china, possibly made by Hertwig & Co. after 1880.

Heubach and his brother Ernst Christian Conrad Heubach, born 1813, were too young to have founded the firm in 1820. It is possible that they were later owners. Gebrüder Heubach made various types of chinaware as well as dolls. From 1863 to 1867 Gottschalk was the Paris representative of the successors of Gebrüder Heubach which indicates that the original brothers were dead or retired. Their trade address was Sonneberg although the factory itself was in Lichte. Presumably other members of the family were Gabriel Heubach who started a porcelain factory at Wallendorf in 1833 (see Heubach, Kämpfe & Sontag), Ernst Heubach of Köppelsdorf near Sonneberg who founded the Köppelsdorfer Porzellan Fabrik in 1887 where he made bisque doll heads and Hugo Heubach of Sonneberg who was listed in the classified directories from 1894 on into the 20th century as a doll maker. He had a London branch from 1897 to 1899 and in 1900 he was one of the Sonneberg group that was awarded a grand prix at the Paris Exposition for their dolls. The Maison Hugo Heubach also won a bronze medal in 1900 at Paris and they exhibited dolls at the 1904 St. Louis Exhibition. In 1891 Gebrüder Heubach advertized that they exported to all countries and had agents in Paris, Brussels, Amsterdam, Copenhagen, Vienna and Bologne. The classified directories listed Gebrüder Heubach, china manufacturers, at the beginning of the 20th century. Another Heubach was the director of the porcelain factory at Closter Veilsdorf, Thuringia beginning around 1822. (see Greiner, 1760)

Gebrüder Heubach Bisque Character Doll mark: see fig. 1.

Photo by G. Angione

Gebrüder
Heubach
Marks

8192

Germany

Gebrüder Heubach

$\frac{8}{0}$

G   H

fig. 1   fig. 2   fig. 3

Ernst
Heubach
Marks

Germany.
275. 11/0.
Heubach-Köppelsdorf.

Heubach.
250·5·
Köppelsdorf
Germany.

fig. 1   fig. 2

HEUBACH, 1833-   Gabriel Heubach, Fredrich Kämpfe and Christian Hutschenreuther (also see Hutschenreuther) started a porcelain factory in Wallendorf, Thuringia in 1833. A few years later this factory became known as Heubach, Kämpfe & Sontag. The Greiners had founded a porcelain factory in Wallendorf in 1764 and the Gebrüder (Brothers) Heubach had founded a porcelain factory in Lichte near Wallendorf in 1820 but a connection, if any, with these factories has not been found. Heubach, Kämpfe & Sontag displayed porcelain dolls at the 1888 Melbourne Exhibition. In 1891 they advertized that they exported bisque figures and "bathing children" to France, England, America, and Australia, They had agents in Paris and Amsterdam. They were listed in directories at least until the 20th century.

HOBBINS, 1856-   John Hobbins of London made wax dolls between 1856 and 1865 according to the London Directories.

HOLBE, 1879-   R. Hölbe of Oberlind near Sonneberg, Thuringia obtained two German patents for a talking doll. The first patent was issued in 1879 and the second in 1881.

HOMER, 1879-   E. B. Homer of Philadelphia, Pennsylvania was listed in the Philadelphia Directories between 1879 and 1881 as a producer of doll materials. Between 1882 and 1883 he was listed as a doll body manufacturer.

HORSMAN, 1865-   Edward Imeson Horsman of New York began a doll assembling business in 1865. In 1901 the business became E. I. Horsman Co. which began to specialize in making rag dolls known by the trade name of "Babyland" rag dolls. Horsman obtained control of the Aetna Doll and Toy Co. in 1909. Aetna manufactured "Can't Break 'Em" composition dolls. Among the best known Horsman dolls were "Billiken", and "Campbell Kids". E. I. Horsman died in 1927 but the firm continued operation and produced dolls after World War II. For further details see "E. I. Horsman, Father of the Doll Industry" in ANTIQUES JOURNAL, Jan. 1963. pp. 21-25.

E.I.H. © 1910

©

E.I.H. CO. INC.

Horsman Marks

HOSPICE DE PEDRO II, 1867   Hospice de Pedro II of Rio de Janeiro,
Brazil exhibited dressed dolls at the 1867 Paris Exposition.

HOTCHKISS, 1875   Arthur E. Hotchkiss of New Haven, Connecticut
secured a U.S. patent in 1875 for walking dolls. The dolls had
clockwork mechanism and large metal shoes with two wooden spools
under each shoe. The patent date was incised on each shoe between
the spools, "Pat'd Sept. 21, 75".

HUGELÉ, 1843   L. Hugelé of Paris was listed in the 1843 Paris
Directory as a maker of kid body dolls.

HURET, 1850-   Mademoiselle Calixte Huret of Paris applied for a
French patent in 1850 for a doll's body that was molded and articulated. She appears to have been the daughter of Leopold Huret who
had won a silver medal at the 1849 Paris Exposition for his children's beds. At the 1855 Exposition Mademoiselle Huret herself
exhibited articulated gutta percha dolls as well as the molds for
making these dolls. She received a bronze medal for this exhibit.
The invention of a swivel neck for dolls has been credited to
Jumeau but actually Mademoiselle Huret appears to deserve the credit,
for in 1861 she patented a porcelain doll's head which terminated in
a spherical part allowing the doll's head any desired movement.
The firm known as Huret & Lonchambron from 1865 to 1867 made articulated bisque head dolls, porcelain dolls and dressed dolls. They
showed jointed gutta percha dolls at the 1867 Paris Exposition. By
1873 the Huret family apparently had departed because Lonchambron
alone was the successor of Maison Huret and he advertized jointed
gutta percha dolls, dressed and undressed. In 1879 the advertizement
included jointed gutta percha bébés as well as dolls. Another
successor, A. Lemoine, had taken over the Huret business by 1885 and
continued to advertize jointed gutta percha dolls
and bébés. Gutta percha ceased to be used soon
thereafter and when Carette succeeded from 1890-   **HURET**
1900 he advertized jointed bébés and dolls. By
1902 yet another successor, Prevost, had assumed   Huret Mark
control of the Huret establishment and once again
children's beds were advertized with no mention of
dolls.

HUTSCHENREUTHER, 1862   Hutschenreuther & Co. of Wallendorf, Thuringia
displayed papier-mâché dolls at the 1862 London Exhibition, Christian
Hutschenreuther had been associated in 1833 with Gabriel Heubach in a
porcelain factory. (see Heubach, 1833)

HYATT, 1870-   John Wesley Hyatt and his brother began to manufacture
celluloid products about 1870 in Newark, New Jersey. The Hyatt firm
took the name of Celluloid Novelty Company. Celluloid had been
discovered by Alexander Parkes of England in 1855. It is made from
cotton, nitric and sulphuric acid, camphor and alcohol. In 1863
Hyatt began to experiment with celluloid for commercial products.
William B. Carpenter was granted a U.S. patent in 1880 for coloring
the eyebrows etc. on celluloid dolls and assigned this patent to the
Celluloid Novelty Co. to use for their doll manufacturing. In 1881
Carpenter and M. C. Lefferts obtained a patent on a celluloid doll
which they likewise assigned to the Celluloid Novelty Co. This

Huret Dolls in Louvre

Second Empire period (1852-1870) costumes

Courtesy Musée des Arts Décoratifs,
Louvre, Paris

Doll on left: molded eyes, blue costume,
toque with a bandeau of feathers, white
mitts, grey satin boots, grey stockings,
19 inches tall.

Doll on right: glass or enamel eyes,
white pique costume, bonnet with large
feathers, black stockings and black
slippers ornamented with pompons.
17 inches tall.

company made both celluloid doll heads and all celluloid dolls,
some with moveable joints. The doll heads were made with either
molded hair or wigs.

I

ILLFELDER, ca.1862-   B. Illfelder & Co. of Fürth, Bavaria was
    established in the early 1860's. At first they handled chiefly
    stationery goods, but by 1890 they specialized in dolls and toys.
    Leopold Illfelder, senior member of the firm, died in 1901. In
    1907 Louis Levy, M. B. Schmidt and Carl Silverman were admitted as
    partners. They had a large New York branch.

INDIA RUBBER COMB CO., 1851   The India Rubber Comb Co. of New
    York used the hard rubber formula patented by
    Nelson Goodyear in 1851 to make doll heads.   I.R. COMB Co.
    Dolls are marked on the back of the neck with   India Rubber
    "I. R. Comb Co." according to DOLL COLLECTORS   Comb Co. Mark
    OF AMERICA, 1946, p. 11.

INSAM & PRINOTH, 1820-   Insam & Prinoth of St. Ulrich, Gröden Tirol
    (Grödnertal), Austria was founded in 1820 when wooden doll making
    was chiefly a cottage type industry and they were probably distrib-
    utors. Insam & Prinoth displayed their wooden dolls at the 1873
    Vienna Exhibition, and at the 1878 Paris Exposition. At that time
    they had agents in both France and England. In 1894 they had a
    London branch. The directories listed Chr. Prinoth & Co. of
    Nürnberg, Bavaria with a Paris branch from 1885 through 1890. This
    company adveritzed indestructible bébés, wax dolls, nankeen (cotton
    body) dolls and in 1890 "bathers". The doll and toy export firm of
    Insam & Prinoth of Nürnberg in the 20th century is probably a succes-
    sor of the earlier Austrian company.

IVES, 1866-   E. R. Ives of Plymouth, Connecticut appeared in the
    1866 Connecticut Business Directory. In 1868 Ives and Cornelius F.
    Blakeslee established the toy firm of Ives, Blakeslee & Co. in
    Bridgeport, Connecticut. Blakeslee had obtained a U. S. patent for
    doll arms in 1865. This company specialized in mechanical toys and
    they produced walking, talking and other mechanical dolls. (see
    Allen) Ives, Blakeslee & Co. had a display at the International
    Philadelphia Exhibition in 1876. In 1880 E. G. Williams of New
    York joined the firm which expanded by opening branch factories in
    New York and Philadelphia. Many patents for mechanical toys were
    granted to Ives and towards the end of the 1880's the firm bought the
    businesses of several other clever inventors, among them Jerome B.
    Secor of Bridgeport and the Automatic Toy Works of New York City,
    the owner of the latter, Robert J. Clay (see Clay) had made excep-
    tionally fine mechanical dolls. At the Chicago World's Fair in 1893
    Ives had an exhibit. Harry C. Ives succeeded his father and the firm
    grew and prospered until the depression of the 1930's.

J

JACOB, 1873   Louis Jacob of Sonneberg, Thuringia exhibited dolls at
    the 1873 Vienna Exhibition.

JAQUET-DROZ, 1774-   Pierre Jaquet-Droz of La Chaux-de-Fonds,
    Switzerland and his son Henri Louis Jaquet-Droz produced three
    automatons as well as a scene with animated characters around 1774.
    These automatons had a clockwork type mechanism which enabled them
    to simulate human movements and accomplish such feats as writing,
    drawing, and playing the piano. Later the Jaquet-Drozes made a
    mechanical doll that could write Chinese characters. These dolls,

although limited in number, are
remarkable for their being mechanical
masterpieces.

JENKINS, 1875   Raymond Jenkins of New York
was assigned the U.S. patent granted to
William Hubbell of New York in 1875. This
was for a toy dancer with a composition
head.

JOBARD, 1855   A. Jobard, according to
the Paris Directory for 1855, made dressed
and undressed dolls.

Example of one of
the drawings
produced by the
Jaquet-Droz
Draughtsman

JONES, 1838-   Robert Jones of London was
first listed as a doll maker in 1838. By
1843 he was classified as a wooden doll
maker, a listing which he held through
1848. In 1852 Henry Jones, a wooden doll
maker, was listed at the same address as
Robert Jones had occupied. Henry Jones was listed until 1855. Richard William Jones at a different London address also made wooden
dolls between 1853 and 1865.

JUDGE, 1875-   E. S. Judge & Co. of Philadelphia, Pennsylvania was
issued a U.S. patent in 1875 for the manufacture of doll heads, etc.
in papier-mâché. Between 1876 and 1878 E. S. Judge & Co. operated by
Edward S. Judge, John P. Judge and John E. Murray sold doll materials and papier-mâché products.

JULLIEN, 1878-   A. Jullien of Paris exhibited dolls and their
trousseaux at the Paris Exposition of 1878. A Paris toy merchant
named Jullien had advertized games and toys as early as 1863. It is
also possible that Jullien, the doll maker, was related to the
Achille & Jullien porcelain manufacturing firm of Limoges who had
won many awards between 1851 and 1869. In 1879 Jullien, Jeune
advertized in the Paris Directory that he made "dressed dolls and
bébés; nankeen dolls and bathers". A lengthy advertizement appeared
in 1885 which stated that Jullien, Jeune made "dolls and bébés, dressed indestructible bébés, deluxe and ordinary; dolls included ladies,
young girls, brides and peasants with stationary or turning heads;
jointed dolls and indestructible bébés with trousseaux; bathers, swimmers and fishermen made to bathe in the sea." At the Paris Exposition
of 1889 Jullien was Foreman of the Jury. In 1892 the trade name
"L'Universel" appeared in the Jullien advertizement. It was a Paris
made indestructible bébé with the "latest perfections" made in four
models: No.1 rigid, No.2 jointed, No.3 with jointed wrists and talking, No.4 was not described. The dolls were described as richly
dressed, less richly dressed and in ordinary dress. The 1895
advertizement further described "L'Universel" as having limbs of
hollowed wood and being the "lightest and most solid
bébé made up to now". This bébé walked, talked, and
had teeth and sleeping eyes. "Mignonettes" were   JuLLieN
advertized by Jullien in 1895. Jullien, Jeune won a
bronze medal for his exhibit at the 1900 Paris Expos-   1
ition. The 1900 advertizement added that their bébé
also bowed. Around 1904 Jullien became a member of   Jullien Mark
the S.F.B.J. (see Jumeau)

JUMEAU, 1843-   Pierre Francois Jumeau founded the Maison Jumeau
about 1843. This date is indicated in the 1842 and 1843 Paris
Directories and affirmed by Jumeau officials according to two different accounts of vists to the Jumeau factory in 1885 and in 1897.
Statements have been made that the Jumeau firm was established earlier
but no verification has been found. In 1888 on the U.S. trademark
application Emile Jumeau stated that the trademark "Bébé Jumeau" had
been in use since 1840. Although this is an official document there

is no other evidence of any French bébés being made as early as this
and Jumeau himself had previously dated "Bébé Jumeau" as much later.
An article by Luella Hart based on a later conference with an official of the Jumeau firm and published in SPINNING WHEEL in August
1957 states that the first Jumeau factory was in 1835 in Paris and
that Jumeau made his first bisque doll heads at Montreuil-sous-Bois
in 1850. Both of these dates seem to be too early judging from
other evidence, which will be discussed later.

In 1843 Belton & Jumeau were listed as makers of dressed dolls at
the rue Salle-au-Compte 14, Paris. The account of the Jumeau factory
given in PEARSON'S MAGAZINE, July 1897, pp.60-65 said that their
dolls in 1843 were "all made of sheepskin stuffed with sawdust and
with china heads".

At the 1844 Paris Exposition of French Industry, Belton and Jumeau
received Honorable Mention for their exhibit. From 1847 to 1867
Jumeau was listed alone as a doll maker at rue Mauconseil 18, Paris.
During this period we learn most about Jumeau dolls from the Exposition reports. At Paris in 1849 Jumeau won a bronze medal. In 1851
at the Great Exhibition in London Pierre Jumeau exhibited dolls and
dolls' wardrobes. Here Jumeau was awarded a prize medal for dolls'
dresses and the Report of the Jury reads: "The dolls on which these
dresses are displayed present no point worthy of commendation but the
dresses themselves are very beautiful". Again Jumeau exhibited dolls
dressed and undressed at the 1855 Paris Exposition and 1862 London
Exhibition and won prize medals at both places.

Jumeau in the 1860 Paris Directory advertized kid body dolls, undressed and dressed in all kinds of attire, and articulated dolls
with porcelain heads. It should be noted that Jumeau did not advertize bébés although other companies were advertizing them at this time.
In the 1865 and 1867 advertizements Jumeau included "talking bébés"
and another new item namely "carved dolls with porcelain heads".
These latter are probably the wooden body Jumeau dolls. Jumeau still
made "kid body dolls dressed and undressed in all varieties and doll
dresses for jointed dolls".

At the Paris Exposition of 1867 Jumeau of rue d'Anjou-Marais, where
he must have recently moved, received a silver medal for his exhibition of dolls, doll lingerie, doll dresses and doll heads. This is
one of the first times that French doll heads are mentioned but the
type of material is not given. Singleton's DOLLS, pp.58-59 quotes
an undated and unnamed "French authority" as saying, "One day the
inventor's (Pierre Jumeau) eldest son thought of an improvement which
would give the head an ingenious articulation. By this means the head
could be moved in any direction, up and down and round and round."
The "one day" was in 1862 or later. However, Mademoiselle Huret had
already applied for her patent for a swivel neck doll head in 1861
which indicates that this invention has been wrongly ascribed to
Jumeau's son.

The 1873 Jumeau advertizement was the same as that carried in the
last half of the 1860's but with the important addition that their
specialty was porcelain doll heads made at Montreuil-sous-Bois. The
French Report on the 1873 Vienna Exhibition devotes several paragraphs
to Jumeau as follows, "M. Jumeau of Paris, the first and the most
important doll making house, has freed us from our former obligation
to have the foreigner furnish us with porcelain doll heads.

"M. Jumeau has established at Montreuil, near Paris, a factory
where he makes doll heads of enameled porcelain with the greatest
perfection. He has surpassed in beauty the products that we used to
buy from Saxony.

"The exhibit of M. Jumeau at Vienna was splendid and the Viennese
merchants were impressed by the good prices at which they could
purchase his products.

"They rendered justice to M. Jumeau when they congratulated him on
his beautiful product and awarded him unanimously the medal of
progress."

At the Vienna Exhibition Jumeau also won a gold medal and a medal
of co-operation went to four representatives of the Maison P. F.
Jumeau, namely, Emile Jumeau, Madame Blanche Pannier, Mademoiselle

Elisa Cadet and Oscar Rinders.
This report of the 1873 Exhibition suggests that few French
porcelain doll heads were made
prior to the 1870 war with Germany. This is also verified by
accounts in the book written in
1885 about a visit to the Jumeau
factory and translated by Nina
Davies, under the title THE
JUMEAU DOLL STORY, pp. 64-66.
Also on these pages Emile Jumeau
is credited with creating "Bébé
Jumeau" around 1875 after working
many years on it which checks
with evidence already cited and
tends to throw further doubt on
the trademark statement that
"Bébé Jumeau" had been used since
1840. The 1873 Exhibition Report
describes the Jumeau doll heads
as being made of "enameled porcelain" which seems to mean
glazed china rather than bisque.

Mechanical Doll
With Music Box,
Bisque head and arms
Lamb's Wool wig.
Mark: see fig. 9

At the Philadelphia Exhibition
of 1876 P. F. Jumeau won a gold
medal for his display of "Doll's
heads and bodies. A fine collection dressed in a most fashionable
style; heads of the finest imitation, superior taste and excellent
workmanship in mechanical construction". Jumeau is the only French
doll maker for whom a record has been found at this important
American exhibition.
    Between 1876 and 1878 Pierre Francois Jumeau retired and his sec-
ond but eldest surviving son became head of the firm. Emile Jumeau
whose influence had already been felt brought the firm to its
zenith. In the 1878 Paris Exposition E. L. Jumeau won the gold
medal for his dolls and bébés over other French competitors such as
Bru, Steiner, Gaultier, Schmitt, etc. The following year, 1879, in
Sydney, Australia Jumeau again won the gold medal.There his dolls were
described as "Artistically made and elegant in style". In 1880 at
Melbourne, Australia Jumeau won the gold medal for his dolls and
bébés and at this exhibition he also won a bronze medal for his
mechanical toys. At New Orleans in 1884 and Paris in 1885 Jumeau
won gold medals. At Antwerp in 1885 he was awarded the Diploma of
Honor. For the first time in 1885 at Paris, Jumeau's superiority
was challenged by Bru who also received a gold medal.
    In the Paris Directories available here in America, the term
"bébé incassable" (indestructible jointed bébé) appeared for the
first time in the 1879 Directory. Later there were always two
separate classifications, one for "Poupées" or Dolls and the other
for "Bébés Incassable". "Bébé Jumeau" appeared under "Bébés Incassables" and Jumeau stated in his 1885 advertizement that "Bébé
Jumeau was put on the market only in 1879. The Jumeau classified
advertizements in the directories from 1879-1885 were similar. In
1879 he advertized that he "makes jointed kid body dolls; jointed
wood body dolls; indestructible jointed bébés of a unique model.
The dolls and bébés are dressed in wool, foulard or silk. Special doll heads in porcelain are manufactured at the factory in
Montreuil-sous-Bois. The finest maisons are furnished with the
newest Paris items". This last statement may apply to the use of
Jumeau dolls as fashion couriers. In 1881 Jumeau also made the
important statement, "Tous marques à son nom" (all marked with his
name). This is most important for doll collectors who are trying
to date a "Bébé Jumeau". Note that it states the name and not
initials are on all products. In 1882 the Jumeau advertizement
also stated that the "Bébé Jumeau from sizes No. 9 to No. 16 have
human eyes, applied ears, wear a pearl necklace of Paris and a comb

in their hair". The 1885 advertizement is still headed "Tous marques à son nom" and it adds a "new creation, talking Bébé Jumeau". Jumeau manufactured his own voice mechanism and his talking bébés were advertized as early as 1865. The advertizement in 1885 also states, "Bébés with kid bodies. These bébés are of a fabrication exactly equal to that of the dolls and consequently have all their defects and are not recommended by my firm which only makes them on command". The description of these doll bodies in the 1885 account of the visit to the Jumeau factory is almost identical with the 1897 description of kid bodies filled with sawdust that Jumeau made when he started in 1843.

The London Directory of 1881 lists Jumeau as a doll maker with a London address but this is the only year in which he appears to have had a branch outside of France.

No patents have been found for Pierre Francois Jumeau but Emile obtained several patents. In 1882 he and Bru jointly obtained a French patent for a mechanical boat. In 1885 Emile Jumeau obtained a French patent for making eyelids drop over the eyeballs rather than to have them move together. Apparently he had trouble with the space left after the eyelid moved up and in 1886 he obtained another French patent to eliminate this space. Also in 1886 he obtained a patent for making dolls of a so-called unbreakable material. In 1887 he obtained another patent for sleeping doll eyes, this time including eyelashes. This was patented both in France and Germany.

Emile Jumeau registered his trademark, "Bébé Jumeau" in France in 1886 and in the United States in 1888. In 1886 he also registered "Bébé Prodige" and "Bébé Francais"in 1896.

At the Paris Exposition of 1889 Jumeau was a member of the Jury and Hors Concours but his exhibit far overshadowed that of Steiner who won the gold medal. The official United States Report on this Exhibition stated, concerning the large central exhibit of Monsieur Emile Jumeau, "It contained large numbers of babies (the name given to the modern doll) of the most incredible richness in every position and so intelligent. These are French dolls unmistakably. The heads are of Sèvres porcelain painted by real artists and having luxuriant and silky hair. Their hats seem worthy of Linn or Virot and their dresses are in the latest fashion and made of rich Lyons silk of the latest style. Perhaps even they have set the fashion sometimes; if so, the best dressmakers of the day need not be ashamed. Little girls could not leave the spot, they were so fascinated."

This is the first and only mention found of a connection between the famous Sèvres porcelain and Jumeau dolls. A letter from Monsieur Bauduy, Director, Manufacture Nationale de Sèvres dated 5 Nov. 1962 states, "In our experimental laboratories there having been studies of the best technical processes for the manufacture of doll heads in order to render service to private industry at the time of the Universal Exposition of 1889 is not impossible. One case of this kind occured in 1915 when the war had stopped the importation of German dolls. (see Sèvres) ... Our archives ... record that a small number of heads of dolls ... were made in our workshops in 1917/18." This letter and the Sèvres doll and doll heads pictured seem to contradict the letter written in 1939 by a staff member of the American Embassy in Paris and quoted by Johl in THE FASCINATING STORY OF DOLLS, pp.51, 57 which states, "No dolls were ever made at Sèvres" and "The ordinary china doll in biscuit or dull china was made in France in the early sixties by one Gautier at Charenton near Paris. This factory was taken over by Mauger who moved it to Montreuil near Charenton. The Jumeaus soon bought him out and the real doll industry was born in France." The second statement seems to be as erroneous as the first one, because Gaultier (see Gaultier) is listed in the Paris Directories as making porcelain doll heads at Charenton as late as 1885 when we know that Jumeau had built and operated his own factory at Montreuil some years previously.

During the 1890's Jumeau had to seek quantity production in place of quality. His advertizements state that in 1881 he made 85,000 bébés; in 1883- 115,000 bébés and in 1884- 220,000 bébés. In the 1897 visit account it states, "There are 17 sizes of heads in all, from

six to seven hundred of each size
are manufactured every day." This
would mean between three and four
million doll heads a year, a tremendous increase. This increase is
readily explained by the Jumeau
advertizement of 1892, "Notice of
Change: The Maison makes two new
models of indestructible jointed
bébés undressed and dressed with
some differences of 20% and 40%,
but with the same irreproachable
quality remaining and not carrying
the Jumeau name. Complete change of
articles in the Maison Jumeau. Ask
for the Catalog.

"Large production of bébés known
throughout the entire world by the
name 'Bébé Jumeau'.

"Races,- French, Mulatto or Negro.

"The Maison Jumeau is not connected
with any supplier and itself produces
all the articles which it sells:-
heads, human eyes, wigs, composition
bodies, lingerie, bonnets, footwear,
all of superior quality and the latest style, and even their boxes and
packing cases, in a word all that
comprises a complete product, this
is also important in order for the
dealer to obtain the highest profit."

Further reductions in price were
indicated in 1895 when the advertizement read, "The Maison makes three
new models of indestructible jointed
bébés, dressed and undressed; without mark with a difference of 40% to
60%.

"New creations, 'Bébé Phonographe',
'Bébé Marcheur' (walking) Examine

Jumeau Talking Bébé

Two pull strings at waist
doll says "Mama","Papa",
voice box marked Jumeau.

Mark on head: see fig. 7

the marks." Doll collectors have often referred to so-called early
unmarked Jumeau bébés but apparently there were a great many of these
unmarked ones made during the 1890's.

There are three published accounts of visits to the Jumeau factory.
The ones in 1885 and in 1897 have already been referred to and Leo
Claretie's LES JOUETS gave an account of another visit around 1894.
An item by item comparison of the changes in the methods employed and
practises over the period recorded during these three visits gives
the reader some fascinating information. For example in 1894 and
1897 the slip was first carefully strained then poured into the
mould and allowed to stand until the desired thickness had hardened
as a crust around the inside of the mould. Then the remaining slip
was poured off. The smaller heads were not as thick as the larger
ones. The process in 1885 was quite different, the slip was of a
paste-like consistency and was kneaded and rolled out like dough to
the desired thickness, then it was cut into squares which were then
pressed onto the two halves of a plaster cast. This indicates that
the customary pouring mould method used today was used in the 1890's
but not in 1885 when instead the clay was rolled out and fitted onto
the moulds. In 1897 the doll heads were baked for 48 hours but in
1885 they were baked only a little over half as long. In 1894 the eyes
were cut out after baking while in 1885 they were cut out before
baking. All accounts state that the larger heads had applied ears
and the smaller ones molded ears. In 1885 Jumeau obtained a patent
for movable eyes that could be worked by a spring so that in the
future "Bébé Jumeau" would sleep, but by 1897 the familiar counter-
weight sleep eyes were being used. These are but a few of the

interesting comparisons that can be made.

Two items in the 1897 account are of especial interest, first, "The most expensive dolls including those sent to England, Spain, and Germany every year as fashion models are fully dressed at the Jumeau warehouse in the rue Pastourelle." This indicates that at least as late as 1897 there were French fashion dolls. The term "fashion" here refers to the doll's function and not necessarily to its type. Both lady dolls and bébés were used as fashion couriers, the latter showing the world the latest French fashion for children. The other item is that Monsieur Emile Douillet who piloted the author of the article around the factory was a partner of Emile Jumeau.

Jumeau exhibited dolls at the World's Fair in Chicago in 1893 but it is not known what award he received there.

In 1896 Jumeau obtained a French patent for movable doll eyes and this seems to be the last official record, other than directories, found for the Jumeau firm before it merged with other doll makers in the Société Française de Fabrication de Bébés et Jouets in 1899. The Paris Directory lists the S.F.B.J. at rue Pastourelle 8 which had formerly been the Jumeau address. The S.F.B.J. were members of the Jury and Hors Concours at the 1900 Paris Exposition. Other companies in the S.F.B.J. included Bru, (see Bru) Fleischmann & Bloedel, (see Fleischmann & Bloedel) Rabery & Delphieu, (see Rabery) and Pintel & Godchaux. By 1904 Jullien (see Jullien) had also become a member and Danel & Co. appears to have joined by 1911. Pintel & Godchaux, recorded in Paris in 1890, made "Bébé Charmant". Danel & Co., recorded in Paris in 1889, made "Paris Bébé" with Eiffel Tower mark. When World War I began Fleischmann, a German, was head of the S.F.B.J. and all his property was sequestered. Henry S. Benjamin, who had been an agent for Gebrüder (Brothers) Krauss in 1887, was the London agent for S.F.B.J. from 1910 to 1920. Dolls carrying the Jumeau name were made after World War I.

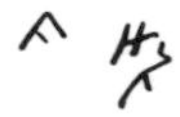

fig. 1
Markings on head and body of a Jumeau doll

fig. 2

fig. 3

fig. 4

fig. 5

fig. 6

fig. 7

fig. 8
Mark on dust ruffle of dresses made by Jumeau

fig. 9

Jumeau Marks

fig. 1

fig. 2

fig. 3

fig. 4 trademark

fig. 5 trademark

S.F.B.J. Markings

K

KELLER, 1878   F. Keller of Paris exhibited bébés in the 1878 Paris Exposition.

KESTNER, 1805-   Johann Daniel Kestner of Waltershausen, Thuringia founded a factory to make papier-mâché toys in 1805. He was an official of Saxony and one of the first doll makers to have his own establishment. He was the founder of the great Waltershausen doll industry which carried a reputation for making the finest grade dolls while at Sonneberg all grades of dolls were made. Johann Daniel Kestner, Jr. succeeded his father. The firm of J. D. Kestner, Jr. expanded with the erection at Ohrdruf, Thuringia of a porcelain factory under the name of Kestner & Co. where the firm was able to make their own china and bisque doll heads. As far as is known Kestner was the only German doll maker who made entire dolls (heads, bodies,etc.). They also sold doll parts separately. In 1891 Kestner advertized china, bisque, and wax doll heads; jointed composition, kid and nankeen (cotton) body dolls, as well as tea services. Adolf Kestner of Waltershausen obtained in 1892 two English patents for doll joints. One of them was for a doll with detachable parts so a new limb or head could easily be substituted for a damaged one. In 1892 and 1893 the firm of J. D. Kestner, Jr. obtained German patents for improved doll joints. At the 1893 Chicago World's Fair they exhibited dolls. Kestner began using their famous trademark "Kronenpuppe" (crown doll) in 1895 and registered it in the United States in 1896. Kestner was one of the firms that made Kewpies when they came out in 1913 and "Bye-lo" doll heads and all bisque dolls in the 1920's.   They also made celluloid dolls and used the celluloid of Rheinische Gummi und Celluloid Fabrik Co. but with their own special J. D. K. marked moulds.

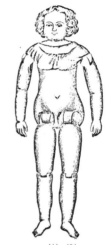

Abb. 10d
Kopf und Körper Papier-
maché, letzterer aber mit
Stoffüberzug. Gelenke Holz.

Doll with head and body of papier-mâché, the latter covered with material, and wooden joints.

These dolls have both the turtle and J. D. K. mark on them. Kestner had a London agent and their exclusive agent in the United States and Canada was George Borgfeldt & Co. For further details on the J. D. Kestner, Jr. firm see ANTIQUES JOURNAL, Aug. 1962 pp. 22-27; and DEUTSCHE SPIELWAREN ZEITUNG, Feb. 1926 p. 28; Aug. 1928 p. 41.

Kestner Character Doll
Bisque head
mark: fig. 1

F. made in Germany. 10
2 11
J.D.K.

fig. 1

44

CENTURY DOLL Co.

Kestner Germany

fig. 4
20th Century Mark

JDK
319
fig. 6

fig. 2
J. D. Kestner Trademark

fig. 5
Kestner-
Rheninische Gummi
und Celluloid
Fabrik Mark

made in
Germany
J. D. K.
2 6 0.

fig. 7

262

Made in Germany.

fig. 3
Mark of Kestner & Co.

made in
K. Germany. 14
J. D. K.
2 1 5.

fig. 8

Kestner Marks

KIETAIBL, 1851   F. Kietiabl of Vienna, Austria won a prize medal
at the 1851 London Exhibition for his collection of 39 automatons.
These dolls were operated by "good metallic clockwork" mechanisms.
They were described as " more expensive than similar manufactures
produced in France, with which unfortunately there is no comparison
in the Exhibition..... This collection was the only one of detached
locomotive figures." (see Theroude) Male and female waltzing figures
were priced at 12 shillings (about $3).

KINTZBACK, 1869   M. Kintzback of Philadelphia, Pennsylvania patented
in 1869 a cloth arm doll with a device so that the china hand would
move.

KIRSCHKAMP, 1867-   J. Kirschkamp, Fr. Gerpott, I. Kirschkamp & Co.
of Dusseldorf, Prussia displayed dolls at the 1867 Paris Exposition.
In 1882 J. Kirschkamp & Co. was represented in Paris by Gottschalk.

KLING, 1836-   Christian Friedrich Kling of Ohrdruf, Thuringia founded a porcelain factory in 1836. This factory began by producing
chiefly figurines and vases, but later it primarily made dolls and
doll heads. They made all porcelain dolls, both the so-called
"Frozen Charlotte" type and jointed all porcelain dolls especially in
smaller sizes. They also made "bathing children". Christian Friedrich
Kling died in 1870 and was succeeded by his son Ernst Kling who in
turn was succeeded by his son Paul Kling who died when only 33.
After the death of young Paul Kling the factory was run under a
trust by Lewis Ortlepp who died in 1897. Ortlepp was succeeded by W.
Straube who in turn was succeeded by his son-in-law, Hugo Schade, in
1920. In 1891 the Kling firm advertized that they had won many
prizes but no record has been found as yet of these prizes. They
exported to all countries and were one of the several firms that
made "Bye-lo" doll heads.

KNIGHT, 1878-   Knight & Co. of Newchwang, China displayed dolls in
silk at the 1878 Paris Exposition. The name Knight seems to be
English rather than Chinese and an Arthur Bertram Knight of Notting
Hill, Middlesex, England was granted an English doll patent in 1893.
In 1894 E. G. Knights & Co. of London were listed ʔs doll makers but
no connection has been found.

KÖHLER, 1862-   L. G. Köhler of Neustadt, Bavaria
won a prize medal for his papier-mâché dolls at
the 1862 London Exhibition. In the 20th century
Georg Köhler of Nürnberg, Bavaria made mechanical
dolls.

Kohler Mark

KÖNIGLICHE PORZELLAN MANUFAKTUR, 1761-   Königliche
Porzellan Manufaktur was the State owned porcelain
factory in Berlin. Earlier the Meissen factory had
also been known as Königliche Porzellan Manufaktur
and used the mark "K.P.M." but it is doubtful if any dolls were made
at that early time. (see Meissen) The Berlin factory was started
by a Prussian named Gotzkowsky in 1761. Frederick the Great of
Prussia made it the State Porcelain factory in 1763. The marks of
this factory have been found on the inside of doll shoulders. For
further information see GERMAN PORCELAIN, by W. B. Honey, pp. 30-32,
42; DOLL COLLECTORS OF AMERICA, 1946, p. 24; 1956/7 p. 36.

fig. 1	fig. 2	fig. 3	fig. 4
sceptre-mark	Red: 1823-1832		1832 onward
from the arms	Blue: 1844 onward		Piece decorated
of Brandenburg			at Berlin

Berlin Königliche Porzellan Manufaktur
Marks

KRAATZ, 1844   W. Kraatz of Berlin in 1844 sent from his waxwork
factory to the Berlin Exhibition wax doll heads, arms and legs as
well as whole wax dolls in glass cases.

KRAUSS, 1863-   Gebrüder (Brothers) Krauss of Eisfeld,
Thuringia advertized papier-mâché, wood and other
material dolls as early as 1863 in French Directories.
They were represented by Gottschalk in Paris. In 1887
they had a London branch with Henry S. Benjamin as
their agent. Benjamin later became the London agent
for the S.F.B.J. of Paris. In the 20th century Gebrüder Krauss advertized dressed dolls.

Gebrüder
Krauss Mark

KRAUSS, 1853-   Samuel Krauss of Rodach near Coburg,
Bavaria displayed papier-mâché dolls with moving heads
at the 1853 New York Exhibition. From 1867 through
1874 he advertized in French Directories that his Paris representative
was Montréer and that he made dolls with movable heads and crèche
figures. Samuel Krauss, Berthold Krauss and Hermann Krauss all of
Rodach showed their dolls at the 1873 Vienna Exhibition.

KUMMER, 1844   K. W. Kummer of Berlin received a silver medal for
his papier-mâché dolls at the 1844 Berlin Exhibition.

L

LACMANN, 1860-   Jacob Lacmann appeared in the Philadelphia Business Directory in 1860 as a doll body manufacturer. He was granted U.S. patents in 1871 for improvements in making doll fingers, and in 1874 for improved methods of making hands and feet for dolls over a papier-mâché core. Jacob Lacmann witnessed the will of Ludwig Greiner in 1872 which indicates that these two famous doll makers were friends and Lacmann probably used Greiner heads. This assumption is verified by a doll with a Lacmann marked body of heavy cotton material and a Greiner marked head. By 1876 Lacmann's son had joined the firm which was then known as J. Lacmann and Son, and they advertized doll materials as well as doll bodies. At the 1876 Philadelphia Exhibition Lacmann showed his products. The last entry found for J. Lacmann & Son was in 1883 when they were still making doll bodies. From 1884 through 1887 Philipine Lacmann was listed as a doll body maker in Philadelphia which suggests that Philipine Lacmann carried on the Jacob Lacmann business.

Lacmann Mark

LACOUCHY, 1863-   D. Lacouchy of Paris was listed as a toy maker in 1863. In 1864 he was granted a French patent for improvements in the making of dolls. Between 1867 and 1873 Lacouchy made dressed kid body dolls, doll clothes and patented metal dolls. By 1879 he was listed as making kid body dolls of fine and ordinary quality.

LACOURTILLE, ca. 1790-   LaCourtille was a porcelain factory in Paris in the late 18th and early 19th century. No data has been found indicating whether china doll heads were made here. However, its mark is very similar to the Meissen crossed swords and should be distinguished from it.

LaCourtille
Mark

LAGROVE, 1873   W. A. P. LaGrove of Brooklyn, New York secured a U.S. patent in 1873 for an automatic toy dancer.

LAMBERT, 1873-   Lambert & Samhammer of Sonneberg, Thuringia displayed dolls at the 1873 Vienna Exhibition and at the 1879 Sidney Exhibition. In Sidney they received commendation for their dolls and doll heads. There was a later Leopold Lambert in Paris who made mechanical toys and an F. Lambert of Hamburg who was a doll maker before 1897 but no connection has been found. It is possible that Samhammer or at least a relative of his was the Philipp Samhammer, a doll maker of Sonneberg, who was listed in the directories from 1888 into the 20th century. He had a branch in London and obtained an English patent in 1888 for applying movable eyes to rag dolls.

L. B.
Mark of
Leopold
Lambert

LANG, 1851-   The heirs of Georg Lang of Oberammergau, Württemberg displayed carved wooden dolls at the 1851 London Exhibition. No doubt one of these was the Erben G. Lange of Oberammergau who showed wooden dolls at the 1853 New York Exhibition and won a bronze medal.

LANG, 1865   Lang & Co. of London were making dolls of India rubber and gutta percha in 1865 according to the London Directory.

LANTERNIER, 1873-   A. Lanternier & Co. of Limoges, France appeared as early as 1873 in the directories as making decorated porcelain. The directories do not mention doll making but bisque doll heads have been found with the mark of this company. In 1915/16 this was one of the three French companies selected by Sèvres for assistance in the manufacture of porcelain doll heads. (see Sèvres) The Lanternier factory was at Limoges and they had a shop in Paris.

China
Doll heads
made at
Sèvres in
1917.

Courtesy of
Musée des Arts
Décoratifs.
Louvre, Paris

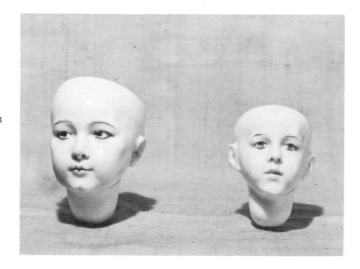

fig. 1

J.E. Masbon
SC
LORRAINE
No
AL & Cº.
LIMOGES

fig. 2

FABRICATION
FRANÇAISE

Al & Cⁱᵉ
LIMOGES

A   1

fig. 3

Lanternier Marks

LEBAS, 1842   Madame Lebas of Paris was listed in the 1842 Paris
Directory as making papier-mâché dolls.

LEBLOND, 1853   J. D. LeBlond of Paris displayed India rubber mannikins at the 1853 New York Exhibition and won a bronze medal for
them.

LEBON, 1863-   Lebon of Limoges, France became the successor to a
Monsieur Chevrot (see Bru) in 1863. And by 1873 Lebon & Co. of
Limoges was manufacturing porcelain toys, some of which were for ex-
port. By 1882 Lebon had been succeeded by Leon Barjaud de la Fond
& Co. They continued making porcelain toys, with some for export.

LECHERTIER, BARBE & CO., 1868   Lechertier, Barbe & Co. of Paris
were granted a French patent in 1868. Their invention dealt with a
new means of articulating the joints and different parts of a papier-
mâché (body) doll by means of elastic placed inside the body.

LECOMTE & ALLIOT, 1866-   Lecomte (Leconte) & Alliot of Paris were
issued a French patent in 1866 for a feeding doll with a reservoir
that could be emptied. The doll was to be called "Marie Jeanne".
In 1888 E. LeConte, a maker of mechanical novelties, was granted a
French patent for a doll in a carriage or wheel chair that moved by
clockwork. This mechanical doll was to be called "Le Petit Bébé".
Although there is a slight variation in the spelling of the name it
is assumed that these men were either the same man or relatives as
their innovations were in the same category and because they also
gave a name to their invention, a rare occurence in patent specifications. H. LeConte & Co. won a bronze medal for their doll exhibit

at the 1900 Paris Exposition. H. LeConte & Co. used the mark "L. C.".

LEE, 1850-   Benjamin F. Lee appeared in the New York City Directories from 1821-1870. Prior to 1850 he was listed as a merchant but in 1850 rubber goods are mentioned specifically. Charles Goodyear, inventor of vulcanized soft rubber or caoutchouc, began to manufacture rubber toys as early as 1839 and he stated in his 1855 book GUM ELASTIC that the manufacture of rubber dolls in the United States was licensed to B. F. Lee. In 1851 Nelson Goodyear, brother of Charles, invented hard rubber. The label "Goodyear's Pat. May 6, 1851 Ext. 1865" has been found on doll heads made of hard rubber. The Goodyear name or initials and/or date appear on both dolls and doll heads. (also see New York Rubber Co.)

GOODYEAR'S PAT. MAY 6, 1851. EXT. 1865.

Goodyear Mark

LEE, 1866   David Thorpe Lee of Birmingham, England obtained an English patent in 1866 for a ball jointed doll strung with either metal or rubber.

LEFEBVRE, 1863-   Lefebvre was listed in the 1863 Paris Directory as a toy maker. In 1869, according to a statement made 50 years later by his son, the father Lefebvre invented the "bébé incassable" or indestructible jointed bébé. However, Leon Casimir Bru (see Bru) had obtained a patent in 1869 for this type doll. The maison Lefebvre exhibit at the Paris Exposition of 1878 was of papier-mâché toys. In 1890 they were advertizing molded papier-mâché toys and indestructible jointed bébés. The display of Alexandre Lefebvre received an Honorable Mention citation at the 1900 Paris Exposition. In 1906 the firm was known as A. Lefebvre & Co. and advertized rubber for doll joints. In 1912 the "Bébés A. L." were advertized. These had papier-mâché bodies and unbreakable heads that were washable. Their new patented joints were designed to sit and kneel. At this time the factory was at Lagny, Seine, & Marne, France. As late as 1919 there were still advertizements by A. Lefebvre & Co. Their dolls came in sizes from 10 inches to 28 inches.

LEJEUNE, 1878-   E. A. Lejeune of Paris showed rubber toys in the Paris Exposition of 1878. In the 1880 exhibition at Melbourne his display of dolls and bébés was awarded a bronze medal. The Lejeune agent at Melbourne was E. Gay, Lamaille & Co. of Paris, London and Melbourne.

LE MONTRÉER, see Montréer

LERCH, 1864-   Philip Lerch was listed in the 1864 Philadelphia Directory as a toy maker. From 1866 through 1870 he appeared as a maker of doll heads. In 1867 Conrad Lang joined Lerch and the firm became known as Lerch & Co. Lerch is not listed in the 1876 Philadelphia Directory but a doll's head of about this period has been found bearing the label "Lerch and Klagg, Philadelphia".

LEROY, 1842-   Leroy of Paris was listed in the Paris Directories from 1842 to 1847 as a maker of papier-mâché dolls.

LIEDEL, 1855   G. Liedel of Hildburghausen, Thuringia displayed papier-mâché dolls at the 1855 Paris Exposition.

LINDNER, 1830-   A. Johann Christoph Lindner was living in Sonneberg, Thuringia in 1830. This name appears in German Directories from 1863 through 1902 as a doll maker. Lindner displayed dolls at the 1873 Vienna Exhibition, the 1880 Melbourne Exhibition and the 1893 Chicago Exhibition. From 1873 through 1882 he had a branch in Paris and was represented by Montréer in 1882. In 1875 he also had a London branch. J. C. Lindner advertized "täuflinge" (baby dolls) and dressed dolls in 1891. Johann Christoph Lindner of Sonneberg, probably a namesake of the 1830 man, was one of the grand prix winners at the 1900 Paris Exposition.

LINDNER, 1863-   Louis Lindner & Son of Sonneberg, Thuringia was listed in German Directories from 1863 well into the 20th century. In the 1860's in Paris he was represented by Gottschalk and in 1873 by Heppet Brodbeck. Louis Lindner & Son displayed dolls at the 1873 Vienna Exhibition; the 1880 Melbourne Exhibition; the 1893 Chicago Exhibition; the 1900 Paris Exposition, where he was one of the grand prix winners; and the 1904 St. Louis Exhibition. In 1911 their New York agent was John Bing.

LOEWENBERG, 1865   Henry Loewenberg of New York City and Emile Granier of Paris were issued an English patent in 1865 for a composition doll head. The ingredients were four pounds of glue; three ounces of nutall and similar substances; eight ounces of glycerine; one pound of acid.

LÖWENTHAL, 1836-   Löwenthal & Co. of the free city of Hamburg was founded in 1836. They displayed papier-mâché doll heads and dolls at the 1844 Berlin Exhibition. The lacquered papier-mâché doll heads had curly or flat hairdos, many of the heads had glass eyes and glass teeth. They represented men and women of many nationalities, among them Turks, Chinese and Scots. A woman doll from this factory which could be dressed and undressed sold for 28 talers ($28) and was described as "very pleasing". The factory employed between 200 and 300 people. At the London Exhibition of 1851 Löwenthal displayed doll heads in wax and in papier-mâché. As late as 1897 James Löwenthal of Hamburg was listed as a doll maker.

Abb. 10c.
Gestopfte
Puppe mit
Papiermaché-
kopf.

LÜTZELBERGER, 1873-   J. N. Lützelberger of Sonneberg, Thuringia showed dolls at the 1873 Vienna Exhibition. In the 1898 German Directory both J. N. Lützelberger and Hermann Lützelberger were listed as doll makers and both were among the grand prix winners at the 1900 Paris Exposition. J. N. Lützelberger had a doll display at the 1904 St. Louis Exhibition. Hermann Lützelberger of Sonneberg was making dolls after World War I.

Stuffed doll with a papier-mâché head such as those made by Löwenthal.

LYON, 1862   Joseph Lyon & Co. of New York was one of the companies (see Cohen) that made the "autoperipatekos" doll patented in 1862 by Enoch Rice Morrison of New York City. The Lyon name appears on an original box in the Museum of the City of New York. Morrison obtained both an English and a U.S. patent for this walking doll with a clockwork mechanism. "Autoperipatekos" dolls have been found with a variety of china, parian bisque, and papier-mâché heads.

M

MACAZAGA & IDARRAMENDI, 1878   Macazaga & A. Idarramendi of Valladolid, Spain displayed dressed dolls at the 1878 Paris Exposition.

MAELZEL, 1823-   Jean Maelzel of Paris, inventor of the metronome, also invented some mechanical dolls. At the Paris Exhibition of 1823, according to a periodical LE BON GENIE, there were dolls which said "Mama" and "Papa" when their hands were touched. These appear to be the mechanical dolls patented by Jean Maelzel in 1824 and described as a talking doll which pronounces by the play of its arms the two words "papa", "mama". Max von Boehn in DOLLS AND PUPPETS, p. 155 states that Maelzel obtained a French patent in 1827 for a doll that said "papa" and "mama" when it was squeezed. No such patent has been discovered and it is possible that von Boehn confused the date of the similar 1824 patent.

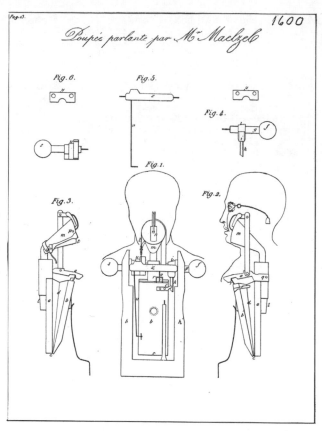

Picture of
Maelzel Patent
drawing of a
Talking Doll

Note the eyes appear
to move with a
counter weight
similar to the later
type sleeping eyes.

MARCHAL, 1863-   Ed. Marchal of Paris was listed as a toy maker in
1863. Marchal & Buffard, doll makers of Paris, were awarded a medal
of merit at the 1873 Vienna Exhibition for their display of mechanical dolls. They were still listed as doll makers in 1879. C.
Marchal was listed as the successor of Maison Schneider in the 1895
Paris Directory. (see Schneider)

MARSH, 1865-   William Marsh, doll maker,
was listed in the London Directory for
1865. Later, from 1878 through 1894,
Charles Marsh, at a different London
address, was listed as a maker of wax
dolls and wax over papier-mâché dolls.
From 1895 to 1901 Charles's wife, Mrs.
Mary Ann Marsh, headed the business.

MARTIN, 1874-   Dexter Martin and his son,
Frank D. Martin, were making wooden toys
in North Springfield, Vermont as early as
1874. In 1878 Martin and Patten were listed as doll makers in North Springfield.
The following year, 1879, the Jointed Doll
Co. was first listed in Springfield as a
manufacturer of patented jointed dolls and
patented multiple tops. In this same year
Frank D. Martin, born 1846, was listed in
North Springfield without his father. Col.
William H. H. Slack, born 1844, treasurer
of the Jointed Doll Co. was listed with

Marsh Marks

J. N. Patten, also an officer of the Company. In 1878 Frank D.
Martin had applied for an American patent which he obtained on
April 29, 1879 for ball and socket joints secured by rivets. The
Jointed Doll Co. appears in the directories from 1879 through 1881
only, but Frank D. Martin was listed as making dolls in North
Springfield as late as 1885. Markings on dolls of this company
show that they used not only the Martin patent but also later
American patents of George W. Sanders, dated Dec. 7, 1880 and of
Col. Charles C. Johnson dated Nov. 7, 1882. Both Col. Johnson
and Col. Slack were Civil War veterans. When Col. Johnson came to
Springfield in 1865 he worked for Joel Ellis in the firm that later
became the Vermont Novelty Works. Charles Johnson had also invented
a toy hoop with a figure inside that walked as the hoop turned.
Sanders assigned his patent to W. H. H. Slack, the treasurer of the
Jointed Doll Co. The Johnson patent for a molded "plastic" (composition) material head over a wooden core is similar to the 1881
patent of Mason and Taylor but sufficiently different to suggest
that the Jointed Doll Co. and Mason may have been rival doll makers.
Dolls were usually 11½" tall but are known to exist as large as 18".
    The mark is a black band around the waist of the doll inscribed
with: "Improved Jointed Doll pat. April 29, '79
        Dec. 7, '80, & Nov. 7, '82."
DOLL COLLECTORS OF AMERICA, 1942, p. 69 shows an advertizement of the
Jointed Doll Co. with an illustration of their doll.

MARTIN, 1863-   Benoit Martin of Paris obtained a French patent for a
    mechanical doll in 1863. Elie Martin of Paris was listed as a doll
    maker in the 1867 Paris Directory. He was most famous for his mechan-
    ical swimming doll bearing the trade name "Ondine". For this mechan-
    ical doll he obtained a French patent in 1876 and a U.S., English,
    and German patent all in 1878. Charles Bertan was the agent who
    obtained this patent in England. Martin was one of the exhibitors
    at the Paris Exposition of 1878 and he received a certificate for
    his display at Melbourne in 1880. His interest in mechanical water
    toys led him to be credited with a French patent in 1879 for an
    "automatic amphibious frog". In France in 1881 he patented a doll
    that jumped rope. His advertizement that year included "a box with
    a religious figure" as well as "Ondine". He won the gold medal at
    Amsterdam in 1883. Elie Martin was named the
    inventor of the swimming doll and the "Lilli-
    putiens" in his 1890 advertizement. Also this
    advertizement credited him with fourteen French
    or foreign patents and gold and silver medal
    awards. After 1890 Elie Martin seems to dis-
    appear from the records and instead we find
    Fernand Martin making mechanical dolls which he
    exhibited in Chicago in 1893; in Paris in 1900,
    where he was a member of the Jury; and in St.
    Louis in 1904. He obtained English patents for
    mechanical dolls in 1899 and 1900. The 1900
    patent was for a clockwork walking doll.

Elie Martin
Mark

MASON, 1852-   Henry Hubbard Mason, born 1821, came to Springfield,
    Vermont in 1844. In 1852 D. M. Smith & Co. was formed with Mason,
    David M. Smith, Aldin Hamlin Whitmore and Albert Brown as partners.
    Joel Ellis (see Ellis) joined this partnership in 1856 but did not
    stay. The company made a variety of products especially the spring
    clothes pins and other items patented by Smith. By 1869 Mason
    joined D. M. Smith to form Smith, Mason & Co. This company, which
    later made mopheads patented by Luke Taylor and other products, was
    still in business in 1894. Luke Taylor, born 1829, came to Spring-
    field in 1872 and operated a wood-turning business in connection
    with the manufacturing of machinery until he died in 1893. Probably
    some of the first machinery made by Taylor in Springfield was used
    by Joel Ellis to manufacture his jointed dolls. After Ellis left
    Springfield in 1878 the D. M. Smith & Co. began to make jointed
    wooden dollsand from 1880 through 1886 they were listed in the

directories as jointed doll makers. Probably Mason was the member of this firm who was most interested in doll manufacturing. Mason and Taylor combined their talents and ingenuity and on May 31, 1881 they obtained an American patent for the improvement in construction of a doll's head and neck joint. This head was made of molded "plastic" (actually a sawdust type composition) over a wooden base. One type was the so-called witch or wizard doll.

The DOLL COLLECTORS OF AMERICA, 1940, p. 16 states that Mason also "tried to use china heads on wooden bodies". The Mason and Taylor joints were very similar to those patented by George Sanders, the previous year. No proof has yet come to light of a connection between the Mason dolls and those of the Jointed Doll Co. (see Martin, 1874) other than the great similarity of construction. The Mason and Taylor dolls appear to have been made on the premises of D. M. Smith & Co. Around 1885 Mason may have severed connections with D. M. Smith & Co. for in that year both D. M. Smith & Co. and H. H. Mason were listed as jointed doll makers. This is the first year Mason appears in the directory as a doll maker. Smith is not listed under "Dolls" after 1886 but Mason continued with a doll listing through 1893.

MAX & SCHUDZE, 1864-   Max & Schudze of Paris were listed in the Paris Directories for 1864 and 1873 as makers of pantins. At the Paris Expositions of 1867 and 1878 M. Schudze of Paris had displays of his dressed mechanical dolls.

MEECH, 1865-   Herbert John Meech, of London, was listed in directories between 1865 and 1887. He was doll maker to the Royal Family. He made both wax and composition dolls. In 1891 H. J. Meech was a doll maker by Royal Appointment.

H.J. MEECH
DOLL MAKER
DOLLS CLEANED & REPAIRED
50 KENNINGTON ROAD
LONDON SE.1.

MEISSEN, 1710-   A porcelain factory was founded at Meissen, Saxony, 12 miles from Dresden in 1710 under the direction of Johann Friedrich Böttger. This was the first porcelain factory in Europe

Meech mark found on a doll with an all wax head.

and one of the most famous. It was also known as Königliche Porzellan Manufaktur, a name later used by the Royal State factory at Berlin. The name Dresden is sometimes applied to the products of the Meissen factory. Luxury porcelain items are still produced at Meissen and Meissen marks have been found on doll heads. The crossed swords Meissen marks have varied through the years and many close imitations of them have been used by other porcelain factories. In some cases original moulds have passed into other hands and were fraudulently used. Actual forgeries were made by Weise of Dresden. "Meissen" is the mark of the modern firm of C. Teichert. The authentification of a true Meissen product requires a skilled expert. For futher details see GERMAN PORCELAIN, by W. B. Honey, pp. 12-16, 37-38, 47.

fig.1   fig.2   fig.3   fig. 4   fig.5   fig.6

Meissen Marks*
*note that incised numerals are mould numbers referring to an inventory started in 1763.

MERLE, 1878   M. A. Merle of Paris displayed dolls called "mignonnes" at the Paris Exposition of 1878.

METROPOLITAN INDIA RUBBER & VULCANITE CO., 1870   The Metropolitan India Rubber and Vulcanite Co. of London was making India rubber dolls in 1870 according to the London Directory.

METZLER, 1864-   Gebrüder (Brothers) Metzler & Ortloff of Ilmenau, Thuringia were listed in directories from 1864 through 1891 as owners of a porcelain factory that made fine doll heads. They had agents in Hamburg and London.

Made in Germany
Metzler.
8 90
E 8 M

Metzler mark

MONROE, 1875   Ansil W. Monroe of Rahway, New Jersey secured a U.S. patent in 1875 for a doll of hard rubber with a round neck which was to be attached to the torso of the doll with an elastic band. The hard rubber head was to have an angora wig.

MONTANARI, 1851-   Madame Augusta Montanari of London won a prize medal for her display of dolls at the Great Exhibition of London in 1851. The report of the Jury reads: "Display of this Exhibitor is the most remarkable and beautiful col- lection of toys in the Great Exhib- ition. It is a series of dolls representing all ages, from infancy to womanhood arranged in several family groups with suitable and elegant model furniture. The dolls have hair, eyelashes, and eyelids

Parian Bisque Doll, ca.1869
Photo by G. Angione

separately inserted in wax....a variety of expressions are given to the figures in regard to the ages and stations which they are intended to represent. The dolls are adapted for children of the wealthy rather than general sale, undressed dolls sell from 10 shillings to 105 shillings (about $2.50 to $26.00), dressed dolls are much more expensive. In a small case adjoining the wax dolls are displayed several rag dolls which are very remarkable produc- tions, considering the material of which they are made. They consist entirely of textile fabrics, and the dolls are well adapted for the nursery, are reasonable in price, varying from 6 shillings 6 pence to 30 shillings (about $1.60 to $7.50) per doll including dresses." The official catalog, besides listing Augusta Montanari as a manufacturer of model wax dolls, the hair being inserted into the head, eyelashes and eyebrows and varying in size, also listed Napoleon Montanari at the same address. His displays included a collection of wax figures and tableaux representing:
    12 civilized Indians of Mexico
    12 savage Indians called Mecos
    4 Blacks at different occupations
    2 statues of Oceola, celebrated Seminole Indian Chief of Florida
    Anatomical specimen portraying the last hour of life in con-
       sumption
    North American Indian preparing to scalp a white traveller
    Indian carrying away a white child
    Indian hunting the tiger, etc.
Another exhibitor was Allessandro Montanari, an architectural dec- orator of Milan, Austria (now Italy), who exhibited an elaborate vaulted library ceiling at the 1851 London Exhibition but his relationship, if any, to Napoleon Montanari is unknown.
   The Montanaris appear to have been a very talented family and it is interesting to note that Napoleon Montanari was listed as Esquire in the London Directory which suggests that they were either of peerage descent or that Napoleon held a public office. At the 1855 Paris Exposition Madame Montanari showed dressed wax dolls and claimed that

the wax would resist temperature of hot countries and being washed
with alkaline water. Napoleon Montanari again showed his wax figures of Mexican and North American Indians. Also at this Exposition
Richard Montanari showed dressed dolls of linen. Only Augusta
Montanari displayed at the London Exhibition of 1862 and the catalog
lists for her "model wax dolls with all modern improvements, model
rag dolls". She appeared in the London Directories as a wax doll
maker as late as 1865 and Richard Montanari was listed as a wax doll
maker in London at least until 1884. At the 1878
Paris Exposition Richard Montanari of London appears to have been the only doll maker from England. *Montanari*
Also at this 1878 Exposition C. Montanari of Paris
exhibited dolls and Indian figures.   Montanari Mark

MONTRÉER, 1867-   Montréer (LeMontréer), a Paris agent for toy and
doll makers in Sonneberg, Nürnberg, Furth, Saxony, Württemberg, etc.,
appears in Paris Directories as early as 1867. His stock included
porcelain goods from Lauscha. The guaranteed talking bébés he carried sold from 25 francs ($5.00) a dozen and up. In 1895 LeMontréer
Frères (Brothers) were listed as a wholesale dealers of toys. And
by 1919 D. LeMontréer was the director of "Comptoir de la Fantasie"
whose mark, "Le Victorieux" had been registered in 1914.

MORODER, 1873-   Gebrüder (Brothers) Moroder of St.
Ulrich, Gröden Tirol (Grödner Tal), Austria had a
display at the 1873 Vienna Exhibition. They showed
wooden dolls at the 1878 Paris Exposition.

MORRELL, 1870-   Horace W. Morrell of London made
dolls in 1870. Beginning around 1878 Charles Morrell
was listed as making dressed and undressed dolls.
                          Meanwhile at the same address
                          Mrs. Jane Arundel Morrell ran
                          a doll warehouse from 1879 to

| CHARLES MORRELL |
| 50 BURLINGTON ARCADE |
| LONDON |

1884. The London Directories
listed Charles Morrell at
least until 1916. In 1894
Charles Morrell sold imports

        Morrell Mark   from France, Germany and Aus-
                              tria and exported goods to all
                              parts of the world.

Peg wooden
doll such as
those made
by Moroder

MOST, 1860-   G. H. Most of Paris was issued a French doll patent in
1860. In 1867 and 1873 he advertized doll heads of German composition; porcelain doll heads and arms; nankeen (cotton) body dolls;
talking bébés and the latest novelties for dolls.

MOTSCHMANN & HÜFNER, 1879-   Motschmann & P. Hüfner of Sonneberg,
Thuringia were commended for their doll display at the 1879 Sidney
Exhibition. In 1886 they obtained a French patent for doll improvements. A German Directory for 1898 lists their products as "täuflinge" (baby dolls) and dressed dolls.

MÖWES, 1844   J. E. Möwes, Jr. of Berlin displayed wax dolls in
costume at the 1844 Berlin Exhibition.

MÜLLER, 1851   C. A. Müller & Co. of Oberleutensdorf, Bohemia,
Austria was cited with an Honorable Mention for their papier-mâché
dolls which they displayed at the 1851 London Exhibition. Their
boxes ranged from 11 pence (23¢) to ten shillings 6 pence ($2.60)
depending on the number and elaborateness of the dolls. The most
costly contained three huntsmen with their dogs, etc.

MÜLLER, 1863-   C. G. Müller & Son of Sonneberg, Thuringia were
listed in directories from 1863 through 1893. They displayed dolls
at the 1873 Vienna Exhibition. In 1898 Carl Müller owned the Sonne-
berger Porzellan Fabrik but his relationship with the above, if any,

is not known. (see J. F. Müller)

MÜLLER, 1873-   Müller Frères (Brothers) of Paris in 1873 were
dealers for German toys. In 1879 A. Müller was making dolls and
bébés in Paris. Müller & Delattre won a bronze medal for their
doll exhibit at the 1900 Paris Exposition.

MÜLLER, 1863-   J. F. Müller & Strassburger of Sonneberg, Thuringia
were listed in directories from 1863 through 1893. Gottschalk represented them in Paris in the 1860's. They displayed dolls at the
1873 Vienna Exhibition and the 1880 Melbourne Exhibition. It is not
known whether Müller & Fröbel of Sonneberg who exhibited dolls at
Paris in 1900 and at St. Louis in 1904 were connected with any of
the earlier Müllers. (see C. G. Müller)

MÜLLER, 1867   T. U. Müller of Detroit, Michigan was making doll
heads of cassia   (cassia is a type of tree or shrub,) in 1867
according to the Detroit Directory.

MUNIER, 1842-   Madame Munier of Paris was listed in the Paris
Directories in 1842 and 1843 as a doll maker.

MUNN, 1863   John Bently Munn of Montclair, New Jersey secured an
English patent in 1863 for an automatic walking doll. Joseph Alvin
Munn and Jonathan Davis Cobb, London merchants, were his agents.

N

NADAUD, 1878   Mademoiselle A. Nadaud of Paris exhibited dolls in the
1878 Paris Exposition.

NATIONAL TOY CO., 1871-   The National Toy Co. of New York City secured an English patent in 1871 for a crawling doll. This doll
which worked with a clockwork mechanism moved its head and made
inarticulate sounds. This firm was listed in the New York Business
Directory in 1872 and 1873.

NEUBRONNER, 1851-   Gustav Neubronner of Frankenthal, Bavaria, doll
manufacturer, displayed six elegantly dressed children's dolls at
the Great London Exhibition of 1851. He appeared in directories as
late as 1908 and specialized in dressed dolls, which he exported.

NEWARK INDIA RUBBER MANUFACTURING CO., 1849-   Around 1849 the Newark
India Rubber Manufacturing Co. of Newark, New Jersey was making rub-
ber toys. But after 1853 they also made dolls according to McClintock
TOYS IN AMERICA, p. 459.

NEW YORK RUBBER CO., 1851-   The New York Rubber Co. of New York City
made rubber dolls under the Goodyear patent of 1851. They obtained
a U.S. patent for improving rubber products in 1854. At the 1876
Philadelphia Exhibition they showed their dolls. The New York Rubber
Co. was listed in the New York Business Directories from 1881 into
the 20th century. In 1915 John P. Rider (1835-1915), President of
the company, died. For dolls marked: "Goodyear's Pat. May 6, 1851
Ext. 1865" see Lee.

NICHOLSON, 1869   Andrew W. Nicholson of Brooklyn, New York was
granted a U.S. patent in 1869 for a walking doll.

NÖTHLICH, 1862   Nöthlich & Otto Richard Falk of Neustadt, Bavaria
won a prize medal for their papier-mâché dolls shown at the 1862
London Exhibition.

NYMPHENBURG, 1753-   The State porcelain factory of Bavaria was
located at Neudeck from 1753 to 1761 when it was moved to the palace

grounds at Nymphenburg. In 1862 it was leased to a private company and it was in existence at least until World War II. As with Meissen there is a need to check the authenticity of products having the Nymphenburg marks. The "C. T." and other Frankenthal marks have been used at the modern Nymphenburg factory. When Frankenthal, near Mannheim, Bavaria closed in 1799 part of its moulds were removed to Nymphenburg.

Nymphenburg Marks

O

OGILWY, 1843   Robert Ogilwy of London was making composition dolls between 1843 and 1848. By 1852 the firm of Ogilwy and Teather were making wax dolls. Then around 1856 the partnership seems to have been dissolved for Robert Ogilwy was making wax and composition dolls until 1860 and George Teather was making wax dolls in 1856 according to London Directories.

P

PANNIER, 1872-   Monsieur Pannier of Paris was issued a French patent in 1872 for a bébé or doll with a metal frame and joints. Madame Blanche Pannier of the Paris Maison de la Pannier was awarded a medal of co-operation for her display at the Vienna Exhibition of 1873. For the same year Madame Pannier was listed in the Paris Directory as a maker of wigs, hats and clothes for dolls. In the 1878 Paris Exhibition Madame Pannier showed doll hats. There was also a Pannier display at the 1883 Amsterdam Exhibition. In 1885 and 1890 the Pannier advertizement stated that they made bébés and dolls.

PARENT, 1872   Ch. Parent was issued a U.S. patent in 1872 for a jointed doll having mechanisms for moving parts.

PAUFLER, 1876-   Emil Paufler & Co. of Schneeberg, Saxony was founded in 1876. During the 1890's this firm advertized unbreakable doll heads of "Masse Holz" and jointed dressed and undressed dolls. Emil Paufler & Co. was listed in the directories through 1907.

PAYNE, 1849   John Edward Payne of London was granted an English patent in 1849. It was for a process of moulding a child's doll out of gutta percha combined with India rubber.

PEACOCK, 1862-   Thomas Peacock of London exhibited wax and composition dolls in the London Exhibition of 1862. He advertized that he always had a stock of 1,000 dolls both dressed and undressed. These included all kinds of composition dolls and wax dolls. He used wax doll heads made by the Pierotti family. (see Pierotti) Peacock's wholesale prices were from one to five pounds ($5 to

Wax over composition heads, glass eyes, wooden limbs, cloth bodies.

$25) for each doll.

PÉAN, 1862-   Laurent Marie René Péan of Paris was granted two patents in 1862. One was an Austrian patent and the other was an English patent for a doll whose movement was initiated by compressed air. The 1863 Paris Directory listed L. Péan as a dealer of tops and toys. In 1885 Péan Frères (Brothers) were members of the Jury at the Antwerp Exhibition and their display was Hors Concours. Again in 1889 at the Paris Exposition Péan Frères (Brothers) were given an Hors Concours for their display. The 1890 advertizement for Péan Frères (Brothers) lists them as successors to Maison Lt. Péan, A. Lambert & Co., Perry Fils (Sons), Guillet Frères (Brothers) and Cuny Radet of Lyon. They manufactured at their factory at Criel, Oise toys in metal, and cardboard, as well as in porcelain and faience. They also carried doll furnishings. Péan Frères (Brothers) was the number one company in the Chambre Syndicale de Fabricants de Jouets Francais, which was formed prior to 1890. (see Chambre Syndicale de Fabricants de Jouets Francais) At this time their mark was "P.F."

PEGARD, 1842-   Pegard was listed in the 1842 and 1843 Paris Directories as a toy maker. By 1847 his listing was that of a doll maker.

PETIT, 1790-   Jacob Petit established a porcelain factory in 1790 at Belleville, France. Later he moved to Paris. In an effort to compete with the German doll heads of porcelain that were appearing on the French market Jacob Petit obtained in 1843 a French patent for the making of porcelain doll heads. He appeared in the Paris Directory as late as 1853, the year in which he also obtained an English patent for an improvement in the manufacture of porcelain. The length of time from 1790 to 1853 suggests the possibility that there was Jacob Petit, Sr. and Jr. From 1863 to 1881 Fred Petit and Widow Petit were listed in the Paris Directories as toy makers but at a different address. Their relationship to Jacob Petit is not known nor is their relationship to Petit & Dumontier (Dumaitier) who had an exhibit at the 1878 Paris Exposition, and who advertized from 1879 through 1890, "Unbreakable dolls, registered models, and talking bébés, unbreakable with jointed hands."

J P

PAR BREVET

Jacob Petit
Mark- found
in blue

PIEROTTI, 1780-   The Pierotti family made wax dolls for over a century in the London area. Dominic Pierotti, the founder of the family in England came there about 1780. He was an artist of architectural ornaments and according to family tradition he also made wax dolls as did his son Enrico. It is believed that Enrico Pierotti made solid wax doll heads with imbedded hair. The London Directory for 1847 listed Henry Pierotti as both a wax doll maker and a composition doll maker. Also in 1847 John Dominic Pierotti was listed as a plaster figure maker but in later directories he is a doll maker. At the London Exhibition of 1862 Henry Pierotti displayed "wax model dolls with inserted hair, dolls and wax figures". Celui Pierotti from the same address displayed "foreign and English toys". The name H. Pierotti has been found on the back of wax doll heads suggesting that in this generation Henry Pierotti was the head of the business and

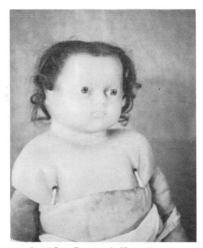

Double Poured Wax Head,
Hair inserted in groups,
Glass eyes,
Photo by G. Angione

other members of the family assisted him. The Pierotti wax dolls
had hairs inserted either singly or several at a time depending on
the quality of the doll. The women of the family are believed to
have made doll bodies which were stuffed with cow
hair. Many well-known doll companies of London
handled Pierotti dolls, among them, Aldis (see Aldis),
Aldred, Cremer (see Cremer), Hamley, Morrell (see
Morrell) and Peacock (see Peacock). The grandchildren
of Enrico Pierotti carried on the doll business until
1935. For further details see article by Lesley
Gordon, "Wax Pierotti", SPINNING WHEEL, Feb. 1957
pp. 14-17.

Pierotti

Pierotti
Mark

PITFIELD, 1875-   William Pitfield of London made wax dolls between
1875 and 1894 according to his advertizements in the London Directory.

PLUMB, 1865   Henry Plumb of London was listed as a maker of gutta
percha dolls in the 1865 London Directory.

PNEAU, 1879-   Pnèau was listed in the 1879 Paris Directory as a doll
maker at the doll shop "Au Petit Noël". It is possible that this is
the doll maker Pineau listed in the 1881 and 1882 Paris Directories.

POLITO, 1867   C. Polito of Vittoriosa, Malta displayed wax figures
at the 1867 Paris Exposition.

POND, 1875   F. L. Pond of Winchester, Connecticut was listed in the
Connecticut Business Directory for 1875 as a maker of doll bodies.

POOLE, 1843-   John R. Poole of London made wooden dolls between
1843 and 1860 according to London Directories.

POOLE, 1852-   William Poole was listed in the London Directories as
a wax doll and composition doll maker from 1852 through 1855. At
another address in London Edward Poole, making wax dolls and composition dolls also, was listed from 1854 through 1865.

POPINEAU, 1855-   Popineau of Paris in 1855 made dolls with rose kid
bodies. According to the Paris Directory he had an assortment of
fine and "half fine" dolls, and he sent dolls to the provinces.
Popineau continued to be listed as a doll maker through 1870.

POPPE, 1844-   Aug. Poppe of Coburg, Bavaria displayed papier-mâché,
mechanical and earthenware dolls at the 1844 Berlin Exhibition. One
of his dolls "represented the famous ballet dancer of the 1830's and
1840's, Fanny Elsler. Other mechanical dolls represented a Tyrolean
marksman with bows and arrows and enchanting clowns." Poppe won a
prize medal for his dolls at the 1854 Munich Exhibition. Again he
displayed his mechanical and papier-mâché dolls, this time at the
1855 Paris Exposition. In 1897 W. M. Poppe was listed as a doll
maker in Neustadt near Coburg but his relationship, if any, to Aug.
Poppe is not known.

POTIERS, 1867-   George Potiers (Potier) of Paris was awarded a
silver medal in 1867 for his doll display at the Paris Exposition.
Then at Paris in 1878 his exhibit won a gold medal. At Melbourne,
1880, he received a certificate for his mechanical dolls. Listed
in the Paris Directory for 1882 as a toy maker Potiers was using the
mark "D. S.".

POULIN, 1861   René Poulin of Paris was issued a French patent in
1861 for making doll heads and limbs. His parts were to be made of
rolled or beaten copper or zinc with or without enamel eyes. The
metal was to be painted. This was probably the beginning of dolls
with heads made of rolled metal.

PRIEUR, 1859-   L. Prieur of Paris founded a doll making firm in

1859. This firm specialized in making doll parts for French and foreign dolls. They claimed that they were the oldest house of this kind in France. They later made indestructible jointed bébés. The firm was listed under C. Prieur in 1890. In 1895 their successor was A. Ayrand. The business was still going after World War I.

PURGER, 1851-   J. B. Purger of Gröden Tirol (Grödner Tal), Austria displayed carved dolls at the 1851 London Exhibition. He carved lay figures of all sizes from pine, lime and maple wood.

Q

QUIVY, 1878-   H. Quivy of Paris showed dressed and undressed dolls in the Paris Exposition of 1878. In the Paris Directory for 1879 he was listed as a doll maker.

R

RABERY & DELPHIEU, 1856-   Jean Delphieu of Paris was granted a French patent in 1856 for the use of pink cloth instead of pink kid for doll bodies. The same year he was listed in the Paris Directory. Alexandre Rabery and A. Delphieu exhibited dressed and undressed dolls in the Paris Exposition of 1878. Then in 1879 they were advertizing that they were manufacturers of jointed dolls of all kinds, some with white or rose kid bodies, some dressed and some undressed. By 1881 they were selling dolls with wooden bodies and white or rose kid, either rigid or jointed, as well as indestructible jointed bébés or bébés with wooden bodies. Their dolls came dressed and undressed. The Rabery & Delphieu display at the 1883 Amsterdam Exhibiton received a silver medal as did the Rabery exhibit at the 1889 Paris Exposition. By 1890 A. Rabery was using the mark "R. D. " for his talking bébés and indestructible jointed bébés. In 1893 Alexandre

Fashion Type Bride Doll
White kid body

Rabery & Delphieu
Mark

Rabery was granted a French patent for a walking-talking doll, and the same year he exhibited dolls at the Chicago World's Fair. In 1898 Gentry succeeded and became head of the Rabery-Delphieu establishment. He advertized "Bébé de Paris" as well as walking, talking and sleep-eyed bébés. According to Esther Singleton in DOLLS, Rabery & Delphieu joined the S.F.B.J. in 1899. (see Jumeau)

RAU, 1844   G. F. Rau of Oberlind, near Sonneberg, Thuringia exhibited little figures of papier-mâché, such as little Swiss maidens, at the Berlin Exhibition of 1844.

RAUCH, 1863-   P. Rauch of Paris was a doll maker from 1863 through 1890. He was designated as P. Rauch, Sr. beginning in 1867. In 1878 he exhibited woolen dolls at the Paris Exposition.

REICHMANN, 1877   Lazarus Reichmann of New York secured a U.S. patent in 1877 for a doll's head. The shell of the head was to be made of bees-wax, paraffin and turpentine with an inner supporting layer of

sawdust, glue and a suitable paste such as flour paste. The doll's
head was to be given a real hair wig.

RHEINISCHE GUMMI & CELLULOID
    FABRIK CO., 1873-
Rheinische Gummi und
Celluloid Fabrik Co. of
Mannheim and Necharau,
Bavaria was founded in
1873, It is the oldest
German factory that made
celluloid dolls but not
as old as the Hyatts of
America. The turtle mark
"Schildkröte" was registered in 1889 by Rheinische
Gummi & Celluloid Fabrik
Co. This turtle mark
represented the long life
and durability of their
products. The earlier
dolls have the words "Schutz-
marke" (trade mark) as well
as the turtle. Some rubber
dolls were made as well as
celluloid. In 1905 they
obtained a German patent
for a celluloid doll head
with glass eyes. They made
celluloid dolls for J. D.
Kestner, Jr. (see Kestner)
from Kestner moulds having
both the Kestner mark and
the turtle on them. Celluloid dolls have also been
found with both the turtle
mark and the mark of Kämmer
& Reinhardt of Waltershausen
which was founded about 1885.

Rheinische Gummi und Celluloid Fabrik
Co. advertizement for celluloid dolls
1934.
Left to right: Inge, Hans, Christel
Bottom: Strampelchen

In the 20th century Rheinische Gummi & Celluloid Fabrik Co. had a
Paris agent for their "bébé celluloid". Dr. P. Hunaeus' celluloid
ware factory merged with Rheinische Gummi & Celluloid Fabrik Co.
in 1930. Their five "Schildkröte"
children of the 20th century were:
Hans, the eldest boy; Cristel, with
short hair and suitable for dressing
as a boy or girl; Barbel, a girl with
braids around her ears; Inge, a bobbed
hair girl also known as Sunbeam; and
Strampelchen (kicker), a baby.

Rheinische Gummi &
Celluloid Fabrik Co.
Marks

RICH, 1853-   William Rich of London was making wax dolls between
    1853 and 1881, according to the London Directories for those years.
    He exhibited model wax and rag dolls at the London Exhibiton of
    1862. As an artist in wax he was a member of the Berlin Repository.

ROBINS, 1843-   Joseph Robins of London made composition dolls be-
    tween 1843 and 1858. He was succeeded by William Robins who made
    composition dolls from 1859 to 1884 at the same address. In 1887
    Mrs. Harriet Robins was listed in the London Directory as a doll
    maker but she is recorded at a different address. In 1899 William
    Robins was making dolls at still a third address.

ROCK & GRANER, 1851-   Rock & Graner of Biberach, Württemberg won
    the following awards for their mechanical and papier-mâché dolls
    and toys: prize medal, 1851 London Exhibition; Honorable Mention,
    1853 New York Exhibiton; Honorable Mention, 1854 Munich Exhibition;

silver medal, 1855 Paris Exposition; prize medal, 1862 London
Exhibition; commendation, 1879 Sidney Exhibition. It is not known
what award, if any, was given them for their display at the 1873
Vienna Exhibition. Their mechanical dancer exhibited at London in
1862 sold for eight florins ($2.00). Charles Mittler & Echardt were
their London agents in 1862.

ROGERS, 1853   Henry S. Rogers of New York displayed a variety of
dressed wax and rag dolls at the New York Exhibition of 1853. For
these he was cited with an Honorable Mention.

ROHMER, 1857-   Mademoiselle Marie
Antoinette Leontine Rohmer of Paris
was issued a French patent in 1857
for articulated joints for kid
dolls with gutta percha arms. In
1858 Mademoiselle Rohmer obtained
a French patent for a new kind of
a doll head with a cord running
through the head and down into the
body to facilitate the turning of
the head in any direction and to
hold the head to the body. This
invention was to be used on dolls
with bodies of kid, cloth and gutta
percha. From 1860 to 1863 it was
Madame Rohmer who advertized patented jointed dolls but after 1867 the
listings are for Maison Rohmer.
Maison Rohmer displayed dolls and
jointed bébés at the 1867 Paris
Exposition. The advertizement of
Maison Rohmer in the 1879 Paris
Directory states that they sold
jointed kid body dolls.

Glazed Doll Head
Head turns laterally
Photo by G. Angione

Kid body
Rohmer mark found on bodies
of similar type dolls.

Rohmer Mark

ROITHNER, 1871-   Hugo Roithner & Co. of Schweidnitz, Schl., Germany
was founded in 1871 and was still in existence at the outbreak of
World War II. They made wooden dolls.

ROOKWOOD, 1880-   The Japanese pottery exhibit at Philadelphia in 1876
inspired socialite Mrs. Maria Longworth Nichols, aunt of Hon. Nicholas
Longworth to start a pottery plant in Cincinnati, Ohio with the help
of Japanese artisans. This Pottery, called Rook-
wood after the Longworth home, was established in
1880. W.W. Taylor became manager in 1883 and head
of the firm in 1890 when Maria retired after mar-
rying Congressman Bellamy Storer. Rookwood won
gold medals at exhibitions all over the world.
For further details see DOLLS, A NEW GUIDE FOR
COLLECTORS, revised, enlarged by Clara Fawcett.

Rookwood
Marks

ROSE, 1866-   William W. Rose of New York secured two English patents.
In 1866 he obtained one for metal or wooden dolls which could assume
different poses by rearranging the pieces. In 1874 he took out
another patent for improvements on the 1866 one.

ROSSIGNOL, 1878-   Charles Rossignol of Paris won a silver medal at
the Paris Exposition in 1878 for mechanical dolls. Then in 1889,

at the Paris Exposition, he was awarded a gold medal for his mechanical dolls. The U.S. report on the 1889 Exposition states, "Mr. Rossignol is another celebrated maker; it is he who by cutting out and mounting machines has succeeded in producing those very cheap mechanical toys. I think they come as low as 8 francs ($2) a gross, breadwomen, commissionnaires etc. which have had such a run and are so popular in the States. His mark 'C. R.' is well known to toy men, and his goods are largely exported to America....." At that time his agent was Ernst Ballu. In 1892 the Société Widow Charles Rossignol & Co. was granted a French patent for a mechanical turning toy. Between 1898 and 1900 the Widow Charles Rossignol & Co. was advertizing mechanical toys in the Paris Directory.

CR
Rossignol
Mark

ROSTAING, 1859   Charles Silvester Rostaing, a citizen of the United States, residing in Dresden, Germany took out an English patent in 1859. This was for a compound of gutta percha with mineral coloring and vegetable substances such as gums, tannin and essential oils to make doll heads.

ROULLET & DECAMPS, 1875-   The firm of Roullet & Decamps was founded in 1875 by Jean Roullet and Ernst Decamps. However, in 1867 Roullet was awarded a bronze medal for his display in the Paris Exposition. Then in the 1878 Paris Exposition J. Roullet won a silver medal for his mechanical dolls. In 1882 Decamps was issued a French patent to improve automatic tumbling figures. Roullet & Decamps were advertizing walking dolls that imitated natural movements in 1890. And in 1892 Roullet and Decamps were issued a French patent for a walking doll with jointed wrists. Again in 1893 Société Roullet & E. Decamps were issued a French patent for a walking doll. In this year they also exhibited at the Chicago Exhibition. Between 1895 and 1898 Roullet & E. Decamps were advertizing a mechanical walking doll with the newest patented works. They claimed it was one of the finest. By 1898 they were advertizing the doll whose name had been trademarked in 1893 by the firm "L'Intrepide Bébé". This bébé had patented mechanical works which allowed it to walk. Roullet & Decamps won a silver medal for their exhibit at the 1900 Paris Exposition. Every year from 1906 to 1909 inclusive Roullet & Decamps were awarded grand prixs for their displays at Paris Expositions. In 1908 E. Decamps's son-in-law became head of the firm. Then by 1910 the Widow E. Decamps was head of the firm. The 1914 advertizement lists the Widow Décamps & Fils (Sons) as selling mechanical toys with music. Jumeau and Simon & Halbig marked heads have been found on mechanical dolls with an "R. D." mark.

R. D.   **L'INTRÉPIDE BÉBÉ**

Trademark

Roullet & Decamps
Marks

ROUSSELOT, 1845   Jean Baptiste Alexes Rousselot was issued a French patent in 1845. This patent was for a mechanical doll which raised and lowered its arms. It was to have a hollow cardboard body with a German head having enamel eyes and teeth and the arms were to be of kid with wire supports in them. Having no legs, this head and torso was to be placed on wheels. The mechanism was to be activated by a spring; there was a copper key to wind it.

RUNGALDIER, 1843-   J. Antoine Rungaldier of Paris had a wholesale toy shop in 1843 when he advertized French and German toys, dolls, with springs, kid body dolls and dressed dolls. The 1873 listing for Rungaldier, as a doll maker, mentions dressed dolls of all kinds and in 1879 he was handling dolls and bébés both dressed and undressed. For 1885 the advertizement entered under the name of Rungaldier & Foucault included dolls and bébés. Rungaldier displayed dolls at the 1889 Paris Exposition and Rungaldier alone advertized in 1889 but in 1890 Foucault was again advertizing with Rungaldier. At this time they were agents for wholesale French and foreign toys.

S

SALLEE, 1865   Lucretia E. Sallee of Decatur, Illinois secured a U.S. patent in 1865 for a method of constructing doll heads from leather covered with composition.

SCAILLIET, 1842-   Scailliet of Paris was listed as a doll maker in the Paris Directories from 1842 through 1847.

SCHAFFT, 1863-   G. Schafft of Waltershausen, Thuringia was listed in directories from 1863 through 1874 as a papier-mâché doll maker. This firm merged with Wislizenus (see Wislizenus) after 1874.

SCHANNE, 1842-   Schanne, Sr. of Paris was listed in the 1842 Paris Directory as a toy maker. But from 1843 to 1873 he was listed as a doll maker. A. Schanne exhibited dolls at the Paris Exposition in 1867 and he was listed as a doll maker from 1879 to 1885 in the Paris Directories. But in 1895 the Schanne advertizement returns to that of a toy maker.

SCHEIFELE, 1853   G. S. Scheifele of New York exhibited mechanical toys from Austria at the 1853 New York Exhibition. His display was cited with an Honorable Mention.

SCHLESINGER, 1875-   Leo Schlesinger & Co. of New York City was founded in 1875. They displayed mechanical toys of tin and pewter at three international Exhibitions: Paris 1878, Sidney 1879, and Melbourne 1880. At Sidney the firm was cited with an Honorable Mention for their well made and cheap products. The firm was in operation at least as late as 1916.

SCHMETZER, 1875-   Louis Schmetzer of Chicago, Illinois, but residing in Rothenburg, Bavaria obtained an English patent in 1875 for a doll. The specifications called for pieces of wood that would fit together to form a jointed doll. Late in 1875 he was issued a French patent for clothing for the jointed doll which would hide the joint pegs. In 1876 he secured an English patent for the clothing.

SCHMEY, 1853-   Gustavus Schmey of Sonneberg, Thuringia founded a doll factory in 1853. The successors of Gustavus Schmey during the 1890's also had another factory at Coburg, Bavaria. In 1895 they made jointed bébés, dressed and undressed, wax dolls and composition dolls. They had a London and Paris branch. J. F. O. Michaelis was their Paris representative. At the 1900 Paris Exposition the successors of G. Schmey were one of the grand prix winners for their dolls. They also had a display at the 1904 St. Louis Exhibition. This firm survived the First World War.

SCHMITT, 1863-   Schmitt of Paris in 1863 dealt with wholesale toys. By 1867 the firm was listed as makers of children's toys. In 1877 Schmitt & Fils (Sons), Maurice and Charles, were granted a French patent for decorating porcelain shoulder heads for dolls and bébés. This was an improved method which would permit any desired shades and colors to be given to a bisque head. Schmitt & Fils (Sons) was awarded a silver medal at the 1878 Paris Exposition for their dolls and bébés. Then in 1879 the firm was issued another French patent

for what may have been the first
jointed all bisque bébés. The next
patent obtained by Schmitt & Fils
(Sons) was in 1883. This was for a
layer of wax to be applied to bisque
doll and bébé heads after they had
left the kilns. It was believed
this would improve their appearance
and make the dolls more durable.
Other patents granted to the Schmitt
firm were for: 1885, eye movement in
dolls; 1887, doll improvements; and
1891, a new method for making doll
heads. From 1879 to 1890 Schmitt &
Fils (Sons), doll makers, advertized
as their speciality, an indestructible
jointed bébé called "Bébé Schmitt".
These were exported as well as being
sold on the domestic market. In 1885
the Schmitt factory was located at
Nogent-sur-Marne, Seine.

Bébé Schmitt on left
S.F.B.J. bébé on right

Courtesy of Kitty Smith

Schmidt- Records have not been
found for any German doll makers
named Schmidt (Schmitt in French,
Schmidt in German) prior to 1880 but
the following list should help to
distinguish German Schmidts from the
earlier Schmitt of Paris. Bruno
Schmidt, 1900- of Waltershausen; C.A.
Schmidt, 1907- of Lichte; Edward
Schmidt, 1904- of Coburg; Franz
Schmidt, 1890- of Georgenthal; H.
Schmidt, 1909- of Coburg; Karl Schmidt, 1907 of Waltershausen; Oscar
Julius Schmidt, 1887- of Sonneberg. There was also a Peter Schmidt,
1880- of Philadelphia, Pennsylvania who made doll bodies.

Mark of Schmitt
of Paris

Mark of Bruno Schmidt
of Waltershausen

SCHNEIDER, 1858-   The Schneider firm (see Serre) of Paris was founded in 1858. Between 1865 and 1873 it was specializing in dolls,
porcelain doll head and doll bodies of rose kid and cloth. Some dolls
were exported. Between 1879 and 1890 their advertizement was similar
to the above except that the dolls were jointed, and the kid bodies
were made in rose and white colors. In 1885 the firm was known as
Schneider Fils. Benoist Schneider Jne. appeared in the 1888 listing and
the mark was "S F". By 1895 C. Marchal was listed as the successor of
Maison Schneider. B. Schneider was listed in the 1896 Paris Directory.

SCHOENHUT, 1872-   Albert Schoenhut established a toy factory in
Philadelphia, Pennsylvania in 1872. He patented circus figures in
the United States in 1903, followed by "Rolly Dolly" in 1908 and
wooden character dolls in 1911. These latter were labled "All Wood
Perfection Art Dolls" and were made until around 1925. In 1911
Schoenhut registered a trademark for "Schnickel Fritz" and "Tootsie
Wootsie". The advertizement for Schoenhut in 1911 states: "Our
extensive plant, the largest in the world devoted exclusively to
the manufacture of toys." They employed from 800 to 1,000
during the busy season. Albert Schoenhut died in 1912 and the firm
A. Schoenhut & Co. was carried on by his sons. One of these sons,

Henry Edison Schoenhut, copyrighted a baby doll's head in 1913. The firm obtained a U. S. patent for doll eyes in 1921. For further details see ANTIQUES JOURNAL, June 1963, pp. 22-24.

Schoenhut Mark

SCHOLZ, 1866-   Paul Scholz of Vienna, Austria headed a firm founded in 1866 which produced papier-mâché products. At the Vienna Exhibition of 1873 Scholz displayed papier-mâché dolls.

SCHÜNEMANN, 1876-   L. Schünemann of Madgeburg, Germany displayed dressed dolls at the 1876 Philadelphia Exhibiton. His products were commended for their fine and various dresses and good workmanship. Schunemann was still in business in 1908.

SCOTT, 1856   William Scott of London was listed in the 1856 London Directory as a maker of gutta percha dolls.

SEHM, 1869-   Matilde Sehm of Guben, Brandenburg (Prussia) founded a doll factory in 1869. In 1891 M. Sehm made dressed dolls and in 1907 she advertized jointed bisque dolls and celluloid dolls. Walter Sehm and his sons, Werner and August Sehm directed the firm in 1928.

SELZEN, 1844   Selzen of Hanover, Prussia showed doll bodies at the Berlin Exhibition of 1844.

SERRE & SCHNEIDER, 1867-   Serre & Schneider (see Schneider) were listed in the Paris Directories for 1867 and 1873 as making jointed dolls, kid body dolls and porcelain heads. In 1904 at the St. Louis Exhibition J. du Serre showed jointed bébés.

SÈVRES, 1738-   Manufacture Nationale de Sèvres was founded in 1738

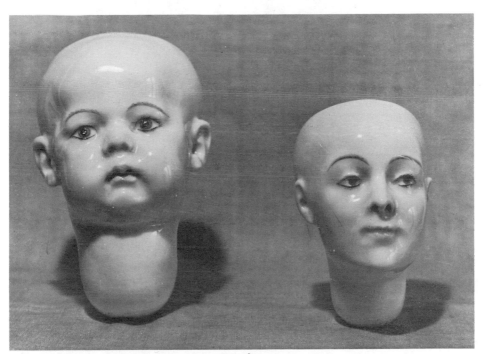

Doll heads made at Sèvres in 1917.

Courtesy: Musée Des Arts Décoratifs, Louvre, Paris

Doll with head of Sèvres Porcelain
Courtesy Musée des Arts Décoratifs, Louvre, Paris

Doll made in 1916, displayed at Exposition of French Art
in 1918, then sent to the Musée des Arts Décoratifs, Louvre,
Paris. Doll head in hard paste porcelain of Sèvres covered
with a glaze. The eyes, the eyebrows and the eyelashes are
painted naturally; cheeks and lips are lightly tinted.

at Vincennes which adjoins Montreuil-sous-Bois where many later doll factories were located. In 1756 the factory was moved to the town of Sèvres which provided its present name. This is the State porcelain factory which includes laboratories for studies of the best technical processes. Commercial dolls in series were never made at Sèvres but French doll companies have used the facilities of Sèvres to improve their products. The official United States Report of the 1889 Paris Exposition describes the Jumeau doll as follows: " These are French dolls unmistakably. The heads are Sèvres porcelain painted by real artists." Monsieur Bauduy, Director of the Manufacture Nationale de Sèvres wrote on Nov. 5, 1962, "At this time, 1915-1916, the benefactors of our counsel were the houses of Verlingue at Boulogne -sur-Mer, Lanternier at Limoges, and Coiffe, Couty & Co. at Limoges, 21 Rue Jules Noriac". The last two companies were old and are discussed in detail under their own names. J. Verlingue built a factory at Boulogne-sur-Mer after World War I had started. This factory produced a large number of porcelain doll heads and mignonettes. By 1919 Verlingue was director of the Société de l'Anc. Faïencerie in Boulogne as well as a factory at Montreuil-sous-Bois. The Bauduy letter continues "Our archives .... record that a small number of doll heads, modeled after certain heads of children of the 18th and 19th century were made in our workshop in 1917/18 as experiments. It was a question then of creating a 'French doll's head' in opposition to the 'German doll's head' which had inundated the European market before the war of 1914-1918.
"These models, sent to the Museum of Decorative Arts in Paris, in 1918 have been kept there, after having been on display in an Exposition of French Art at the Pavillion of Marsan in Paris in 1918." (See Coiffe and Lanternier for additional pictures of these Sèvres doll heads.)

SHIELDS, 1843-   John Shields of London made composition dolls between 1843 and 1848. In 1852 and 1853 Mrs. M. Shields is found in the London Directories as a maker of wax dolls. Both these Shields worked at the same address. Later in Philadelphia, Pennsylvania Joseph R. Shields was recorded as a maker of toys in the directories for 1860 and 1861.

SICHLING, 1876   Heinrich Sichling of Nürnberg, Bavaria, showed dressed dolls at the 1876 Philadelphia Exhibition. His dolls, designed for the wholesale trade, were commended for their fine finish, their cheapness and variety.

SIMAR & FLANTIN, 1842-   The firm of Simar & Flantin of Paris was making doll moulds between 1842 and 1847. By 1855 the Widow Flantin had become head of the company.

SIMON, 1867-   G. Simon of Hildburghausen, Thuringia displayed dolls at the 1867 Paris Exposition. In 1897 Wilhelm Simon & Co. of Hildburghausen was listed as a porcelain factory specialising in dolls. It is possible that these Simons of Hildburghausen were related to Simon of Simon & Halbig, a famous firm in Gräfenhain near Ohrdruf, (about 25 miles from Hildburghausen) which also specialized in porcelain doll heads. Early types of bisque heads have been found marked "S. H." but no documented reference to Simon & Halbig prior to 1890 has been discovered as of yet.

S11 H719 DEP

// S H 1039   S & H

DEP   1160   SIMON & HALBIG

Simon & Halbig Marks

SIMON, 1847-   P. Simon of Paris was listed in 1847 and 1855 as the successor of Roulez & P. Simon, an establishment which had dealt in German and French dolls and porcelain doll heads.

SIMONNE, 1863-   F. Simonne, listed in the Paris
Directories from 1863 through 1873 as a maker of
dolls and dressed bébés, was an exhibitor at the
Paris Exposition of 1867 where he displayed mechanical dolls. Simonne was credited with an Honorable
Mention for this display. Simonne also showed dolls
and bébés at the Paris Exposition of 1878.

Simonne Mark

SLAUGHTER, 1763   Mary Slaughter of London was recorded in the London
Directory for 1763 as a modeler of portraits in wax.

SMITH, 1763   Joachim Smith of London was listed in the 1763 London
Directory as a modeler of portraits in miniature in wax.

SMITH, 1856   Sampson Smith of Longton, Staffordshire, England was
listed as a china toy manufacturer in an 1856 Directory. Doll heads
would seem to be a principle type of china toy. (see Townsend)

SNOWBALL, 1855   Mrs. S. Snowball of London was listed in the 1855
London Directory as a wax doll maker.

SORET, 1847   Jean Pierre Soret of Paris was granted a French patent
in 1847 for making papier-mâché heads for bébés and for "modistes"
(milliners) model dolls. Up to this time, the patent paper stated,
French products of this sort had been inferior to similar German
products. Soret was found in the 1847 Paris Directory but not under
the doll classification.

SPAYD, 1877   Benjamin F. Spayd of Philadelphia, Pennsylvania secured
a U.S. patent in 1877 for a toy dancer.

STEINER, 1855-   Jules Nicholas
Steiner founded the Steiner doll
making firm in Paris in 1855. Like
Bru he obtained many patents but
the Steiner patents seem to pertain
more closely to dolls than those of
Bru. In 1862 Steiner obtained a
French patent for an automatic talking bébé and in 1863 a French patent for a mechanical doll. A
mechanical Steiner doll has been
found with a label dated Dec. 6,
1867 which suggests that the firm
obtained another patent at that
time. From 1864 through 1873
Steiner advertized that he specialized in patented talking, mechanical
and jointed dolls and bébés. At
the 1878 Paris Exposition Steiner
showed mechanical talking bébés.
Like Bru, Steiner received a silver
medal for his exhibit about which
the Jury in its official report
wrote, "We must not forget to cite
the talking bébé. The manufacturer
who is almost the only one in
France to produce this toy has
turned out bébés perfectly made and
amazingly lifelike.
"We notice also among the products
of this manufacturer of dolls and
bébés, some made chiefly of rubber.
We are persuaded that there would
be in this case a great improvement
if they were able to apply hard
rubber to a certain extent and thus

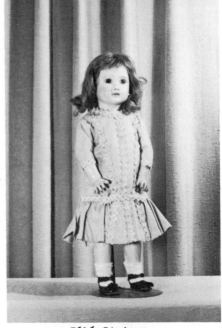

Bébé Steiner
Closed Mouth
Unjointed Wrists

Courtesy of Kitty Smith

produce dolls having the advantage of being solid." Steiner continued his efforts to improve his dolls and his applications for patents
poured in. He obtained in 1880 both French and German patents for
moving eyes in dolls and bébés which he claimed was an improvement
over the counterweights which had been used up to that date. In 1881
there was another French patent for improving doll eyes. In 1884
Steiner obtained a French patent for a method of molding dolls and
bébés out of pasteboard by the use of compressed air. In 1889 he
obtained a patent for improving porcelain and bisque heads for indestructible jointed bébés and dolls. At the Paris Exhibition in
1889 Steiner received a gold medal for his exhibit which "followed
in the same lines as M. Jumeau". Also in 1889 Steiner registered as
a French trademark the girl with a banner. The following year,
1890, at the Paris Exposition Steiner received the Diplome d'Honneur.

The 1890 Steiner advertizement in the Paris Directory states that
he was the inventor of the Bébé in France. But this allegation
might be questioned because Soret of Paris mentioned bébés in his
1847 French patent and Fr. Alph. Greffier from Nantes, France had
exhibited bébés in the 1855 Paris Exposition, the year in which the
Steiner firm was founded. In 1890 Steiner advertized, "'Mama' and
'Papa' talking dolls, mechanical dolls, indestructible jointed bébés
with eyes that move when it pleases and jointed wrists. All these
bébés are put together with excellent articulation, lightness and
incomparable build. It is impossible to confound them with dolls of
German make." The last patent found for Steiner was in 1890 when he
obtained a French patent for walking dolls with clockwork mechanism
which he named "Bébé Premier Pas" (Baby First Step) and "Bébé Marcheur". The last record found for an exhibit by Steiner was the
Paris Exposition of 1891 where he was honored with Hors Concours as
a member of the Jury. Unlike Bru all of the awards and honors seem
to have come to the Steiner firm while the founder Jules Nicholas
Steiner was in charge.

By 1892 Amedee Lafosse had succeeded as the head of the Steiner
firm. He advertized in the Paris Directory that the firm owned
twenty-four patents and made five categories of indestructible bébés,
talking and ordinary, sleeping eyes, jointed wrists, mechanical and
walking. These bébés had heavy bisque heads "unbreakable" and were
named "Le Parisien" and "Premier Pas". The factory was at 60 Rue d'
Avron, Paris. Lafosse registered the trademark "Le Parisien" in
1892. In the same year, 1892, he obtained a French patent on talking
bellows for dolls. Lafosse appears to have died shortly after be-
coming head of the Steiner firm for in 1893 it is the Widow Lafosse
who obtained a French patent for a walky-talky doll. The maiden
name of Madame Lafosse was Marie Lambert. It is possible that she
was related to Leopold Lambert of Paris who made mechanical dolls,
1888-1894 and used "L. B." as his mark. In 1894 Widow Lafosse was
granted a French patent for a walking doll with a head that moved.
By 1895 she was using the French trademark "Bébé Phenix". This
trade name had been used by Henri Alexandre in 1890 and by his successor, Tourrel, in 1892 which suggests that Widow Lafosse may have
taken over the Alexandre business. In 1897 Widow Lafosse obtained
another French patent for a kiss throwing and talking doll and the
following year she was granted yet another French patent for improving doll heads and limbs. At this time she advertized that the
Steiner firm owned thirty patents.

Jules Mettais succeeded the Widow Lafosse in 1899. He may have
been the Mettais, woodcarver, found in the Paris Directories for
1890-1898. Mettais used the trade names "Le Parisien", "Le Phenix"
and "Liege". These names, of course, can also appear as "Bébé Le
Parisien", etc. In 1900 Mettais used the trade name "Poupée
Merveilleuse". The 1900 Directory advertizement still stated that
the Steiner firm made five categories of indestructible jointed
bébés and described the dolls as ordinary, speaking, sleep eyes,
jointed wrists and mechanical. They also advertized negro and
mulatto bébés and that the factory was still located on Rue d'Avron.
Jules Mettais won a silver medal for his exhibit at the 1900 Paris
Exposition. In 1901 Mettais registered the trademark "Bébé Modele".

Mettais used the trade name "Mascotte" which indicated that the Steiner firm had probably obtained this from their neighbor, the May Frères (Brothers). (Both companies had been located on rue Saintonge.)

In 1904 E. Daspre had a doll and bébé factory at Montreuil-sous-Bois and in 1906 he was listed in the Paris Directory as head of the Steiner firm. He advertized in 1908 "La Patricienne", a worldly doll.

Doll heads have been found with the name Bourgoin as a Steiner successor. A man of this name was listed in the Paris Directories as a porcelain manufacturer around 1904. It is not known whether Bourgoin preceeded or succeeded Daspres.

Steiner,- Records have not been found for any German doll makers named Steiner prior to 1880 but the following list should help to distinguish the later German Steiners from the earlier Steiner of Paris: Albin Steiner, 1913- Sonneberg; Georg Steiner, 1926- Sonneberg; Heinrich Steiner, 1898- Schalkau; Hermann Steiner, 1924- Sonneberg; Louis Steiner, 1910- Sonneberg; Nicol Steiner 1915- Neustadt; Rudolph Steiner, 1889- Sonneberg; Victor Steiner, 1903- Sonneberg; Willi Steiner, 1926- Freiburg. There was also Edmund Ulrich Steiner of New York City whose trademarks "Majestic" and "A scroll with an eagle perched thereon and the word 'Liliput' appearing on the scroll" were both registered in 1902 but had been used since 1894.

fig. 1	J. STEINER Ste SGDG PARIS Fie AE A 11 fig. 2	STEINER .S.G.D.G. PARIS A 11 fig. 3

Jules Steiner Marks

BÉBÉ "LE PARISIEN"
MÉDAILLE D'OR.
PARIS

A 17
PARIS
Le PARISIEN

fig. 5

A3
Le PARISIEN
SGDG
fig. 4
Lafosse- Steiner Mark
found on head and body

LE PARISIEN
fig. 6
Lafosse Trademark

Lafosse-Steiner Marks

BÉBÉ PHÉNIX
fig. 7
Alexandre Mark
used by Widow Lafosse

fig. 9
Steiner Mark of 1890
under Mettais

H & A
fig. 8
Alexandre Mark

"BÉBÉ MODELE"
fig. 10
Mettais
Trademark

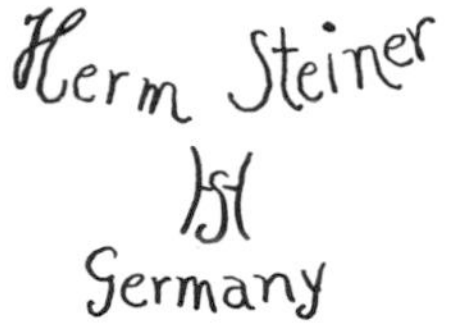

Herm Steiner

HSt

Germany

fig. 10
Hermann Steiner Mark

Majestic 2 Regd

fig. 11
Edmund Steiner
Trademark

STEUBER, 1878-   Mary M. Steuber of Philadelphia, Pennsylvania obtained a U.S. patent for doll legs in 1878. The following year, 1879, Daniel Steuber was listed in the Philadelphia Directory as handling doll materials. Mary and Daniel Steuber were, no doubt, close relatives. From 1882 through 1888 Daniel Steuber was listed as a doll body manufacturer.

STEVENS & BROWN, 1870-   The Stevens & Brown Manufacturing Co. of Cromwell, Connecticut displayed mechanical toys at the 1873 Vienna Exhibition. (see Brown)

STRASBURGER, 1863-   Isidore Strasburger of Paris, according to the Paris Directories from 1863 through 1865, was making doll bodies of cloth and kid. Strasburger also made doll clothes.

STROBEL, 1864-   Charles Strobel and his brother Lewis Strobel of Cincinnati, Ohio began manufacturing pocket books in 1860. By 1864 George Wilken had joined the business which became known as Strobel & Wilken Co. and by 1864 they had begun to handle toys. As soon as overseas trade was resumed after the Civil War they imported dolls from Europe. Strobel & Wilken were represented in the 1875 Cincinnati Exhibition. By 1882 Emil S. Strobel appears to have taken the place of the older Strobels in the firm which was growing rapidly. In 1886 the firm opened a branch in New York City. This immediately became one of the largest doll firms in New York and handled some of the finest German dolls such as the Royal Line of Kämmer and Reinhardt, Heinrich Handwerck and Jubilee dolls. The latter appear to have been made especially for Strobel & Wilken for they carried the Strobel & Wilken mark, "S. W.". Strobel & Wilken registered their trademark "American Beauty" in 1902 but they had used this mark since 1895. They registered their "Royal" trademark in 1903. Also in 1903 they began selling metal doll heads called "Diana" made by Alfred Heller of Thuringia, Germany. Strobel & Wilken were among the first to introduce character dolls in America. In 1910 they advertized "Baby" (now referred to as "Kaiser Baby"), as well as "Marie", "Peter", "Elsa", "Carl", "Gretchen", "Hans", "Elise", and "Walter", all different character children made by Kämmer & Reinhardt of Waltershausen. Strobel & Wilken continued their doll business for many years.

fig. 1
Strobel & Wilken

fig. 2
Strobel & Wilken

fig. 3
Kämmer & Reinhardt

fig. 4
H. Handwerck

HANDWERCK
7½

fig. 5
Handwerck Mark

69 - 12 x
Germany
HANDWERCK.
4

fig. 6
Handwerck Mark

29

fig. 7
Handwerck Mark

K.  R.

fig. 8
Kämmer & Reinhardt Mark

T

TALRICH, 1855- Jules Talrich of Paris was awarded a medal at the Paris Exposition of 1855. He exhibited figures in wax and crèche figures. He had a similar display at the London Exhibition of 1862. In the 1867 Paris Directory Talrich was listed as a modeler in wax, making crèche figures, infant Jesus, etc. At the Paris Exposition in 1867 Talrich again had a display. He was still listed in the Paris Directory of 1881.

TEMPIER, 1843 Tempier of Paris was listed in the Paris Directory for 1843 as a doll maker who also made doll trousseaux.

TESTARD, 1842- Mademoiselle Testard of Paris in 1842 was making dressed dolls, and dolls with rose or white kid bodies. She was selling at this time German dolls that would bend, dolls dressed in the latest fashion and dolls with springs. In 1843 she was only advertizing dolls with rose or white kid bodies. Louis Testard was cited with an Honorable Mention at the 1849 Paris Exposition for his doll display. He exhibited dolls again at the Paris Exposition of 1855.

THÉROUDE, 1842- Alexandre Nicholas Théroude of Paris was listed as a toy maker in the Paris Directory at least as early as 1842. In 1843 he advertized that he made mechanical dolls with perfect spring works. He also made dolls with ordinary kid bodies and with jointed kid bodies. His products were sent to the Provinces and abroad. At the Paris Exposition of 1849 he won a bronze medal. Théroude was granted an 1852 French patent for a mechanism to be put inside a doll to give it movement and sound. In 1854 he obtained a French patent for a mechanical doll that said "Cuckoo", raised its arms and opened and closed its eyes. The following year, 1855, he was awarded a silver medal at the Paris Exposition. His advertized specialties in 1855 were automatons and mechanical toys. At both 1862 London and 1867 Paris Exhibitions, A. N. Théroude was awarded prize medals. Then there is a gap in Théroude records for over a decade. In 1881 Théroude, father and son are listed. It seems likely that a new generation of Théroudes had grown up for the Théroude, Sr. was to be active for another decade or so. One would hardly expect the active head of a business to span over 50 years, but it is possible. In 1890 Théroude, Sr. obtained a French patent for a new type of jointed doll. From 1890 to 1895 the Théroudes advertized that they made automatons

A. THEROUDE
PARIS

Théroude
Mark

and mechanical toys for museums and displays.

Mechanical Walking Doll with Théroude Mark
Papier-mâché head, glass eyes, teeth, mohair wig, original clothes.
Doll moves arm and head as she rolls along on 3 wheels, key in lower
right corner.   Photo by G. Angione

THILEN, 1852-   Moritz Thilen of Vienna, Austria founded his doll
   establishment in 1852. He displayed dressed dolls at the 1873
   Vienna Exhibition, and in 1878 at the Paris Exposition he showed
   dolls.

THORPE, 1866   David Lee Thorpe of Birmingham, Warwickshire, England
   was issued an English patent in 1866 for a ball jointed doll. The
   doll was to be strung either with metal or rubber.

THORPE, 1856   Joseph Thorpe of London was recorded in the 1856
   London Directory as a wax doll maker.

THUILLIER, 1879-   A. Thuillier of Paris, according to the Paris
   Directories for 1879 through 1890, made jointed dolls with wooden
   or kid bodies. These were sold either dressed or undressed.
   Thuillier also made indestructible jointed bébés.

TIFFANY, 1856-   Anson B. Tiffany of Hartland, Connecticut was listed
   in the 1856 New England Business Directory as a doll manufacturer.
   In 1865 he was still handling dolls.

TOWNSEND, 1856   George Townsend of Longton, Staffordshire, England
   was making china toys and figures in 1856 according to Kelly's Post
   Office Directory for 1856. Doll heads would seem to be a principal
   type of china toy. Townsend and Sampson Smith were the only two
   china toy makers listed in the Staffordshire Directory.

TREBECK, 1851   Thomas Frederick Trebeck of London exhibited dolls
   and miscellaneous toys at the London Exhibition of 1851.

TROGNITZ, 1844   F. Trognitz & Co. of Ohrdruf, Thuringia was described as a new doll making firm in 1844 and the only important papier-
   mâché factory in the Dukedom of Gotha at that time. They sent to the

1844 Berlin Exhibition, a boy's head with glass eyes and a doll dressed as a Hungarian official.

TUTTLE, 1853   George W. Tuttle of New York showed dressed dolls at the 1853 New York Exhibition

U

ULHENHUTH, 1876-   Henry Ulhenhuth & Co. of Paris was awarded an Honorable Mention for its display at the Paris Exposition of 1876. In the Paris Exposition of 1878 J. Ulhenhuth entered an exhibit of articulated dolls in kid, and bisque which were dressed and undressed. At the Paris Exposition of 1879 Henry Ulhenhuth & Co. again displayed dolls and a medal was awarded to the firm for its products. This firm also had an exhibit at the Liverpool Exhibition of 1886 and won a medal there. By 1890 the Henry Ulhenhuth factory was located at Lagny, Seine and Oise where they made an indestructible jointed bébé which they called "Bébé Merveilleux".

♣

Ulhenhuth
Mark

V

VALET, 1855-   Valet of Paris, in 1855, was making dolls with movement which he sold at reasonable prices. In 1873 his listing in the Paris Directory was that of a doll maker.

VERDAVAINNE, 1843-   Alph. Verdavainne of Paris in 1843 was making dolls with leather bodies and dressed dolls. In 1863 he was classified as a toy maker but by 1867 he was again listed as a doll maker.

VEY & KREITER, 1873-   Vey & Kreiter of Waltershausen, Thuringia made a talking and crying doll for export in 1873 and 1874.

VICHY, 1862-   G. Vichy of Paris was granted a French patent in 1862 for mechanical dolls. In 1863 Vichy, Jr. was listed in the Paris Directory as a toy maker. G. P. Vichy Fils (Sons) were awarded a silver medal for their mechanical dolls with music which were displayed as the Paris Exposition of 1878. At Cherbourg in 1879 the Vichy exhibit won another silver medal but at the 1880 Melbourne Exhibition their display won a bronze medal. At the 1884 New Orleans Exhibition G. Vichy was awarded a gold medal. Gold medals were awarded G. Vichy at the 1888 Melbourne, and 1889 Paris Exhibitions. The U.S. report on the 1889 Exposition states;"The very excellent mechanical toys sent by Mr. Vichy. All our large American stores contain mechanical toys made by this ingenious and careful maker. The smoking figures and the beautiful waltzers, keeping time to the music, which have so delighted our young lads and our fair girls alike, are all his make." The 1890 Vichy advertizement in the Paris Directory states that he sold bébés, artistic shoulder heads as well as mechanical dolls. G. & H. Vichy exhibited mechanical dolls in the Chicago Exhibition of 1893 and won a grand prix at the 1900 Paris Exposition.

Vichy
Mark

VIDELIER, 1843-   Videlier of Paris was listed as a doll maker in 1843. The Paris Directory for 1863 includes a Widow Videlier who was listed as a toy maker.

VILLARD & WEILL, 1834-   The firm of Villard & Weill of Paris was founded in 1834. They exhibited dolls in the 1878 Paris and 1879

Sidney Exhibitions. In 1889 they were represented at the Paris
Exposition with a doll display that won them a gold medal. Henri
Villard & Weill had a factory at Luneville, Meurthe & Moselle in
1890. In 1900 at the Paris Exposition Villard & Weill displayed
their products where they were awarded a gold medal and in 1904 the
firm won a grand prix for their exhibit at St. Louis. The Soc.
Anon, des Anc. Etab. Villard & Weill displayed toys at the 1905
Exposition held at Liege.

VIRNICH, 1874-   B. H. Virnich founded a doll firm in Cologne, Germany in 1874. He was known as "The Doll King". In 1902 he was
succeeded by his son P. H. Virnich and the firm survived the first
World War.

VOGEL, 1879-   Fritz Vogel of Sonneberg, Thuringia was commended for
the "useful and cheap" toys which he exhibited at Sidney in 1879.
He obtained German patents for dolls and doll heads in 1880 and 1882.

VOIGHT, 1879-   Friedrick Voight of Sonneberg, Thuringia founded a
doll factory in 1879. B. Voight of Sonneberg obtained a German
patent for a talking doll in 1891. The successors of Friedrick
Voight operated the doll factory until
World War II. It is not known whether the
Sonneberg Voights were related to the
Voight Porcelain Factory founded in 1850
in Sitzendorf, Thuringia or to Edwin Voight
of Rodach, Bavaria who made dolls beginning
about1907.

F. Voight Mark

VOIT, 1835-   Andreas Voit of Hildburghausen, Thuringia made papier-
mâché doll heads in the 1830's. He had already
become famous for his fine products by 1844 when
he won a bronze medal at the Berlin Exhibition for
his display of 12 single doll heads. The Sonneberg Museum reports that Andreas Voit also made
a rather heavy plaster doll head that looked as
if it were stamped out of clay. Voit exhibited
papier-mâché doll heads at the 1855 Paris Exposition.

VOIT & FLEISCHMANN, 1844.   Voit & Fleischmann of
Nürnberg, Bavaria were awarded a silver medal at
the 1844 Berlin Exhibition for their dolls. At
that time the firm claimed that they made 360,000
doll heads a year.

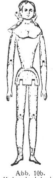

Abb. 10b.
Holzgelenkdocke
m. Papiermaché-
kopf, schon 1825
erwähnt.

W

WAGNER, 1879-   D. H. Wagner & Son of Grünhainichen,
Saxony were commended for the "ingenious and well
made" toys which they exhibited at Sidney in 1879.
They also had a display at the 1880 Melbourne
Exhibition. In 1926 at the Leipzig Fair they were
showing mechanical dolls with motion and music.

Jointed wooden
body   doll
with papier-
mâché head,
ca. 1825.

WALKER, ca.1855-   Izannah Walker of Central Falls,
Rhode Island secured a U. S. patent in 1873 for a
rag doll with painted features. According to a
statement made by Mrs. Sheldon of the Chase Doll
Factory in DOLL COLLECTORS OF AMERICA, 1940, p. 11, Izannah Walker
made her rag dolls as early as around 1855.

WEIR, 1866-   Robert H. Weir while living in Cohoes, New York in
1866 obtained a U.S. patent for a toy walking figure. In 1880,
when a resident of Philadelphia, Pennsylvania, Robert H. Weir was

issued a second U.S. patent.   This was for a method of working leather over a cast or relief to form a figure.

WICKS, 1853-   Henry Wicks of London was listed in the London Directory between 1853 and 1865 as a composition doll maker. Working at a different address but in the same city was James W. Wicks also a composition doll maker listed in the 1853 and 1854 London Directory.

WIEGAND, 1876-   Carl Wiegand of New York City in 1876 obtained a U. S. patent for a doll's head molded of two or more layers of fabric with an intermediate layer of paper. In 1881 Carl Wiegand was listed as a toy maker at one address while at another address the firm of Martin & Rippel was listed as makers of improved model wax dolls, wax doll heads, etc. Carl Wiegand moved to the premises occupied by Ernst Martin and Henry C. Rippel in 1882 and the firm was listed in the Directories for 1882 and 1883 as the National Doll & Novelty Company as well as Wiegand, Martin & Rippel. Unfortunately this company appears to have had only a brief existence. Their sole agent was Aloys Meisel who had imported German, French and English dolls since 1864. (see Meisel)

WIESENTHAL, SCHINDEL & KALLENBERG, 1858-   Wiesenthal, Schindel & Kallenberg of Waltershausen, Thuringia was founded in 1858/9. Later they made wax dolls and baby dolls in bisque, china, papier-mâché, etc. Between 1863 and 1874 Schindel & Co. was listed as making papier-mâché dolls. By 1891 Wiesenthal, Schindel & Kallenberg advertized their products as first quality ball jointed dolls. They displayed their dolls at the 1893 Chicago Exhibition.

WILD, 1870-   George L. and Louis P. Wild of Washington D.C. secured a U.S. patent in 1870 for a dancing toy. Between 1884 and 1891 Lewis Wild was a London agent for foreign manufacturers of wax, composition, china and patented indestructible dolls.

WILSON, 1854-   Thomas Francis Wilson of London was making wax dolls from 1854 through 1891. Working at the same London address from 1856 to 1865 was George Isaac Wilson who also made wax dolls.

WISLIZENUS, 1851-   Adolf Wislizenus of Waltershausen, Thuringia founded a papier-mâché doll factory in 1851. In 1873 the firm was represented by Montréer in Paris and shortly thereafter they took over the G. S. Schafft (see Schafft) doll making firm. In 1891 they advertized "Gobelin-dolls" apparently named for Gobelin tapestries. Their successor at the end of the 19th century was Hans Heincke, from which their mark "H. & Co." was probably derived, however the name Wislizenus still appeared in the directories after World War I. Luella Hart in SPINNING WHEEL, Sept. 1954, p. 18 states that this was the company that made dolls marked "Viola".(Hamburger & Co.of Berlin 1891 trade mark)

Made in Germany 8 Viola

Wislizenus Mark

WITTHAUER, 1862-   Christopher Witthauer (Wittbauer) of Neustadt, Bavaria exhibited papier-mâché dolls at the London Exhibition of 1862. His display won a prize medal. In 1910 Carl Otto Witthauer, also of Neustadt, was a doll maker.

WOLF, 1870-   Louis Wolf & Co. of Sonneberg, Thuringia and Boston, Massachusetts was established in 1870. They also had listings in New York City directories as early as 1889. They handled German and American made dolls and assembled dolls including those with Armand Marseille bisque doll heads. Armand Marseille of Köppelsdorf was established about 1894. Louis Wolf & Co. of Boston and New York registered in 1897 their trademark "Cinderella" which they had used since 1892. At the 1904 St. Louis Exhibition, Louis Wolf & Co. of

Sonneberg displayed dolls. In 1907 they advertized "Columbia" and "Superba" kid body dolls; "Young America", dressed dolls; "Mangolin" unbreakable dolls and "Minerva" metal doll heads. In 1910 they obtained U.S. registration of their trademark "Queen Louise" and in 1911 of their trademark "My Companion". They advertized Steiner walking and sitting dolls in 1910. It is not known whether this refers to the French Steiner or the American Steiner both of whom had patented walking dolls but their use of the trade name "Majestic" suggests the latter. In 1914 they advertized "the celebrated 975/ line, our own manufacture medium priced character babes".

Germany

Queen Louise

fig. 1
Wolf Trademark

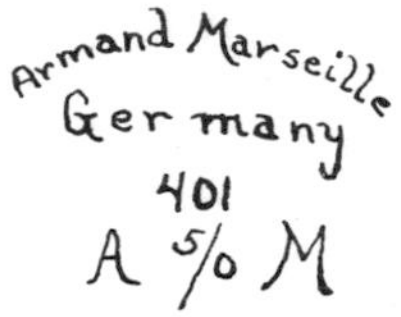

Armand Marseille
Germany
401
A ⁵⁄₀ M

fig. 2

Columbia

fig. 3

Marks
on Dolls
Assembled
by Wolf

Amand Marseille
Germany
990
A 9/0 M

fig. 4

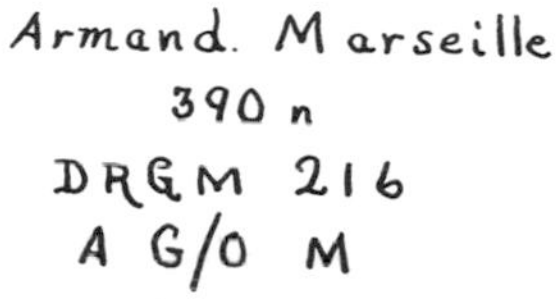

Armand. Marseille
390 n
DRGM 216
A G/0 M

fig. 5

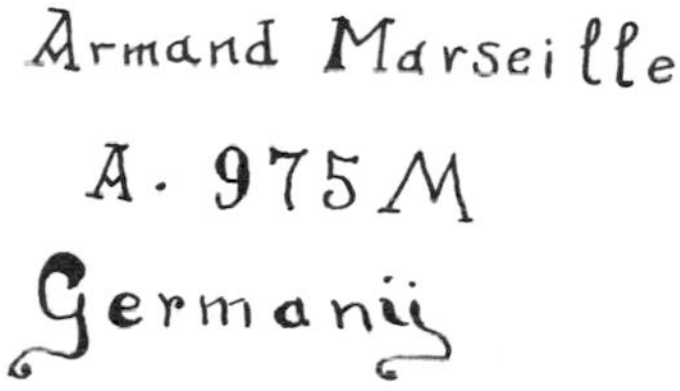

Armand Marseille
A. 975 M
Germany

fig. 6

WORK, 1873   Henry C. Work of Brooklyn New York secured a U. S. patent in 1873 for a walking doll.

Y

YAMAGAWA, 1878   Y. Yamagawa of Tokyo, Japan had a display of dolls at the Paris Exposition of 1878.

Z

ZAMMIT, 1867   E. Zammit of Floriana, Malta displayed wax figures in national costume at the Paris Exposition of 1867.

French Doll, end of the 18th Century, 24 inches tall
Courtesy Musée des Arts Décoratifs, Louvre, Paris

Jointed doll of "carton bouillei et tissus" with wig.
Dress of figured blue-green silk with the design of trefoil shaped
leaves. The dress is trimmed with an edging of silver lace and with
buttons and pendants of silk floss. The doll is ornamented with
jewels; a diadem, necklace, bracelet and a chain of silver pearls
wound around the wrist.
    The first London Classified Directory in 1763 defines a French
Merchant as a merchant who imports wines or toys (including dolls),
which indicates the importance of the French doll industry at that
time.

EXHIBITIONS

1823 PARIS

Award unknown
    France: Maelzel

1839 PARIS

Silver Medal
    France: Giroux

1844 BERLIN

Silver Medal
    German States: Kummer; Sonneberg Group; Voit & Fleischmann
Bronze Medal
    German States: Fleischmann; Rau; Voit
Award unknown
    German States: Grossmann; Kraatz; Löwenthal; Möwes; Poppe;
        Selzen; Trognitz

1844 PARIS

Honorable Mention
    France: Belton & Jumeau; Brouillet & Cacheleux; Dumont
Award unknown
    France: Francois; Greffier

The Official Report of this Exposition states that it is well
known that the Germans furnish toys to the whole world. France imports
over 600,000 dolls a year from the German States. However, Paris does
make many dolls, for example, those of Monsieur Francois and MM.
Belton & Jumeau.

1849 PARIS

Bronze Medal
    France: Jumeau; Théroude
Honorable Mention
    France: Testard

Monsieur Natalis Rondot reported on this Exposition, "The Parisian
workmen have no rivals in the making of doll's clothes; they understand
how, with a marvellous nimbleness, and skillfulness of finger, to
create with the tiniest pieces of material a most elegant trousseaux.
The cloak and the dress of a little doll costing but a franc (20 cents)
are perfectly correct reproductions of our newest fashions. --- The
doll is hurried off to the Provinces and often to foreign lands as
patron of the fashions; she has even become an indespensable accessory
for all the latest novelties and it is now the case that without a
doll merchants would find it difficult to sell their wares. The first
cloaks that were sent to India were worn on their heads, like mantillas,
by the ladies of Calcutta, until the doll-models arrived to show the
fashion."
    The REPORT OF THE JURY states about dolls, "Increasing business in
this industry has brought about a division of work and in the last few
years, thanks to these intelligent efforts, the price of dolls has lowered, their construction has improved, and their sales have increased."

1851 LONDON

Prize Medal
    Austria: Haller; Kietaibl
    England: Montanari; Spurin (mechanical, see Fleischmann, 1844)
    France: Alix; Jumeau
    German States: Fleischmann; Rock & Graner
Honorable Mention
    Austria: Müller
    England: Bouchet
No Award
    Austria: Purger
    England: Trebeck
    German States: Albert; Bahn; Lang; Löwenthal; Neubronner

    This was the first World Exhibition

1853 NEW YORK

Bronze Medal
    France: LeBlond
    German States: Lange
Honorable Mention
    Austria: Scheifele
    German States: Fleischmann; Krauss; Rock & Graner
    United States: Brunswick; Rogers; Tuttle

1854 MUNICH

Prize Medal
    German States: Helm & Wellhausen; Poppe; Gross
Honorable Mention
    German States: Hawsky; Rock & Graner

1855 PARIS

Silver Medal
    France: Fessard; Jumeau; Théroude
    German States: Rock & Graner
Bronze Medal
    France: Huret
    German States: Gross
Award unknown
    England: Montanari
    France: Alix; Arnaud; Dartheny; Greffier; Guillard; Talrich; Testard
    German States: Liedel; Poppe; Voit

    The OFFICIAL CATALOG of this Exposition describes Monsieur
Greffier's exhibit as including dolls and bébés but there is no description of the type of bébés. Later Jules Steiner advertized that
he had made bébés since 1855.
    Shortly after 1855 Monsieur Natalis Rondot wrote, "In 1855 a French
exhibitor at the Exposition, M. Fr. Greffier, showed some Japanese
dolls called by the names of 'bébés'. They were of good models, of
excellent manufacture, and of low price; and at this Exposition dolls
perfectly jointed and of an entirely new style, were shown by several
French manufacturers."
    Max von Boehn in DOLLS AND PUPPETS, page 156 (rev. ed.) states,
"About 1850 the limbed baby doll, or 'Gelenktäufling' was introduced
from England into Germany. This term signifies a baby doll of flesh-
coloured papier-mâché dipped in a wax solution to give an impression
of the human skin. The limbs are movable, and the dress is only a
little chemise. In 1855 at the Parisian world exhibition these baby
dolls were for the first time introduced to a large public. Since then
they have won great popularity, and have almost entirely ousted the
dolls representing women."

1862 LONDON

Prize Medal
    France: Jumeau; Théroude
    German States: Benda; Fromann; Gross; Köhler; Nöthlich & Falk;

German States: Rock & Graner; Witthauer
Honorable Mention
German States: Hawsky; Helm & Wellhausen
Award unknown
England: Burley; Cremer; Montanari; Peacock; Pierotti; Rich
France: Talrich
German States: Hutschenreuther
Russia: Han

1867 PARIS

Silver Medal
France: Jumeau; Potiers
Bronze Medal
France: Caron; Roullet
Medal
France: Théroude
Honorable Mention
France: Simonne
Award unknown
Brazil: Hospice de Pedro II
England: Cremer
France: Bereux; Bontemps; Dehors; Fialont; Giroux; Guillard; Huret
& Lonchambron; Rémond; Rohmer; Schanne; Max & Schudze;
Talrich
German States: Duffner; Frank; Kirschkamp; Simon
Malta: Polito; Zammit

The OFFICIAL CATALOG of this Exposition states that the greater number of French dolls are made in Paris. The making of doll clothes alone occupies several hundred women, half of whom work at home for wages of less than fifty cents a day. Men receive a dollar a day. Few doll makers employ more than twenty people. The makers deliver their finished dolls to retail dealers and export agents. "A number of dolls are made whose trousseaux show so much taste and are so elegant that they are constantly used by dress and bonnet makers as types of Parisian trousseaux."

Monsieur Natalis Rondot wrote, "A reporter of the Exposition of 1867 was horrified to see an India shawl worth seventy five dollars on the shoulders of a doll!"

1868 PARIS

Silver Medal
France: Caron

1873 VIENNA

Gold Medal
France: Jumeau (medals of cooperation were given to four members
of Maison Jumeau)
Medal of Merit
France: Bontemps; Giroux; Marchal & Bouffard; Pannier
Diploma of Merit
France: Guillard
Awards unknown
Austria: Insam & Prinoth; Moroder; Scholz; Thilen
England: Cremer
Germany: E. Bischoff; Chr. Bischoff & Co.; Dorst; Cuno & Otto
Dressel; Dressel, Kister & Co.; Engelhardt; Escher;
A. Fleischmann & Co.; J.P. Fleischmann; Hachmeister &
Franz; Jacob; Krauss; Lambert & Samhammer; Joh. Chr.
Lindner; Louis Lindner & Son; Lützelberger; C. G. Müller;
F. Müller; Rock & Graner
United States: Stevens & Brown; Vermont Novelty Works (Ellis)

British Report on Toy Exhibitions,-
France: Nearly all the exhibitors received medals.
Germany: 42 exhibitors, the majority of whom received medals or
honorable mention.

Japan: Toys show taste and exact workmanship.
United States: Exhibited some unnoticeable toys.

French Report on Sonneberg exhibit:
"Sonneberg has sent a collective entry of its products which is
very remarkable. What an effort to raise this manufacturing in 30
years, to its present height in a country poor and without resources.
Today 30 firms send their goods all over the world. This export business raises nearly $30,000,000. The principal articles made are the
'bébés', papier-mâché animals, doll heads, etc. This inductry provides
livelihood for a large part of the population. But it is not only at
Sonneberg but all the province of Thuringia from Coburg to Gotha that
is occupied in this industry. It is everywheres there that are made
the toys in porcelain, the doll heads and the dolls in porcelain, the
dolls dressed and undressed. Germany furnishes these dolls to the
entire world."

French Report on French exhibit:
"France has excelled in beautifully dressed dolls and since the
Prussian War we are freeing ourselves from the need to buy doll heads
from Saxony. Paris is forcing herself to be self sufficient with an
industry that is both active and intelligent. M. Jumeau of Paris, the
first and the most important doll making house, has freed us from our
former obligation to have the foreigner furnish us with porcelain doll
heads.
"M. Jumeau has established at Montreuil, near Paris, a factory
where he makes doll heads of enameled porcelain with the greatest perfection. He has surpassed in beauty the products that we used to buy
from Saxony. ---
"We have great confidence in the spirit and inventiveness of the
makers and workers of Paris and we hope that soon we shall equal the
German products and even surpass them."

Monsieur Natalis Rondot wrote slightly earlier:
"Most doll heads are made of papier-mâché. Saxony furnishes them
but we get our wax heads from England. We have had the idea of making
porcelain heads in France and this manufacture, neglected by us, has
been introduced in Bavaria, Prussia and Austria; it has developed
greatly in Coburg, Sonneberg and Nürnberg. The heads that come from
these places are very well executed. The back of the head is hollowed
out because this kind of porcelain has to pay custom dues of nearly
$1.00 per kilogram so we are obliged to reduce the weight of these
objects as much as possible. Heads of size No. 4 cost in Coburg about
$2.50 a dozen and the dozen weigh about 2 kilograms. The cost of trans-
portation is about 75¢ a dozen. In France good painters of porcelain
consider it derogatory to paint doll's heads and this is the reason we
have to go to Coburg and Sonneberg, which have a right of custom of 7%."

1875 CHILE

Prize
    Germany: Fischer, Naumann & Co.

1875 CINCINNATI

Award unknown
    United States: Philip Goldsmith; Strobel & Wilken

1876 PARIS

Honorable Mention
    France: Ulhenhuth

1876 PHILADELPHIA

Gold Medal
    France: Jumeau
Award unknown
    Germany: Cuno & Otto Dressel; Schünemann; Sichling
    Norway: Gram
    United States: Althof, Bergmann & Co.; American Mechanical Toy Co.;

Ives; Lacmann; New York Rubber Co.

1878 PARIS

Gold Medal
    France: Jumeau; Potiers
Silver Medal
    France: Bontems; Brujeune & Co.(sic); Caron; Choumer & Collet; Derol-
        land; Gaultier; Rossignol; Roullet; Schmitt; Steiner; Vichy
Bronze Medal
    France: Blampoix
Honorable Mention
    France:Borreau; Pannier
Award unknown
    Austria: Insam & Prinoth; Moroder; Thilen
    Bolivia: Artola
    China: Knight
    Denmark: Brix; Hansen
    England: Montanari
    France: Bereux; Dehors; Devanaux; Estivalet & Martin; Guillory;
        Jullien; Keller; Lefebvre; Lejeune; Martin; Merle; Montanari;
        Nadaud;Petit & Dumontier; Quivy; Rabery & Delphieu; Rauch;
        Schudze; Simonne; Uhlenhuth; Villard & Weill
    Guatemala: Mayorga
    Japan: Yamagawa
    Spain: Macazaga
    United States: Grandperret; Schlesinger

REPORT OF JURY INTERNATIONAL on Dolls, Bébés and Accessories:
    " The making of dolls is essentially Parisian. It is one of the
most important branches of the toy industry and has accomplished the
greatest progress since 1867. There are 21 exhibits representing 57
doll makers and they comprise:
    Undressed dolls and bébés, in leather, linen, wood, papier-mâché,
        porcelain, bisque, wax, etc.
    Dressed dolls and bébés of all kinds.
    Mignonettes in porcelain, in bisque, dressed and undressed.
    Trousseaux of dolls and of bébés in all varieties.
    Accessories of dolls, wigs, hats, shoes, jewelry, etc.
    "The once common doll in papier-mâché and the old-fashioned pou-
pard, although it is true that these articles had a very modest price,
are now forsaken because people prefer others that are better made and
not very much more expensive. The linen doll was considered a medium
doll but the doll in rose linen once very common which sold quite easily because of its low price has entirely disappeared.
    "Many doll makers have shown us in their fine dolls, the most
beautiful specimens known. The finished article shows the great effort
required to maintain the place they now occupy. It is necessary to add
that for the making of these toys, the best French taste must be used
to reproduce as exactly as possible both the lady and the child to the
point of perfection of modeling of body, facial expression and movement.
    "We are happy to affirm that no other country is able to rival
France in the skill of imitating nature so perfectly, we congratulate
our principal manufacturers who with their great care have brought this
industry to perfection. The bébé which best suits the taste of children
tends to supersede the doll and it doubtless appears to us that if the
bébé had been produced as inexpensively as the doll the sales would
have increased considerably.
    "Although there are some quite important manufacturers special-
izing in undressed bébés, nevertheless these are only to take care of
the demand.
    "Some models of bébés in composition have also been presented,
they were a tentative and cheap product. We regret that these efforts
have not until now given the best results. We heartily encourage our
manufacturers to force themselves to fill this gap as promptly as possible with attention to this everyday item for a large number of which
we are dependent on foreign manufacturers.
    "In carrying his researches towards the desired end, the manufac-

turer who attains this goal will be able to assure himself of a considerable portion of business. Assuredly the difficulties to be over-
come are numerous but they are not insurmontable.
" We must not forget to cite the talking bébé. The manufacturer
who is almost the only one in France to produce this toy has turned
out bébés perfectly made and amazingly lifelike. (Probably Steiner)
"We notice also among the products of this manufacturer of dolls
and bébés, some made chiefly of rubber. We are persuaded that there
would be in this case a great improvement if they were able to apply
hard rubber to a certain extent and thus produce dolls having the advantage of being solid.
" We have not enlarged on the merits of the clothing of the dolls
and the bébés. The makers who specialize in this must follow the pre-
vailing styles exactly and portray also the dress of the couturiers
for the socially elite, We have been able to satisfy ourselves with
the pretty styles shown at the Exhibition and are assured that they
will meet the demands of the foreign dressmakers who use these little
models which are so easy to transport elsewhere in order to spread
the latest French fashion. Moreover, these dolls have sufficient articulation to take and keep any desired pose.
"We have seen also a great variety of costumes on dolls and bébés
including the most luxurious and the most current; but we regret that
these collections are not complete, because they do not include the
inexpensive.
"Dolls in wax were represented by some models but the price of
these toys, which are perishable is too high. The several specimens of
muslin dolls that we have seen although well made have not been success-
ful in France. This toy is expensive and becomes worn quite rapidly.
If these dolls were able to be manufactured more cheaply, we believe
they would find a ready market.
"One manufacturer who has shown some heads and some dolls in porcelain merits special mention. He is the first to establish in our
Country the doll mignonette in porcelain called 'the bather'. (Probably
Merle) Thanks to the precision of form and finish of these dolls that
heretofore we have been buying abroad, this industry has spread and is
struggling to gain the advantage over competitors.
"In speaking of the mignonette it should be recalled that many
more companies have dressed these toys. Their coquettishness and at-
tractiveness show all the care and taste that have been dispensed on
them. ---
"Production, for France $300,000 (only 1% of the Sonneberg export
business reported in 1873); for export $200,000. There are 57 entre-
preneurs and 988 employees making dolls in France. Men workers receive
$1.50 a day and women workers receive 50¢ to 85¢ a day."

"Austria: mechanical dolls, pantins, etc., wooden dolls and mannikins
         from Gröden, Tirol (Grödner Tal).
 Japan: papier-mâché dolls satisfactorily made. The costumes are lux-
         urious. However, the examples which we have seen are ex-
         pensive.
 China: figurines in wood and in papier-mâché, various models, but we
         have been unable to resign ourselves to the price.

"The principal toys imported into France are Sonneberg bébés of
all kinds."

1879 CHERBOURG

Silver Medal
    France: Vichy

1879 PARIS

Bronze Medal
    France: Guimmoneau
Medal
    France: Ulhenhuth

1879 SIDNEY

First Degree Merit
    France: Jumeau
Honorable Mention
    United States: Schlesinger
Highly Commended
    France: Villard & Weill
    Germany: Fischer, Naumann & Co.
Commended
    Germany: Lambert & Samhammer; Motschmann & Hüfner; Rock & Graner;
            Wagner

1880 BRUSSELS

Bronze Medal
    France: Gaultier

1880 MELBOURNE

Gold Medal
    France: Jumeau (dolls, bébés)
Silver Medal
    France: Bru (dolls, bébés); Falck
Bronze Medal
    France: Bontems; Jumeau (mechanical); Lejeune; Vichy
    Germany: Fischer, Naumann & Co.; Unger, Schneider & Co.(mechanical)
    United States: C. W. F. Dare (mechanical)
Certificate
    France: Bru (mechanical); Martin; Potiers
    Germany: Wagner
    United States: M'Laughlin Bros. (mechanical)
No Award
    Germany: Dorst; Cuno & Otto Dressel; Fleischmann Bros.; R. Heinze;
            J. C. Lindner; L. Lindner & Sons; Müller & Strassburger
    Japan: T. Hayashi; Koshokuwaisha Kiriu & T. Akiyama
    Queensland: P. Thomle (mechanical)
    United States: Schlesinger

The Exhibition lists are incomplete because details have not been found for all the awards given at the smaller exhibitions. It should also be noted that many of the porcelain manufacturers who made doll heads had displays in the exhibitions, but are not included in the above list because their products were primarily other types of porcelain than dolls. For further details on the prize-winning doll makers and their exhibits, see the alphabetical text. A few doll makers who exhibited in 1880 but for whom no earlier data have been found, were not included in the alphabetical text.

Dolls with Unusual China Heads
Photo by G. Angione

The dolls shown in the picture are types that probably were shown at mid-nineteenth century exhibitions. The doll on the left has brown painted eyes with lower lashes. She is 17 inches with a 5 inch head. Doll on right is pink "lustre", three part mould, with ears completely showing. She is 15 inches with a 4 inch head. Both dolls have homemade cloth bodies.

ADDENDA

A

ADAMS, 1878 (see p. 1)   Samuel W. Adams of Boston in 1878 was the patentee of a mechanical rope jumping doll.

ALT, BECK & GOTTSCHALCK, 1854-   Alt Beck & Gottschalck was founded in 1854 as Porzellanfabrik von Alt. There is a "c" before the final "k" in Gottschalck which is not found in Gottschalk & Co. (see p. 25)

ALTHOF, 1848- (see p. 1)   Louis Althof was listed in the New York City Directory of 1848 as well as Frederick Althof. Both were in the toy business but at different addresses. Frederick Althof was the successor to the widow of Gustavus F. Meyers. Directories as early as 1839 listed Gustavus F. Meyers. By 1858 Louis Althof was a member of the firm Althof, Bergmann & Co. which also included Charles Althof, Frederick Althof and Hermann Bergmann. Frederick Althof lived in Europe at that time. The 1867 New York Directory lists Augustus Bergmann as a toyman at the same address.

Doll advertized by Althof, Bergmann & Co. in 1867.

The 1867 Christmas issue of HARPER'S BAZAR (see AGE OF DOLLS, pp. 8-9) shows a picture drawn from the actual dolls displayed by Althof Bergmann & Co.

The initials, "A.B.C." appear to have been used as their trademark.

In 1874 Louis Althof with Hermann Thomass of Brooklyn, N. Y. obtained a U. S. patent for a

Althof, Bergmann & Co. Trademark, 1872-

mechanical doll with a bell and hoop. The 1874 catalog of Althof, Bergmann & Co. shows this patented mechanical doll as well as others including the 1868 walking girl patented by William Farr Goodwin and a boy riding a tricycle. (see AGE OF DOLLS, by Coleman, pp. 19-20)

B

BACULARD, 1860-   Monsieur Baculard obtained a French patent in 1860 for the use of gutta percha in making doll heads. Baculard appears in Paris Directories through 1876. In the 1870's the name is listed as Favier & Baculard.

BÄHR & PRÖSCHILD, 1871-   Bähr & Pröschild (Baer & Proeschild) porcelain factory was founded in 1871 in Ohrdruf, Thuringia. In 1898 they advertized that they made doll heads, bathing children and figurines. They registered a German trademark in 1910 for dolls made of a celluloid-like material.

Dupont

fig. 1
1910

B&P
800

624

6

Bähr &
Pröschild
Marks

BP

585

13

Germany Germany
fig. 2   fig. 3

BARROIS, 1846- (see p. 3)   Madame Barrois appeared in Paris Directories as early as 1846 and E. Barrois was listed in the 1858 Paris Directory.

BAWO & DOTTER, 1838- (see pp. 3-4)
Bawo & Dotter, established in Bavaria, Germany in 1838, made fine
Bavarian porcelain according to
Jervis, A BOOK OF POTTERY MARKS, p.
58. In 1862 Francis H. Bawo and
Charles T. Dotter were living in
New York and Directories recorded
them as "clerks". They established
the New York importing firm of Bawo
& Dotter in 1864; the "Elite" porcelain factory in Limoges, France in
1872; a porcelain factory at Fischern
near Carlsbad, Austria (now Czechoslovakia) in 1883 and a white china
factory at Limoges in 1896. The earlier factories may have been decorating works rather than complete porcelain manufactories. Bawo & Dotter
also controlled the output of the
the porcelain factory at Klosterle,
Austria (now Czechoslovakia).

China Doll Head marked
"Pat. Dec. 7/80"

Bawo & Dotter in 1897 were referred to as of New York and Limoges.
Charles T. Dotter of New York, the
patentee of the Dotter corset body
with a corset printed on the body,
retired in 1888 and was succeeded by
C. F. W. Bawo. Both Strobel & Wilken
Co. and Hamburger & Co. (see Wislizenus) used "Carlsbad" as part of their
marks which suggests a connection
with the Carlsbad factory of Bawo &
Dotter. Bawo & Dotter were agents
for the English porcelain makers;-
W.H. Goss who made dolls and W. T.
Copeland who originated "Parian"
ware in the 1840's.

China Doll Head marked
"B. & D."

The above information is largely
from the books of William P. Jervis,
the introduction to whom is thanks to an article in the April 1966
issue of SPINNING WHEEL MAGAZINE, p. 33, by Brice Garrett.
Both china head and bisque head dolls have been found marked "B.
& D.". (see TOY TRADER, Dec. 1959, p. 13)

Bawo & Dotter Marks

| Bavarian | Limoges | Carlsbad | Klosterle, Vienna | Mark on bisque head |

| Made for Hamburger & Co. Carlsbad | Made for Strobel & Wilken Co. Carlsbad |

BATES, Mid 19th century   Reuben Harlow Neal Bates of Providence,
Rhode Island, was a pattern maker who made an iron two-piece mold
for a doll's head around the middle of the 19th century. Both the
mold and the rag doll made from it are pictured in Johl, YOUR DOLL
AND MINE, p. 39. There may have been a connection between Bates
and Izannah Walker. (see p. 75)

BEAGUE, 1750   André Beague of Lille, France created several walking automata before 1750 according to Chapuis and Droz, AUTOMATA,
p. 316.

BELTON, 1842- (see p. 4)   DOLL NEWS, Aug. 1962, p. 8, notes a "fashion" type doll body with the word "Belton" written in heavy black
letters across the chest.

BEUCHIN, 1600   Barbara Beuchin of Nürnberg, Bavaria made and sold
dolls in 1600.

BLAKSLEE, 1865-   Charles F. Blakslee of New York City obtained a
U. S. patent in 1865 for making leather doll arms by using two layers of unsplit leather, gluing the cut fingers of the layers together and stuffing only the hand and arm. The following year,
1866, Leonard Blakeslee witnessed the Darrow patent for leather
dolls. (see p. 14) Later the Blakeslees were associated with Ives.
(see p. 36) Although it was not Charles Blakslee but Cornelius
Blakeslee who was a member of the Ives firm, they may have been related, since the spelling of names varied somewhat at that time.

BONTEMPS, 1838- (see p. 6)   In 1868 Blaise Bontemps had nearly
succeeded after 30 years of work in producing a talking automaton
according to Chapuis and Droz, AUTOMATA, p. 324

BORCHERDT, 1865   Richard Borcherdt and Henry Bergman of Thompkins-
ville, New York obtained a U. S. patent in 1865 for a composition
to be used in making the bodies of little dolls. The ingredients
of the composition were: glue, sugar or honey, glycerine and powdered chalk.

BOUCHET, 1851- (see p. 6)   Ad. Bouchet of Paris won a silver medal
at the 1889 Paris Exposition and gold medals at Paris in 1895,
Rouen in 1896 and Brussells in 1897. He was listed in Paris Directories from 1892 through 1898. The trade names of his dolls were:
"Bébé Géant", priced from 10 centimes to 1 franc, 95 centimes (40¢);
"Gentil Bébé" with a porcelain head selling from 60 centimes up
(12¢); "L'Indestructible", imitation porcelain; "Bébé Tête Mobile"
with interchangeable heads and fingers; "Le Seduisant";
"Bébé Parlant"; "Bébé Dormeur" in all sizes; "Bébé
Hamac" (doll in hammock) from 1 franc, 45 centimes   *AB*
up (30¢-); and "Les Parisiennes à la Mode", doll parts
that were interchangeable among various dolls. In 1894   Bouchet
Bouchet obtained a French patent for a new mounting for   Mark
doll heads and limbs.

BRAITLING, 1869- (see pp. 6-7)   The Braitling
kid doll bodies in 1902 were made in sizes 1
to 20 and measured from 8 inches to 28 inches.
The 1907 Braitling body shown in the picture
was made in kid or muslin. Note the two lines
of stitches between the hips and the thighs.
Also note the row of stitching across the top
of the foot. Braitling discontinued the manufacture of doll bodies in 1916. (see Strasburger and Pfeiffer for more data on doll
bodies)

BROCK, 1867- (see p. 7)   William E. Brock was
listed in the New York City Directory of 1867
as a clothier. In 1873 William Brock applied
for four U. S. patents all relating to woven
fabrics: (1) the fabric was saturated with
liquid quartz and coated with marble dust;
(2) the fabric was saturated with glue, var-
nish and whiting and coated with sawdust; (3)   Braitling
same as #2 shellaced; (4) the leather doll   Body

heads to be stiffened with a backing of woven fabric saturated with glue. All four of these patents were granted in 1874.

BROOMAN, 1848-   Richard Archibald Brooman of London secured a U. S. patent in 1848 for making articles, including busts, from gutta per- cha by moulding, stamping or embossing. This patent states that gut- ta percha resembles caoutchouc (India rubber) but differs in the following ways: (1) free from stickiness when dry; (2) not affected by atmospheric heat or by unctuous oils; (3) workable by means of hot water alone; (4) being fibrous. In 1858 Brooman was the London agent for André Francois Émile Robert of Paris in obtaining an Eng- lish patent for making a doll of vulcanized rubber and inserting ar- ticulated wooden or metal limbs.

BROWER, 1873 (see p. 8)   Henry L. Brower of New York City assigned his patent of 1873 for a dancing doll to Josephine De F. Brower of Yonkers, New York.

BROWN, 1857- (see pp. 8, 71)   The Stevens and Brown Manufacturing Co., also known as the American Toy Co. published a price list of their products in 1870. The American Toy Co. was listed in the New York City Directories at least from 1867 through 1874. George W. Brown of Forestville, Conn. filed an application in 1873 and in 1874 obtained a U. S. patent for an automatic hoop doll.

BRU, 1867- (see pp. 8-10)   Monsieur Anton Bru started the doll bus- iness according to Fawcett, DOLLS, A NEW GUIDE FOR COLLECTORS, p. 112. Edouard Fournier, HISTOIRE DES JOUETS ET DES JEUX D'ENFANTS, wrote around 1866, "Some establishments with over 30 employees are occupied exclusively in the making of dresses, pinafores etc. for dolls. One of these establishments located on the rue Saint Denis (Bru was listed on the rue Saint Denis in the 1868 Paris Directo- ry) works especially for the American trade and sells these emigrants all decked out for from 5 to 30 francs a dozen (1 franc = 20¢) One other establishment, even larger is located on the rue Mauconseil. (Jumeau was listed on rue Mauconseil 1848-1866. In 1867 Jumeau had moved to the rue Anjou-Marais) This firm does an annual business of over 120,000 francs ($24,000) and sends dolls as far away as China. Occasionally one of the great Parisian couturiers will stoop to compete with the dressmakers of dolls but the prices that they charge are exorbitant.--- nearly $100 in one instance."
Luella Hart, COMPLETE FRENCH DOLL DIRECTORY, pp. 17- 18 quotes the 1868 Paris Directory, "Bru Junior, and Co., b.s.g.d.g. Maker of dolls of all kinds in pink or white kid, straight or jointed, crying or talking. New doll in rubber. New doll in porcelain. New doll in hardened paste. (It's pate in the French.) New doll in carved wood with joints (such as those at feet and hands) giving it a specially graceful look. Big workshops for making dressed dolls made always with new materials and in new styles; trousseaux. Maker of dolls' heads in bisque, rubber, or hard- ened paste. Commission agent. Exporter. 374, Rue St. Denis."
   The following year, 1869, Leon Casimir Bru was issued a French patent for a ball jointed compo- sition type doll body but it was held to-gether with pegs or pins and not elastic. The elastic strung ball jointed doll bodies appear to have been invented by Parent (see pp. 56, 112) in 1871.
   An illustrated advertizement for a Bébé Bru in 1890 is shown in Coleman, AGE OF DOLLS, p. 94.

BÉBÉ   BRU

FABRIQUE ET MAGASINS

1890

BRUGUIER, 1815-   Charles Abram Bruguier of London made several mech- anical walking dolls from 1815 through 1821 according to Chapuis and Droz, AUTOMATA, p. 318.

C

CANNON, 1852-   James Cannon was listed as a doll maker in the London Directories from 1852 through 1855.

CARLIN, 1879   Wayland Carlin of New York City obtained a U. S. patent for a doll or puppet that could walk or dance by having fingers inserted in its legs.

CAVELL, 1868   Monsieur Cavell obtained a French patent in 1868 for improvements in making mechanical dolls.

CHALTÉ & LEBORGNE, 1861- (see p. 11)   Chalté & Leborgne in the 1861 Paris Directory advertized that they made small, flexible dolls without clothes; porcelain heads and dolls' trousseaux.

CHAMSON, 1868   Mademoiselle Chamson of Paris secured a French patent for a type of composition to be used in making dolls.

CHAUVIÈRE, 1848- (see p. 12) Jacques Chauvière of Paris was in the doll business from 1848 through 1852 according to Paris Directories. A doll with the "Au Nain Bleu" mark on its body has been found with a French Steiner marked head.

CHECALIER & VENARD, 1850   Checalier & Venard of Paris in 1850 were issued a French patent for the mechanism by which the parts of a doll could be put into any desired position.

CHECKENI, 1866- (see p. 12)   On one of Dominico Checkeni's patents, his name was spelled "Cheeckeni".

PROSOPOTROPE

PATENTED FEB. 20, 1866

MANUFACTURED & SOLD

BY

OZIAS MORSE

WEST ACTON, MASS.

SOLE AGENT FOR PATENTEES

A four faced waxed over composition doll head in the museum of Mrs. Homer Strong has a label pasted inside the shoulder which reads as shown opposite. The New Haven, Connecticut Directories for 1883 through 1885 list both Dominico Checkeni, toymaker, and Ozias Morse.
    Dominico Checkeni in 1866 assigned his doll patent to himself and to George N. Thompson.

CHINNOCK, 1865- (see p. 12)   Charles Chinnock of Brooklyn, New York obtained a U. S. patent in 1865 for a doll that he made to dance by a spring. Chinnock's doll patent of 1878 was assigned to Ives, Blakeslee & Co. of New York City. (see p. 36)

CHOUMER & COLLET, 1878-   Choumer & Collet won a silver medal for their doll display at the Paris Exposition in 1878. They were listed in Paris Directories through 1890. (also see Derolland p. 16)

CLAY, 1868- (see pp. 12, 36)   The creeping doll patented by Robert J. Clay of New York City in 1871 has a smooth edged wheel with four spokes, to propel the doll. A few months later in 1871, George Pemberton Clarke patented a creeping doll with a solid, serrated edged wheel, to propel the doll. This patent was witnessed by Robert J. Clay and most known creeping dolls appear to have been based on this second patent. The following year, 1872, Robert Clay patented an improvement in the creeping doll which included the imitation of a

The Creeping Baby
Shown in Catalog of
THE AUTOMATIC
TOY WORKS, 1882

child crying. Both of Clay's patents were assigned to himself and
Tasker H. Marvin of Brooklyn, New York. George P. Clarke was list-
ed as a machinist in the 1874 New York City Directory. The 1882
Catalog of the Automatic Toy Works (see AGE OF DOLLS, p. 54) showed
the creeping baby. The same type creeping baby was shown in the
Ives, Blakeslee & Williams Co. Catalog some years later.

CLEMENT, 1866-   Pierre Victor Clement of Paris was issued a French
patent in 1866 for making dolls entirely of embossed leather. V.
Clement appears in Paris Directories as making jointed leather dolls
from 1870 through 1875.

CLOUGH, 1858-   Isaac S. Clough was listed in the New York City Directories in 1858 as an agent, in 1862 under Hardware and in 1867
with his home in Brooklyn. Isaac S. Clough of Brooklyn and Vincent
Fountain Jr. of North Shore, New York, obtained a patent for a dancing automaton in 1864.

COHEN, 1862- (see p. 13)   Daniel S. Cohen appeared in New York Directories as an importer in 1858, under Fancy Goods in 1862 and under Trimmings in 1867. This suggests that he may have been the as-
sembler and distributor rather than the manufacturer of the "Autoperipatekos".

COUSIN, 1870- (see p. 14)   E. Cousin at "Aux Amis de l' Enfance"
was listed in Paris Directories from 1870 through 1875 as making
jointed dolls.

COX, 1760-   James Cox of London in 1760 made automatons which he
displayed in his museum. Many of Cox's automatons were exported to
China. He died in 1788.

CRANDALL, 1875- (see p. 14)
Charles M.
Crandall applied
for his U. S.
patent for doll
joints in 1875.
Jointed wooden
Crandall dolls
were advertiz-
ed in the 1876
Strasburger &
Pfeiffer of   H. Jewitt & Co.
New York Cata-   Mark
log and in the
1881 Millikin and Lawley of
London Catalog in which the   Crandall's Acrobats as advertized
British patent for Crandall's   by Strasburger, Pfeiffer & Co., 1876
acrobats was ascribed to H.
Jewitt & Co. of London. Besides the acrobats, Crandall also made
the wooden dolls for "The District School".

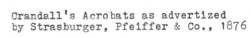

CREMER, 1862- (see p. 14)
Henry Cremer operated one of the finest toy shops in London during
the last quarter of the nineteenth century. His description of his
visit to the Leipsig Fair in 1873 is given in Lesley Gordon's PEEP-
SHOW INTO PARADISE, p. 59.

CROW, 1863- (see p. 14)   Thomas and James Crow of Motthaven, New
York were granted a U. S. patent for their dancing doll in 1863.

D

D'AUTREMONT, 1858   Monsieur D'Autremont of Paris obtained a French patent in 1858 for a rubber doll. A doll has been found with a "D'Autrement" (sic) elliptical label on its body according to Hart, COMPLETE FRENCH DOLL DIRECTORY, p. 93.

DAVIS, 1872-   Albert D. Davis of New York City was the assignee of a U. S. patent filed by Isaac F. Eaton in 1872 for an improvement in an automatic swimming doll. This patent was granted in 1873, three years before Elie Martin patented his famous swimming doll, "Ondine". (see p. 51)

DEHAIS, 1836- (see p. 15)   Louis Marie Renou was granted a French patent in 1905 for a mechanical doll with a music box inside the doll.

DEFOSSE, 1833-   Defosse, maker of dolls of all kinds, was listed in Paris Directories from 1833 through 1852.

DERNHEIM, KOCH & FISCHER, 1860-   The Dernheim, Koch & Fischer porcelain factory in Gräfenroda was established in 1860. They specialized in bisque figures with "Dresden" type flowers which were popular into the 1890's.

DKF

Dernheim (Dornheim) Koch & Fischer Mark

DESCHAMPS, 1847-   F. Deschamps was listed under Dolls in the Paris Directories for 1847 and 1848. Mademoiselle Deschamps appears in Paris Directories from 1863 through 1895. Her mark, "Maison DESCHAMPS, 5 Rue de l'Echelle" has been found on Jumeau's portrait doll,"Eleanor of Austria". It is believed that Mademoiselle Deschamps made the elaborate costume for this doll.

DORST, 1839- (see p. 16)   In 1895 Julius Dorst of Sonneberg registered a trademark to be used on papier-mâché toys, täuflings, dolls and doll heads of wood and "holz masse" (composition). This mark appears to have been used since 1879.

Dorst Mark

DRESSEL, 1700- (see pp. 16-17)   In 1906 Cuno and Otto Dressel of Sonneberg began to use the trademark "Jutta" which they registered in Germany in 1907. At that time they described their factory as making jointed dolls and the trademark was to apply to "double jointed"dolls of composition. "Jutta" bisque heads have been found which were made by Simon & Halbig. (see p. 67) Cuno and Otto Dressel registered in Germany their trademark, "Bambina"in 1909; and "Poppy Dolls" for stuffed dolls in 1912.

$\mathcal{B}$AMBINA

Cuno & Otto Dressel Tademark, 1909

The elliptical mark,⬭, shown on page 17 belongs to Cuno and Otto Dressel and NOT to Dressel & Koch.

DRESSEL, KISTER & Co., 1840- (see p. 17) Dressel, Kister & Co. established a porcelain factory in 1840 at Passau, Bavaria. Allegedly Karl Hagen obtained permission to build a kiln at Passau in 1776. He made porcelain dolls and other porcelain objects according to the data of Eva Kaiser printed in the Kimport, DOLL TALK, March-April 1962, page 8.

Note the "Dresden" type rose in the hand of the pincushion head shown here with the mark illustrated in figure 1. This mark is in blue,on the inside of the base of the pincushion head.

Dressel, Kister & Co. marked pincushion head

Dressel,
Kister & Co.
Marks

fig. 1

fig. 2

DUBRAY, 1840   Dubray was listed in the 1840 Paris Directory as a
doll maker.

E

ECK, 1876   Berthold Eck of Unterneubrunn, near Eis-
field, Thuringia registered his trademark in 1876 for
use on täuflings and dolls.

EDISON, 1878- (see p. 18)   Edison Phonograph dolls
were exhibited at the 1889 Paris Exposition. In 1889
the body of the Edison Phonograph doll was made of
tin and the head of bisque. The entire output of two
German bisque doll head factories was required. The
arms and legs were made of wood by an American firm.
In 1891 the size of the phonograph was enlarged so
that it's playing time was increased from approximately 15 seconds to one minute.

Berthold Eck
Trademark

EDWARDS, 1852- (see p. 18)   John Edwards was listed in the 1868 London Directory as an inventor of the Exhibition wax model dolls, wax
and composition dolls, also Exhibition rag dolls. His dolls were
dressed or undressed and he sold them wholesale and for export.

ESCHER, 1863- (see p. 19)   E. Escher Jr. of Sonneberg
in 1881 registered his trademark to be used on wooden
or porcelain dolls, doll heads or täuflings. The
1896 renewal mentioned doll arms and legs also.

ETEDI, ca. 1871   A wax doll head of about 1871,
marked "C. P. Etedi" is pictured in Fawcett, DOLLS,
A NEW GUIDE FOR COLLECTORS, p. 206.

EVANS, 1868-   Joseph Evans & Sons are listed as toy
makers in the 1868 London
Directory and as doll makers
in the 1881 London Direct-

Evans' Mark

ory. Wax dolls with the Evans' mark, showing the 1868 address, are described in Gerken, WONDERFUL DOLLS OF WAX, pp. 57, 93.
Dolls with papier-mâché heads in 12 sizes
and often used for Pedlar type dolls were
made by Evans & Cartwright of Wolverhampton,
England in the middle of the 19th century
according to Gwen White, DOLLS OF THE WORLD, pp. 178, 227.

Escher
Trademark

F

FIALONT, 1867- (see p. 20)   Madame Fialont was listed in Paris Directories under dolls, from 1867 through 1870.

FISCHER, NAUMANN & CO., 1852- (see p. 20)   In 1907 Arno Fischer
founded a porcelain factory at Ilmenau, Thuringia.
See picture on the following page of a doll body patented by
Fischer, Naumann & Co. in England in 1860.

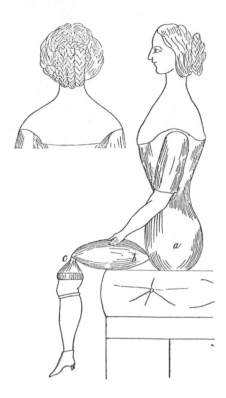

PAF
fig. 1   fig. 2

Arno Fischer Marks

1860 Patent Drawing
of a
Fischer, Naumann & Co.
Doll Body

Note:
  Heels on shoes
  Small hands and feet
  Long neck and shoulders
  Hair-do with 3 vertical and one
    horizontal braids worn as a
    bun on the back of the doll's
    head.

FLEISCHMANN, 1844- (see pp. 20-21)   The tableau of Gulliver among
  the Lilliputians which enjoyed acclaim at the Great London Exhibition in 1851 and at the New York International Exhibition in 1853
  is pictured below. This toy was made by Adolf Fleischmann of
  Sonneberg out of papier-mâché and is 4 feet by 2 1/6 feet in size.
  After the Exhibitions it was displayed in the Sonneberg Museum.

Gulliver among the Lilliputians made by Adolf Fleischmann

A.Fleischmann & Crämer of Sonneberg
in 1881 registered a trademark to
be used on täuflings, dolls and doll
heads of wood or porcelain.

FLEISCHMANN & BLOEDEL, 1873- (see
p. 21)   Fleischmann & Bloedel, a
doll factory of Furth, Bavaria, in
1891 registered "Eden Puppe" as a
German trademark for their dolls.
   Fleischmann & Bloedel of Furth,
Germany and Paris, France in 1892
were the assignees of a patent by
Claude Joseph Simonot of Paris for
a walking doll whose head turned as
the feet moved. This patent was
obtained in France, Germany and England in 1892; in Spain, Italy, Austria and the United States in 1893.

Fleischmann & Crämer
Trademark, 1881

FORSTER, 1844   Thomas Forster of
Streatham, Surrey obtained an English
patent in 1844 for a composition of
rubber and the coating of surfaces of
leather and woven fabrics to make doll
heads, arms and legs by casting them
in moulds.

FRANÇOIS, 1811- (see p. 22)   Mademoiselle
François appeared in French Directories
under dolls, from 1846 through 1858.

Fleischmann & Bloedel
Trademark, 1891

G

GALIBERT, 1860   Galibert of Marseille, France obtained a French
patent in 1860 for a mechanical doll.

GAUTIER (GAULTIER), 1751- (see p. 22)   P. Gautier created a walking
doll which is dated 1751 and signed "P. Gautier" according to
Chapuis & Droz, AUTOMATA, p. 318, picture p. 317.

GERARBON (GIRARBON), 1874   Monsieur Gerarbon of Paris was granted
a French patent for a multi-faced doll in 1874.

GERARDIN, 1874   Monsieur Gerardin obtained a French patent in 1874
for a sleeping eye adapted for dolls made of rubber.

GILLET, 1833-   Gillet was listed in Paris Directories from 1833
through 1836 as a maker of small automatons.

GIROUX, 1839- (see p. 23)   Chapuis & Droz, AUTOMATA, p. 262 pictures
and describes a mechanical tight-rope walker of about 1840, on which
there is a brass plate with the inscription , "Chez Alph. Giroux, 7
rue du Coq, St. Honore, Paris". In 1885 N. Giroux was listed at
140 rue du Temple, Paris. This was an address occupied by Pannier
(see p. 56) and Rauch (see p. 59) a few years earlier.

GOEBEL, 1871-   Franz Detlev Goebel, who was descended from a long
line of china makers, established in 1871 the Goebel porcelain factory. This factory later became known as W. Goebel of Oeslau, Thuringia when William Goebel, son of Franz succeeded him in 1879. The
mark ⚲ was used from 1879 on and has been found on bisque doll

heads and china pincushion
heads. Around 1900 the
Goebel factory made only
porcelain figures and
dolls. M. I. Hummel star-
ted the earthenware "Hum-
mel" figurines in 1934.

GOLDSMITH, 1870- (see
   pp. 23-24)   The Gold-
smith body shown here
has a red corset made
of material inserted in
the front and back of
the body. Red stockings
and shoes of leather
match the red corset.
Both the corset and the
shoes have adjustable
tan laces. The shoes
are decorated with tas-
sels. Elbow length
brown leather arms end
with fingers indicated
by stitching. Across
the chest in blue block
letters is stamped:

PATD. DEC. 15, 1885

This body is 16½ inches
long, which was the larg-
est size according to an 1887 advertizement
which reads as follows: "Patent Corset
bodies (no head), entirely new, with seat,
kid arms, colored stockings, shoes with
tassels, and adjustable lace corsets".
These bodies came in three sizes, 10 inches
for 24 cents, 13½ inches for 32 cents and
16½ inches for 48 cents.

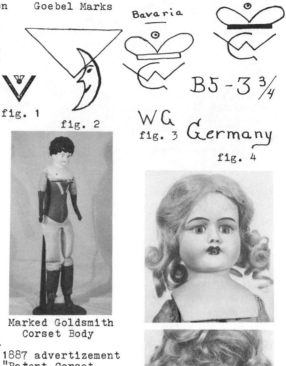

Goebel Marks

fig. 1

fig. 2

Marked Goldsmith
Corset Body

fig. 3

fig. 4

Goss Doll Head
Courtesy of Margaret Strong

GOODWIN, 1870   William C. Goodwin of Ham-
den, Connecticut obtained a U. S. design
patent in 1870 for mechanical dolls operated by a flow of hot air.

GOSS, 1858-   William Henry Goss of Stoke-on-Trent, Staffordshire,
England established in 1858 the pottery known as Goss & Co., for the
production of Parian and "Ivory" porcelain busts. Their bisque doll
heads, made in the early 20th century, were marked "GOSS". Most of
these were shoulder heads. Bisque limbs were also made. The doll
parts were assembled by the Potteries Toy Co. The bodies were made
of pink cambric and stuffed with brown wool fibres according to re-
collections of employees. An oval shaped ink stamp has been found
on the back of a body. Various types were made, including babies
and various sizes up to 36 inches high were made. 18 inches was the
most popular size. The heads generally had moveable eyes and the
lips were usually painted a dark red. In 1942 Goss China Co. Ltd.
and T. S. Harrison obtained an English patent for casting movable
doll eyes from porcelain. Goss also used the crest of a falcon as
a trademark but it is not known whether this mark was ever used on
any Goss doll head.

GREEN, 1855   Thomas Green was listed in the 1855 London Directory
as a doll maker.

GREINER, 1760- (see pp. 25-28)   The porcelain factory at Ilmenau was
founded in 1777. The "i" mark was used by Christian Nonne from 1792
through 1808; the "N&R" mark has been used since 1808. In 1888 Gal-

luba & Hofmann took over the factory.

The porcelain factory at Grossbreitenbach, Thuringia was founded in 1780. In 1869 it was taken over by H. Buhle & Son.

Galluba & Hofmann Marks

H. Buhle & Son Marks

China doll head with fig. 1
Rauenstein mark

Mark on china   Mark on bisque
doll head   doll head
fig. 1   fig. 2
Rauenstein Marks

The Limbach porcelain factory registered a German trademark for dolls in 1919. (see mark p. 27)

The trefoil mark has been used at Ilmenau, Grosbreitenbach and Limbach since 1788 and at Closter Veilsdorf since 1797.

Ilmenau Marks

Bisque doll head with fig. 2
Rauenstein mark

GUILLARD, 1842- (see p. 29) Guillard was listed in Paris Directories as early as 1842. However, he was not located on the rue Neuve des Petits-Champs, as indicated by his mark, until 1847.

H

HANDWERCK, 1876- Heinrich Handwerck of Waltershausen, Thuringia established a factory in 1876 for making wooden doll bodies and he died in 1902 according to records published by Patricia Schoonmaker in RESEARCH ON KÄMMER AND REINHARDT DOLLS. Heinrich Handwerck registered German trademarks for his eight pointed star in 1891 with French wording and in 1895 with German wording. He registered in Germany the name "Bébé Cosmopolite" in 1895; the name "Heinrich Handwerck" and the name "Bébé Réclame" in 1898; and the name "Bébé Superior" in 1913. A German Directory of 1891 lists Heinrich Handwerck of Waltershausen as a maker of ball jointed dolls. He obtained a German patent in 1897 for ball jointed dolls (see following page) and he also obtained a German doll patent in 1900. An ink stamp on the right thigh of a doll reads, "Heinrich Handwerck D R Patent # 100297". This is the number of his 1897 patent. After Heinrich Handwerck died in 1902, the Handwerck factory was taken over by Kämmer and Reinhardt. Strobel and Wilken (see pp. 71-72) handled Heinrich Handwerck dolls.

The relationship to Max Handwerck of Waltershausen is not known. Max Handwerck registered in 1901 his German trademark "Bébé Elite" which he had used since 1900. The mark on the doll's head which is

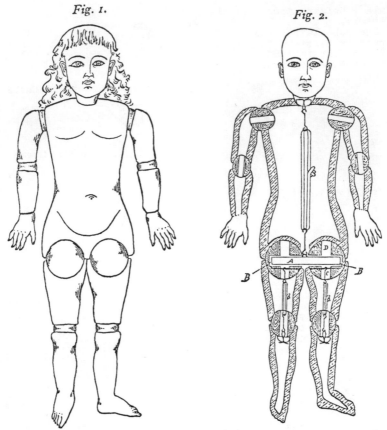

Fig. 1.

Fig. 2.

Patent drawing of Heinrich Handwerck's ball jointed doll, 1897

pictured, indicates that Max
Handwerck used a bisque head
made by William Goebel. Handwerck dolls exhibited at Seattle, Washington in 1910 were
described as, "Dolls from the
master hands of Handwerck who
produces only dolls of quality"

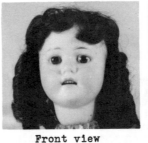

Front view   Rear view

Max Handwerck's "Bébé Elite"

79.

10.

Germany
HANDWERCK
fig. 1

.H.
fig. 2

fig. 3
Heinrich Handwerck trademark
Handwerck Marks

Max
HANDWERCK
Germany
fig. 4

Germany
HANDWERCK
HALBIG
fig. 5

Handwerck Marks, cont. (see pp. 71-72 for additional marks)

HARMUS, 1873- (see p. 30)

HARSDORFER, ca. 1600   Georg Philipp Harsdorfer, a native of Nürnberg, Bavaria
around 1600 created mechanical craftsmen
such as a barber, a painter, a butcher and
a baker, according to Chapuis and Droz,
AUTOMATA, p. 335. This might be a spell-
ing variant of Philipp Hainhofer (see p. 30) mentioned by Max Von
Boehn.

Harmus
7   M
fig. 1   fig. 2

Harmus Marks

HARWOOD, 1862- (see p. 30)   William A. Harwood appears in New York
City Directories as early as 1862 as a manufacturer.

HAWKINS, 1862- (see p. 31)   In 1862 George Hawkins was listed in
the New York City Directory under "Bonnets". The 1867 New York City
Directory lists George H. Hawkins as a manufacturer of "Excelsior
bonnet frames". It is interesting to note that papier-mâché doll
heads have been found marked "EXCELSIOR".

HERLAND, 1865   Augustin Marie Herland obtained a French patent in
1865 for a mechanical doll that would skip rope to the sound of
music.

HEUBACH, 1820- (see pp. 32-33)   Ernst Heubach
was allegedly a brother-in- law of Armand
Marseille.

HIGGS, 1733   William Higgs of London in 1733
made jointed wooden babies (dolls) which he
turned on a lathe. His wife dressed the babies.
His apprentice, Joseph Phips, painted faces.
The dolls were sold to shops for 2½ pence each
(5¢) according to Early, ENGLISH DOLLS, p. 90.

Ernst Heubach Mark

HOFFMAN, 1873   Joseph Hoffman of Waterbury, Connecticut patented
in the United States in 1873 a mechanical rope skipping doll.

HORSMAN, 1865- (see pp. 33-34)   Horsman used the trademark shown on the right from 1897 on. In the early
decades of the twentieth century Horsman obtained a large
number of copyrights and trademarks for dolls. These
will be given in detail in Volume II.

Horsman
Trademark

HUBBELL, 1874-   William L. Hubbell of Brooklyn,
early in 1874 patented in the United States waltzing dolls operated by a clockwork mechanism, which he
called "Hubbell's Grand Jubilee Dancers". Later
in 1874 Hubbell filed for an improvement in the joints of his dancers and assigned this patent to Raymond Jenkins (see p. 37) of New
York who also purchased in 1874 and registered in 1875 the U. S.
trademark, "Jubilee". The second patent was granted in 1875. In
1876 William Hubbell obtained two more U. S. patents which he also

assigned to Raymond Jenkins.
These were both for mechanical
dolls operated by clockwork
movements. The 1879 New York
City Directory listed William L.
Hubbell under toys. See page
71 for "Jubilee" dolls handled
by Strobel & Wilken Co.

```
┌─────────────────────────────────────┐
│          HUBBELL'S                   │
│      Grand Jubilee Dancers,          │
│  PATENTED. { FEBRUARY 17th. 1874.    │
│            { FEBRUARY 2d. 1875.       │
└─────────────────────────────────────┘
```

Trademark of Hubbell and Jenkins

HURET, 1819- (see p. 34) Leopold
Huret won silver medals at the   Paris Expositions of 1819, 1823,
1827, 1834, 1839 and 1844 as well as 1849 but they appear to have
been for dolls' and children's furniture. In 1851 Leopold Huret advertized all kinds of jointed dolls of a new type with porcelain
heads. In 1857 he was advertizing patented jointed dolls.

HYATT, 1870- (see pp. 34, 36) An English patent of 1877 indicates
that Isaiah Smith Hyatt of Newark, New Jersey was the brother of
John Wesley Hyatt. In 1881 William B. Carpenter of Newark, New
Jersey obtained an English patent for moulding dolls and doll heads
of celluloid. A similar U. S. patent was obtained in 1881 by Carpenter and Marshall C. Lefferts.

I

ILLFELDER, 1862- (see p. 36) The 1862 and 1867 New York City Directories list Leopold Illfelder with his home in Europe. The 1867
and 1874 Directories list as Stationers both Leopold Illfelder and
Bernard Illfelder Jr. at the same place of business, but Leopold's
home was in England in 1874 while Bernard lived in New York City.
In 1893 when Francois Edmond Hèron and Carl Cràmer of Sonneberg obtained their U. S. trademark, "BABY RUTH", they stated that Cràmer
& Hèron was late of L. Illfelder & Co. Heron was a British subject
in 1893. Max Illfelder registered as his trademark "ROSEBUD" in
Germany in 1902; "LITTLE SWEETHEART" in Germany in 1902 and in the
U. S. in 1905; and "MERRY WIDOW" in Germany in 1908. In 1905 the
firm, B. Illfelder & Co., was composed of Max Illfelder and Sigmund
Levy, both United States citizens, living in New York City. Max Illfelder, exporter of Furth, Bavaria registered in 1909 in Germany
the trademark, "BUMBLE PUPPY" to be used on dolls and doll heads.

INDIA RUBBER COMB CO., 1851- (see p. 36) The India Rubber Comb Co.
appeared in the New York City Directories for many years. In 1876
they registered "IMPERIAL" as their trademark in the United States.

IVES, 1866- (see p. 36) In the 1880's Ives made walking lady dolls
according to Hertz, THE HANDBOOK OF OLD AMERICAN TOYS, p. 96. The
1875 U. S. patent of Edward R. Ives and Joseph W. Pilkington relates
to an animal that rolls on three little wheels by a clockwork mechanism. It is possible that the walking doll that rolls on three
wheels as shown in one of the Paintings of the Index of American Design and in HOBBIES, March 1950, p. 40, might have been made by Ives.
J. J. Mott at one time belonged to the Ives firm. Jerome Burgess
Secor made automatons from 1877 to 1882 before joining Ives. The
Bridgeport City Directory listed Jerome Secor as a manufacturer of
mechanical toys and clock movement toys in 1879.

J

JAQUET -DROZ, 1773- (see pp. 36-37) The Musician, Draughtsman and
Writer of Jaquet-Droz first appeared in 1773. In 1782 Jean Frederic
Leschot, an apprentice of Pierre Jaquet-Droz, became a partner of
the son, Henri Louis Jaquet-Droz. After the death of Pierre in 1790

and Henri in 1791, Jean Frederic Leschot became manager of the
Jaquet-Droz & Leschot firm and created various automatons. From
1784 to 1792 Henri Maillardet was manager of the London branch of
the Jaquet-Droz firm. After 1792 he worked for himself and made
some famous Draughtsmen and Writer automatons. Two brothers of
Henri Maillardet, Jean David Maillardet, Jacques Rodolphe Maillardet
and a nephew, Auguste Maillardet created "Magician" automatons in
the early part of the 19th century. Jean David and his son, Auguste
Maillardet exhibited an automaton with two shepherdesses in 1809.
In 1840 Auguste Maillardet exhibited in Switzerland a mechanical
spinning girl according to Chapuis and Droz, AUTOMATA, pp. 337, 340.

JOHNSON, 1860-   Johnson Brothers
Ltd. of Birmingham, England was
established in 1860 and later became The Chad Valley Co., Ltd.
They trademarked in England in
1923 the name "LA PETITE CARESSE".
In 1924 they obtained patents for
doll heads made of stiffened material with glass eyes. Some
of the most famous Chad Valley
dolls were their portrait dolls
made in 1938 of Princess Elizabeth, Princess Margaret Rose
and Prince Edward.

Chad Valley, Princesses
Elizabeth and Margaret
Portrait Dolls

JOLIET, 1867   Nicholas Joliet
in 1867 obtained a French patent
for a doll or bébé with two faces. One of which was hidden by the
adjustable hair. The limbs of the doll moved into various positions by hidden joints.

JUDGE, 1867- (see p. 37)   Edward S. Judge was listed in the Baltimore Directory of 1867. In 1868 Edward S. Judge of Baltimore,
Maryland,obtained a patent for producing an extra surface on papier-
mâché by coating the surface of the mould with glue and whiting.
Mrs. E. W. Rasberry has a doll with a papier-mâché head marked:

   JUDGE'S PATENT INDESTRUCTIBLE DOLL HEAD, No. 3, March 24th, 1868

Johl in YOUR DOLLS AND MINE, p. 13 shows a papier-mâché doll head
marked:
            JUDGE & EARLY, No. 5, Patd. July 27, 1875

This Judge and Early mark is in a rectangle with a flower design at
each corner.

JULLIEN, 1875- (see p. 37)   Jullien, Jeune (Jr.) advertized in the
Paris Directory of 1875 that he made dressed bébés, dolls called
"Mignonettes" of nankeen (cotton cloth bodies), dolls called "Zou-
aves" (soldiers)and dolls called "Marottes" (whirling musical dolls
on a stick).

JUMEAU, 1842- (see pp. 37-42)   Dolls have been found marked "J".
According to Monsieur Moynot, formerly President of the Jumeau
Company, they used the "J" mark until about 1875 (DOLL NEWS, Feb.
1964, p. 6). Probably this "J" was used up until Emile Jumeau
became head of the firm in the second half of the 1870's. There is
a question as to the authenticity of some of the dolls marked with
a "J". (see SPINNING WHEEL, Jan.-Feb. 1964, p. 27)
   In 1885 (see p. 41) the method of making doll heads by applying
the clay paste onto a mould is described for the Jumeau factory.
This method would generally make a thicker head and rougher on the
inside than those made later by pouring slip. This fact may help
in the dating of doll heads. Some of the later Jumeau Bébés were
modeled by the master sculptor, Carrier-Belleuse. See Coleman, THE
AGE OF DOLLS for advertizements of the Jumeau Bébés from 1882-1897.

Emile Jumeau registered in 1891 a
French trademark to be stamped on Jumeau shoes. (see fig. 1) This trademark
was renewed by the Société Française de
Fabrication de Bébés et Jouets (S. F. B.
J.) in 1906. BÉBÉ FRANÇAIS was regist-
ed in France in 1896 by E. Jumeau. The
S. F. B. J. registered BÉBÉ PARISIANA in
1902; BÉBÉ MODERNE and LE SEDUISANT in
1903. EDEN BÉBÉ, the Fleischmann and
Bloedel trademark of 1890 was renewed by
the S. F. B. J. in 1905. The BÉBÉ PARIS-
IANA trademarked in 1902 by S.F.B.J.;
POUPÉE PARISIANA and POUPON PARISIANA
were all registered as trademarks in 1905
by the Société Anonyme de Comptoir General de la Bimbeloterie, Paris. In the
same year, 1905, the Société Française
de Fabrication de Bébés et Jouets registered a trademark with the letters
"S F B J" in a different form. The S.
F. B. J. registered their trademark in

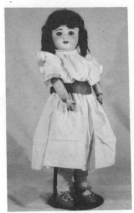

S. F. B. J. Doll
Mark: fig. 7

England in 1910. In 1911 the S. F. B. J. renewed the French registration of the trademarks: BÉBÉ JUMEAU, BÉBÉ FRANÇAIS, BÉBÉ PRODIGE,
and PARIS BÉBÉ. The first two had been Jumeau trademarks and the
last two were previously trademarked by Danel & Co.

Around 1907 the S. F. B. J. factories made 4½ million dolls a
year. By 1912 they were producing 5 million dolls a year. In 1921
6 million Bébé Jumeaus were produced. (see pp. 40-41 for production
in earlier years) This should be compared with the 1903 output of
Sonneberg porcelain factories which was around 20 million doll
heads.   There were over 20 million papier-mâché doll heads made in
Sonneberg in 1903.

Fashion experts dressed the French dolls and prizes were offered
each year for improvements. Women all over the world helped to design the dolls' clothes which is one reason for the excellence of
French dolls. (also see Deschamps, p. 92)

In 1893 P. H. Schmitz of Paris registered his trademark, BÉBÉ
MODERNE.   This trademark was renewed in 1903 by S.F.B.J. which indicates that Schmitz had joined the S.F.B.J. by 1903.

BÉBÉ MODERNE   "BÉBÉ PARISIANA"   (UNIS FRANCE)

fig. 2
Schmitz, 1893
S.F.B.J., 1903

fig. 3
S.F.B.J., 1902

fig. 4
S.F.B.J.

PARIS

DÉPOSÉ
fig. 1
Jumeau, 1891
S.F.B.J., 1906
Mark on shoes

LE SÉDUISANT
fig. 5
S.F.B.J., 1903
TÊTE DÉPOSÉ
PARIS BÉBÉ
11
fig. 9
Danel, 1889
S.F.B.J., 1911

fig. 6
S.F.B.J., 1905

S. F. B. J.
60
PARIS
fig. 7
Mark on
doll pictured

fig. 8
S.F.B.J.
1910

Société Française de Fabrication de Bébés et Jouets Marks (see p. 42)

K

KEEP, 1867-   J. M. Keep & Co. is listed in an 1867 New York City
Directory as a manufacturer of small toys. In 1868 James M. Keep
applied for a patent on the improvement in the dancing motion of a
toy figure. This patent was granted in 1869.

KESTNER, 1805- (see pp. 43-44) Around 1845 Kestner was manufacturing dolls with either kid or muslin bodies. A history of the firm
states that their dolls of this period had wooden limbs and papier-
mâché heads which are currently referred to as "milliner's models"
or "coiffure dolls". Dolls dressed in a chemise, shoes, stockings
and a hood were introduced by Kestner in 1845. In 1860 when Kestner
acquired their porcelain factory in Ohrdruf, Thuringia they began to make porcelain heads and wax over papier-mâché heads. Some
of these dolls contained a squeak box and had sleeping eyes. The
Kestner kid bodies were stuffed with sawdust, cork or hair. In 1896
Kestner made jointed composition and cloth body dolls as well as kid
body dolls. Around 1900 Kestner used slip casting for making bisque
doll heads. It is not known how long this method had been used by
Kestner. The Kestner dolls at the 1910 Exposition in Seattle, Washington were described as "dolls from the master hands of Kestner
who produces only dolls of quality". J. D. Kestner, Jr. of Waltershausen copyrighted in the United States in 1914 "HILDA", the head
of a child laughing and showing two front teeth.

DOLL MARK AND SIZE TABLE

Mark on Doll Head	Approximate Circumference of Doll Head
made in	
A Germany 5	8 inches
B " 6	8½ "
C " 7	9 "
D " 8	9½ "
E " 9	10 "
F " 10	10½ "
G " 11	11 "
H " 12	11½ "
J(I) " 13	12 "
K " 14	12½ "
L " 15	13 "
M " 16	13½ "
N " 17	15 "

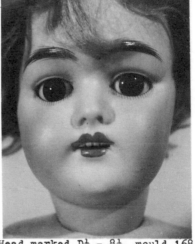

Head marked D½ - 8½, mould 168
Courtesy of Genevieve Angione

Kestner appears to have
used the above incised marks
on bisque heads of dolls to indicate the size of his dolls. The aver-
age measurement applies to socket type doll heads and is taken around
the head above the ears. There is some variation in head sizes probably due to differences in where it is measured and the amount of
shrinkage in firing. In addition to the numbers shown above there
are also half numbers, for example, D½ - 8½, E½ - 9½, Kk - 14½, etc.
Hildred Brinkley has a pair of identical twins, both mould number
146; one is marked "L - 15" and the other "L½ - 15½" with the latter
about ¼ inch larger in head circumference. Shoulder heads belonging
to this series appear to have the size number in the center back just
under the crown. The letter of the alphabet and the "made in Germany"
are along the edge of the back shoulder plate. The sizes of the shoulder heads seem to run slightly larger than the socket heads but the
differentials follow the same general pattern. A few lower case letters have been found but an insufficient number to draw any conclusions. Appreciation goes to Genevieve Angione for introducing this
study and calling attention to the fact that the heads in this series
seem to have a characteristic mouth with squared-off ends on the upper lips and the appearance of having been drawn with a stencil. all
of the sample studied show plaster-like pates and heavy decal eyebrows. One of these size markings, "C - 7" (mould No. 152) appears
on a bisque doll head without the "JDK". This head is on a walking
body with red marks stamped on the sole of the feet. On one foot is:
DRP   This refers to the German patent No. 66543 which Adolf Ascher
66543   of Berlin obtained in 1892 for mechanically pressing hollow
1 1/2   doll bodies out of a single piece. On the other foot is the

"Linon" mark registered in 1895 by
Herrmann Landshut & Co. of Waltershausen
and used since January 1894 (see picture
of doll). The head appears to be original on this doll and if so, indicates
that these size markings were used at
least from the 1890's until after 1910.
The fur eyebrow doll, several of which
were included in the sample on which the
table is based,was patented in 1910. The
character babies such as the one pictured
on page 43 were not made until around 1910.
The heads in this series which are also
marked "JDK" generally came from moulds
numbered around 200 or more.

Dolls with the num-
bers 171, 180, 186,
187 and 195 do not
have "JDK" on their
heads but are known
to be Kestner heads
of 1910 or later.
The first four mould
numbers are found in
an original box at the
Mary Merritt Museum and

Doll Head Marked
as in fig.1
Landshut Doll Body
Patented by Ascher
Raised Foot with
"Linon" Mark

were advertized in PLAYTHINGS, Jan. 1910, p.12.
The 195 is on a fur eyebrow head on a Kestner
marked body. Figure 8, p. 44 is the mark on a
Kestner fur eyebrow doll also which shows that
various moulds were used to make these dolls.
In studying mould numbers, it should be remembered that several firms often used the same
number.

Kestner Character
Dolls advertized in
PLAYTHINGS Jan. 1910

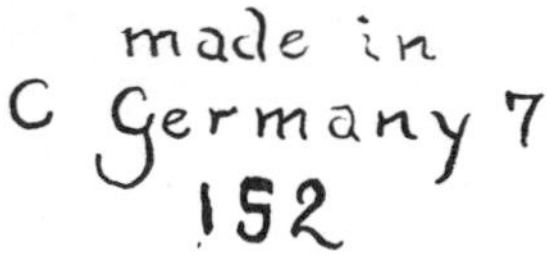

made in
C Germany 7
152
fig. 1

fig. 2
Marks on doll pictured above

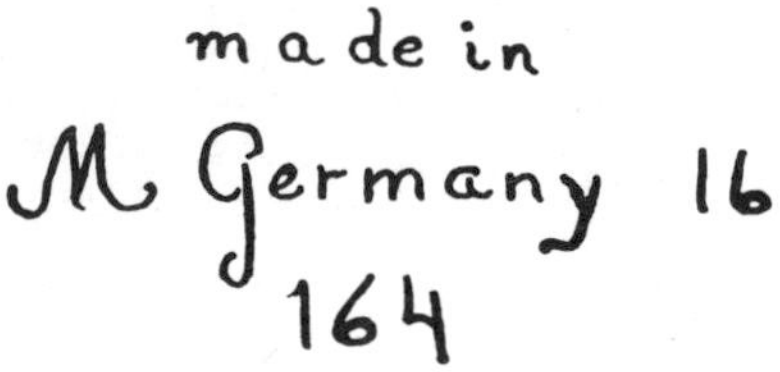

made in
M Germany 16
164
fig. 3

Hilda
©
J.D.K. Jr.190
Ges gesch
madein 1070
Germany

fig. 6
Kestner's HILDA Mark
1914

Made in
3½   Germany   10½
171
fig. 4
Size Marks

fig. 5
Kestner
& Co. Mark

In June 1892 the J. D. Kestner firm obtained a German patent for stringing a jointed composition doll. This was patented in England in August 1892 and Luella Hart pictures it in her DIRECTORY OF BRITISH DOLLS, p. 18. An amended patent was

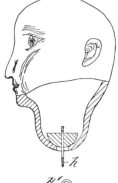

Zu der Patentschrift

№ 70685.

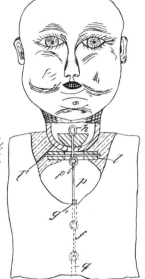

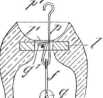

obtained in Germany in January 1893 which is shown in the accompanying patent drawings.

KLING, 1836-   (see p. 44)

Kling china head doll
Height of doll 10½ inches
Height of head 3 inches

Germany
189 🔔 2/0

Incised mark on rear shoulder
of doll shown above

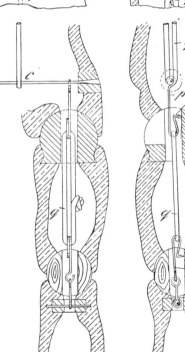

Front view   Side view
Kestner German Patent, 1893

L

LACMANN, 1860- (see p. 46)
The name of Jacob Lacmann's
son who also made doll bodies was J. P. Alfred Lac-
mann. A doll body made from
the 1871 Lacmann U. S. patent is shown in the AMERI-
CAN GERMAN REVIEW, Decem-
ber, 1959, page 31.
A Lacmann body made from
the 1874 U. S. patent and
stamped in blue ink on both
upper arms and in black ink
on both rear thighs is pictured here. The
arms are cloth but of a darker color than
the rest of the body which is stamped "8"
on the rump. The head is a French type
bisque with cork pate, applied and pierced
ears, stationary paperweight eyes and closed mouth.

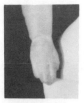

Enlargement
of Lacmann
hand

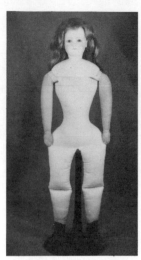

Lacmann body
Body 23 inches
Doll 27 inches
mark, see p. 46

LA GROVE, 1873 (see p. 46)   William A. P.
La Grove assigned his 1873 U. S. patent
for an automatic toy dancer to himself,
to Charles O'Kemp of Brooklyn and to Henry
H. Webb of Newark, New Jersey.

LAMORLETTE, 1839-   Madame Lamorlette was listed in Paris Directories
as a maker of dolls from 1839 through 1846.

LANG, 1865- (see p. 46)   The 1868 London Directory states that Lang
& Co. made dolls with India rubber faces. In the Paris Directory of
1869 Lang advertized rubber dolls and rubber doll heads.

LANTERNIER, 1873- (see pp. 46-47)   A. Lanternier Jr. learned the
pottery business in England under Wedgewood. Lanternier doll heads
have been found with the names "FAVORITE" and "LA GEORGIENNE" on
them.

LEE, 1850- (see p. 48)   Charles Goodyear obtained a U. S. patent in
1853 and an English patent in 1855 for moulding toys of India rubber
and gutta percha. The U. S. patent was issued to Charles Goodyear
and Robert Haering of New Haven, Connecticut, with Charles Goodyear
as assignee.

LEGRIP, 1833   Madame Legrip appeared in the 1833 Paris Directory
as a doll maker.

LE MAIRE, 1829-   Le Maire, a maker of kid dolls, was listed in
Paris Directories from 1829 through 1852.

LETORT, 1849   LeTort of Paris obtained a French patent in 1849 for
detachable feet and heads on dolls.

LEVERD, 1869   Leverd & Co. obtained a French patent in 1869 for an
improvement in making jointed dolls.

LUCAS, 1832   Richard Cockle Lucas in 1832 created a wax portrait
doll of the Marchioness of Blandford according to Gerken, WONDERFUL
DOLLS OF WAX, p. 115. In 1832 the Marchioness of Blandford was Jane
Spencer-Churchill an ancestress of Sir Winston Churchill.

LUGUET, 1877-   A. Luguet of Paris obtained a French patent in 1877
for a mechanical doll which would wave a flag. This doll was to be

sold as a souvenir of the 1878 Paris Exposition.

M

MAELZEL, 1808- (see pp. 49-50) Monsieur Maelzel made musical automatons as early as 1808. At Vienna in 1809 he exhibited an "Automatic Trumpeter" which played various marches and bugle calls.

MARCHAL, 1863- (see p. 50) The 1871 Paris Directory lists the shop
of Marchal and Buffard as "Aux Bébés Sages".

MARSEILLE, 1865-   Armand Marseille established a porcelain factory,
according to Jervis, A BOOK OF POTTERY
MARKS, p. 51, in Köppelsdorf, Thuringia
in 1865. Tradition says that he came from
Riga, Russia. In Germany Armand, his son
and his grandson were also known as Her-
man, but the surname suggests that either
the family did not originate in Russia or
they changed their name. German Directories list Armand Marseille as a maker of
porcelain doll heads in the 1890's. Armand Marseille made the following doll
heads as well as many others: FLORODORA
for Borgfeldt in 1901; BABY BETTY, 1912;
DUCHESS, 1914; DREAM BABY, 1924; KIDDIE-
JOY, 1926; JUST ME, 1928; COLUMBIA and
probably QUEEN LOUISE. Louis Wolf & Co.
(see pp. 76-77) used Armand Marseille
doll heads. As late as 1935 Armand Marseille still employed a large number of
people to make doll heads. Most of their
heads are marked with a mould number;
370 for shoulder heads and 390 for socket heads seem to be the two most frequently found. Numbers such as 1894, 1900,
1908, etc. could represent the year in
which the model was first used but this
has not been proven. For further information on Armand Marseille dolls, see the
series of articles by Genevieve Angione
in SPINNING WHEEL, beginning March 1966.
  In 1888 Francois Emile Marseille, doll
maker at Maisons Alfort, County of Seine
(Paris area) registered a French trademark,
LE PETIT FRANÇAIS.

Armand Marseille Doll
Original costume, 1932
Head marked as in fig. 3
Height of doll, 9 inches

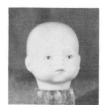

Armand Marseille baby
Marked as in fig. 7
circumference of head
8 3/4 inches

fig. 1*

fig. 2

Armand Marseille
Germany
390
A 12/0xM
fig. 3
1932

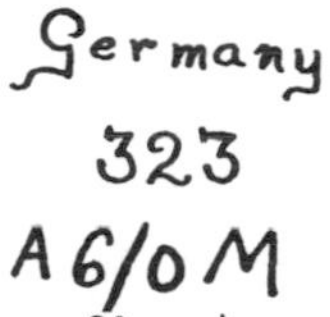

Germany
323
A 6/0 M
fig. 4

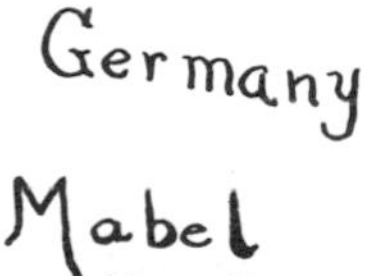

Germany
Mabel
fig. 5

A ⬡ELLAR M

Germany
2.K.
fig. 6

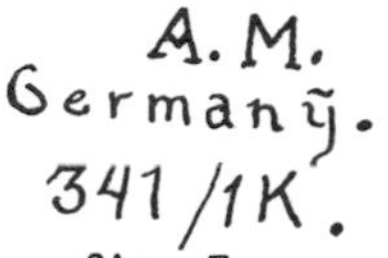

A.M.
Germany.
341/1K.
fig. 7
1924

Armand Marseille Marks

* Mark attributed to Armand Marseille by DOLL COLLECTORS OF AMERICA,
1946 Manual, p. 21. Ernst Heubach also used a horseshoe mark.

Made in Germany.

Armand Marseille
256
A 3/0 M

Maar
fig. 8

Made in Germany.

Armand Marseille
390
A. 9 M
fig. 9

Germany.
971
A 5 M
DRGM 267/1
fig. 10
Baby head
circum. 11 inches

1894
A.M. 0 DEP.
Made in Germany
fig. 11, Doll 13 inches

AM
Germany
351. 14K
fig. 12

3200
AM 8/0 DEP
fig. 13
Doll 11 inches

Germany
310
A 8/0 M
fig. 14

Made in Germany
A 4 M
Z
fig. 15

A M
Germany
341/3K
fig. 16

Floradora
A.M. 5½. DRP.
made in Germany.
fig. 17, 1901-, Doll 24 inches
fur eyebrows

Florodora
A-4-M
Made in Germany
fig. 18, 1901-

Made in Germany
A   M
DRGM
fig. 19, 1912-

Baby
O
Belly

Duchess
germany
A M
fig. 20
1914-

Duchess
A.6 M.
Made in Germany
fig. 21, 1914-

Germany
Kiddieioy
372
A 1. M
fig. 22, 1926-

Just ME.
Registered.
Germany
A 310/7/0. M
fig. 23, 1928-
eyes look sidewise

253
9 B
Germany
AOM
fig. 24

G. 253 B.
Germany
A 11/0 M
fig. 25

Armand Marseille Marks

MARSH, 1865- (see p. 50)   The London Directories list Mrs. Mary Ann Marsh, doll repairer, through 1910. From 1911 through 1913 Miss Jessie Marsh was listed in the doll business at the same address.

MARTELET, 1829-   Martelet, Jeune (Junior)was listed in Paris Directories as a maker of moulds for dolls from 1829 through 1836.

MARTIN, 1874- (see pp. 18-19, 50-51)

CHAS. MARSH MANUFACTURER 31+32 CORINTHIANBASAAR ARGYLL ST. LONDON W DOLLS REPAIRED

WARRANTED TO STAND ANY CLIMATE

Marsh marks

Front view   Side view
Wooden dolls made by Jointed Doll Co. (blonde, 12 inches) and Co-operative Manufacturing Co. (brunette 12½ inches)

"Ondine"
20th century version
Courtesy of Kitty Smith

MARTIN, 1863- (see p. 51)
"Ondine", the clockwork swimming doll invented by Elie Martin in 1876, was advertized in the 1881/2 Catalog of Millikin & Lawley of London, p. 96. The price was 18s.6d. ($4.65)
From about 1900 to 1930 Fernand Martin made large quantities of automatons about 6 inches high, including "The messenger boy", "The little pianist", "The barber", "The violinist", and "The man breaking plates". In 1929 "Ondine" was being mass-produced by a member of the Martin family, according to Chapuis and Droz, AUTOMATA, pp. 165-166.

"Ondine" patented by Elie Martin
1881 advertizement

MARTIN & RUNYON, 1862-   Martin & Runyon of London were English makers of the Enoch Rice Morrison "Autoperipatekos" doll patented in 1862. A doll box in England states that H. Martin was the sole agent for "Autoperipatekos" dolls. London Directories list Martin & Runyon in 1865. (also see Cohen, p. 13 and Lyon, p. 49)

MATHIEU, 1766-   Father Jean Mathieu built automatons for the Emperor of China between 1766 and 1787 accord-

Autoperipatekos with china head

ing to Chapuis and Droz, AUTOMATA, p. 315.

MAYORGA, 1878   J. Mayorga of Guatemala exhibited dolls dressed in native costumes at the Paris Exposition of 1878.

MEISEL, 1862-   The 1862 New York City Directory lists Aloys Meisel as a Toyman and also a member of the importing firm of Meisel, Lampe & Co. His partner was Edward Lampe and they dealt in German, French and English toys. In 1878 Aloys Meisel of Brooklyn resistered a U. S. trademark to be used on toys. (also see Wiegand p. 76)

MESS, 1465   H. Mess of Nürnberg was recorded as a doll maker in 1465 according to Max Von Boehn.

METZLER, 1864 (see p. 53)

Meisel Trademark

Metzler & Ortloff Mark

MEYLAN, ca. 1800   Philippe Samuel Meylan of Geneva, Switzerland made Magician automatons by himself and later around 1811 with Isaac Daniel Piguet of Geneva. They made a great number and variety of automatons at least as late as 1828.

MONTANARI, 1851- (see p. 53)   Jo Elizabeth Gerken, the wax doll expert, has found "Montanari" marks only on doll bodies and not on doll heads. One mark is in brown ink on the lower front of the torso. All of the marked Montanari dolls which she has found have bunches of hair inserted in slits and not single hairs inserted with a needle.

MORRELL, 1870- (see p. 54)

MORTYN, 1860-   James Mortyn of London was listed in the London Directories as a doll maker from 1860 through 1879.

MOST, 1852, (see p. 54)   G. H. Most, doll maker, in 1852 was the successor to Mademoiselle Benoist. He used German-made doll heads.

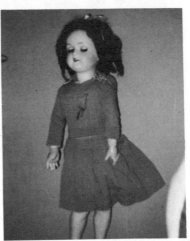

Metzler Doll; mark, see p. 53
Courtesy of the Newark Museum

Morrell Mark

MÜLLER, 1863- (see pp. 54-55)   Andrew Müller of Sonneberg, Thuringia registered his German trademark in 1896 which he had used since 1894. This mark was used on doll bodies (not made of porcelain) on waxed and poured wax and wooden jointed dolls. According to Gwen White, DOLLS OF THE WORLD, p. 233, Leopold Emil Jacob of London, importer of toys used this mark in 1893. This is three years before the mark was registered and one year before it was reported

Müller Trademark

as used by Müller.

MUNIER (MUNNIER), 1834- (see p. 55)
The widow Munier, doll maker, was
listed in Paris Directories from
1834 through 1852.

Maison Munnier

*Passagon Janpsoz
n° 15817.
Paris*

Mark on Munnier Doll

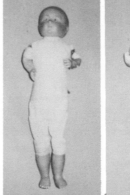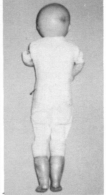

Front   Back
Munnier Doll, marked on back
Courtesy of the Newark Museum

N

NATIONAL TOY CO., 1871- (see p. 55) The 1871 English patent papers
of the National Toy Co. of New York City show a crawling doll with
a large serrated wheel like George Pemberton Clarke's crawling doll
also patented in 1871. (see Clarke p. 12 and Clay p. 90) The English
patent appears to have several small wheels in the front while
Clarke has only one under each arm.

NEUBERGER, 17th century   Daniel Neuberger of Augsburg, Bavaria in
the 17th century, according to Joachim Von Sandrart, made wax dolls
which were as hard as stone and so marvelously colored that they
seemed to be alive.

NEW YORK RUBBER CO., 1851- (see p. 55) The New York Rubber Co. of
New York City obtained a U. S. patent in 1859 for hollow elastic
dolls with reed, whistle or other squeaking device inserted in the
body. These dolls were advertized in the 1876 Catalog of Strasburger, Pfeiffer & Co. (see p. 116)

NOONAN, 1874-   Timothy Noonan of Boston, Massachusetts obtained a
U. S. patent for improvement in an automaton that smoked either a
pipe or a cigar. In 1876 Timothy Noonan and William Emerson Baker
of Wellesley, Massachusetts, obtained a U. S. patent for improvements
in a mechanical bubble blowing doll. This patent was assigned to
William Baker.

NUNNS, 1864   William Nunns of New York City obtained a U. S. patent
in 1864 for an automaton dancer operated by a pianoforte action.

NYMPHENBURG, 1753- (see p. 55) A doll marked with a pattern of
lozenges on an irregular shield (see p. 56, mark on right) is pictured on the cover of DOLL NEWS, May 1963.

O

OTT, 1413   Ott of Nürnberg was recorded as a doll maker in 1413.

P

PANNIER, 1872- (see p. 56)   In the
1870's Pannier is listed at the same
address as Rauch. (see p. 59)
    A doll with the head incised "C9P"
and the sole of the foot marked Mme.
Pannier is described and pictured in
DOLL NEWS, Nov. 1965, pp. 6-8.   Charles Pannier was listed under dolls in
the 1881-1882 Paris Directories.   The
1892 Paris Directory lists Madame
Pannier as making bébés and dolls and
Pannier Frères (brothers) engaged in
the porcelain business.

Mme. Pannier   C 9 P.

Doll head marked "C9P."
    Mark on sole of foot   Mark on head   on doll 22 inches
            Marks on doll pictured

PARENT, 1871- (see p. 56)   Charles Louis Parent of Havre, France
    obtained a French patent in 1871 and a U. S. patent in 1872 for a
    ball jointed doll strung with elastic.   The head and waist swivel
    on a complete ball, the wrist, elbow, shoulder, hip, knee and ankle
    joints have the lower member rounded at the top so that it fits in-
    to the cavity of the adjoining socket.   The construction of the
    body is somewhat similar to the 1869 Bru patent. (see p. 89)

PERONNE, 1864-   Mademoiselle Peronne was listed in Paris Director-
    ies under dolls for 1864 and 1865. At the same address, 21 rue de
    Choiseul, Madame Lavallée - Peronne was then listed through 1884.
    Apparently Mademoiselle Peronne married in 1865 for the JOURNAL DES
    POUPÉES published in 1865 appears to be an advertizement for "La
    Poupée de Nuremberg", the Paris shop of Madame Lavallée - Peronne.
    The 1870 Paris Directory states that Madame Lavallée- Peronne spe-
    cializes in dolls' trousseaux and is recommended by JOURNAL DES
    DEMOISELLES ET LA POUPÉE MODELE.   A wooden body French fashion
    type doll has a label on the chest,"À LA POUPÉE DE NUREMBERG, 21
    rue de Choiseul, Lavallée - Peronne, Trousseaux complets, Repara-
    tions, Paris". (see Hart, COMPLETE FRENCH DOLL DIRECTORY, p. 36)

PLUMB, 1865- (see p. 58)   H. Plumb was listed in the 1868 London
    Directory as a doll maker.

POOLE, 1843- (see p. 58)   L. Poole, wooden doll maker, was listed
    in the 1852 through 1855 Directories at the same address in London
    as John R. Poole.

R

RABERY & DELPHIEU, 1856- (see p. 59)
    Both Rabery & Delphieu and Roulet &
    Decamps (see p. 62) used "R. D." as
    their mark. It seems logical that the
    mechanical dolls marked "R. D." would
    be made by Roulet & Decamps since that
    was their specialty. The non-mechan-
    ical dolls marked "R. D." were prob-
    ably made by Rabery & Delphieu.

R.4.D

Mark on 28 inch doll pictured

Doll head marked "R. 4 D."

RECHSTEINER, 1840-   Rechsteiner of Germany and Switzerland created a smoking doll in 1840 and in 1842 made a talking doll that
said, "Papa, Mama "according to Chapuis and Droz, AUTOMATA,
pp. 324, 332.

RESTIGNAT, 1868-   Madame Restignat, née Filliol appears in Paris
Directories from 1868 through 1872. She made doll bodies and dressed
dolls as well as making trousseaux of all kinds. In 1869 she obtained a French patent for a jointed cork doll body, with a head
that could turn completely around.

RICHARD, 1853-   Monsieur Richard, toymaker, of the environs of Paris
obtained a French patent in 1853 for a type of composition comprised
of malleable paste of lime, plaster, stearic wax, tallow and whiting.
Doll heads made of this composition were known as "Buste Richard".
Richard claimed that his doll heads were more durable, superior and
cheaper than those formerly imported from Germany.

RIDGEWAY, ca. 1800   At the end of the 18th century Job Ridgeway founded a pottery in Staffordshire, later carried on by his sons, John
Ridgeway and William Ridgeway. Their products were marked "J. R."
or "J. RIDGEWAY". After John Ridgeway retired in 1859, Messrs.
Brown-Westhead and Moore took over the Company and used the initials,
"B.W.M. & Co." for their mark as late as the first decade of the
twentieth century. For some years this firm was known by the name,
Cauldon Potteries. Fragments of doll heads have been discovered on
the Cauldon premises but the marks that were used on the doll heads
have not been identified. Cauldon Potteries took over the pottery
of S. Hancock & Sons, also known as Corona Potteries; some of whose
wares from 1891 on were marked "S.H. & S.". S. Hancock & Sons (Cauldon) are known to have made dolls and used the trademark "CORONA"
in the 1930's. During the 1930 decade Cauldon Potteries were acquired
by Crescent Potteries, also known as George Jones & Sons, who had
been in the pottery business since 1862 and used the mark "G.J. &
Sons". According to a manager of Coalport China Ltd., "Corona" dolls,
"were made in several sizes and decorated in natural and black, and
supplied either with fixed or moveable eyes".

ROBERT, 1858   André Francois Emile Robert, toymaker of Paris, in
1858 obtained both a French patent for a crying rubber doll and an
English patent for moulding vulcanized rubber dolls. His London patent agent was Richard Archibald Brooman (see p. 89) who in 1848 had
obtained a U. S. patent for moulding busts of gutta percha.

ROCHARDE, mid 19th century   Two doll heads signed, "Ed Rocharde"
are pictured in Fawcett, DOLLS, A NEW GUIDE FOR COLLECTORS, pp. 59,110.
One of these is an early china head with long curls and the other
is a bisque head with glass eyes. No E. Rocharde has been found in
Paris Directories but the Breveté and S.G.D.G. found on the doll
heads suggest that he was French.

ROCHAT, ca. 1810-   The brothers, Ami Napoleon
Rochat and Louis Rochat created numerous automatons and "magiciens" in Brassus and Geneva,
Switzerland during the first quarter of the
19th century and as late as 1829.

Ed Rocharde

Depose

Breveté

S.G.D.G.

Rocharde Mark

ROENTGEN AND KINTZING, 1780   Roentgen, a cab-
inet maker, and Kintzing, a watchmaker, made one
of the most famous lady musicians about 1780.
The lady plays a dulcimer and was acquired for Queen Marie Antoinette according to Chapuis and Droz, AUTOMATA, pp. 279, 285.

ROSSIGNOL, 1878-   (see p. 61)   Charles Rossignol obtained a French
patent for perfecting a walking doll in 1888.

ROULLET & DECAMPS, before 1871-   (see p. 62)   The firm of Roullet
& Decamps was founded in the second Empire period by Jean Roullet

whose daughter married Monsieur Decamps of Paris. Chapuis and Droz,
AUTOMATA, pp. 262-263 describes and pictures the first automaton de-
vised and created by Decamps, namely a woman snake-charmer. Around
1890 Jean Roullet made a negro piper. In the twentieth century
Gaston Decamps and Georges Decamps made automatons. Georges Decamps
called his mechanical dolls, "Chansons de France" which included the
chef lifting the lid off of a pot in which he is cooking a cat.
    Dolls marked "E.D." are often identified as made by Ernst Decamps.
This may be correct but the fact should not be overlooked that both
E. Denamur of Paris (see p. 15) and E. Dumont of Paris (see p. 18)
were also making dolls and bébés in the second half of the 19th century. Moreover, Ernst Decamps was the junior member of the firm
Roullet & Decamps that used the mark "R.D." according to Paris Directories of the period.

ROUSSELOT, 1845- (see p. 62)   The Paris Directories from 1846 through
    1852 list Rousselot.

S

SCHMITT, 1863- (see pp. 63-64)   Franz Schmidt & Co. of Georgenthal,
    Thuringia, makers of dolls, doll heads, doll bodies and
    jointed dolls in 1902 registered their trademark in Ger-
    many. As seen in the picture, their trademark has cross-
    ed hammers similar to those found on French Schmitt dolls.   Schmidt
                                                                  Mark

SCHOENAU, 1854-   Gebrüder (Brothers) Schoenau,
    Swaine & Co., a porcelain factory in Köppels-
    dorf, Thuringia,was founded in 1854. The rela-
    tionship is not known to the Schoenau & Hoff-
    meister Porcelain factory which was founded in
    1901 in Burggrub, Bavaria.

fig. 1   fig. 2   fig. 3   fig. 4   fig.5
    Gebrüder   Schoenau, Swain & Co.   Marks

fig. 6

4000
fig. 7

PORZELLAN
FABRIK
BURGGRUB
169
A/0
Germany
    fig. 9
    Schoenau & Hoffmeister Marks

4000-8
fig. 8

Schoenau & Hoffmeister
Doll with bisque head
Height 23 inches
Mark fig. 6

Porzellanfabrik - Burggrub
769
8/0
Germany
    fig. 10

SIMAR & FLANTIN, 1829-   (see p. 67)   Simar and Son made doll moulds
    as early as 1829. Flantin appears as a doll maker in the 1840 Paris
    Directory.

SIMONNE, 1839- (see p. 68)   Simonne appeared in Paris Directories as
    early as 1839. The listing was at rue de Rivoli 188 in 1863 which
    is the address given in the mark . This mark has been found stamped

in turquoise blue ink on the chest of a doll.

SMITH, 1846- (see p. 68)   Sampson Smith used the mark "S.S"
from 1846 through 1858 and "S.S. Ltd." from 1860 on. During
the 19th century his figures were formed by hand-pressing
bats of clay into moulds while in the 20th century casting
was done with slip.

Smith
Mark

SOUTY, 1862   Madame Hortense Vincent Souty obtained a French patent
for a jointed doll body made of painted pumice stone in 1862. The
head and arms of the doll could be of porcelain, bisque or pipe clay.

STEINER, 1855- (see pp. 68-71)   May Frères
(Brothers), later part of the Society Steiner,
registered BÉBÉ MASCOTTE as a French trademark
in 1890. Jules Mettais registered the following French trademarks in 1899: PHÉNIX BÉBÉ,
BÉBÉ LIÈGE and POUPÉE MERVEILLEUSE; and in
1901 BÉBÉ MODELE.

STEINER B^TE SGDG S^TE C·6 BOURGOIN
fig. 1

MARQUE DÉPOSÉE
ARTICLE
FRANCAIS
N° 13
BÉBÉ "PHÉNIX"
ARTICULE BREVETE SGDG
fig. 2

BÉBÉ-LIÈGE
fig. 3

PHÉNIX-BABY
fig. 4

Steiner Marks

Bébé Steiner
Mark: fig. 1
Height 28 inches

STENEVARD, before 1850   Monsieur Stenevard
of Hauteville, France,made automatons in the
first half of the 19th century according to
Chapuis and Droz, AUTOMATA, p. 255.

STEUBER, 1878 (see p. 71)   Mary Steuber patented in the U. S. in 1878 a commercial doll leg
made by sewing the stocking to the leg and the
boot to the stocking before sewing up the back
seam so that there is only one thickness of material. Thus obviating the method formerly used of
making a foot and leg, then making separate stockings and separate boots. Dolls with the type of
legs patented by Mary Steuber usually are found
with cloth bodies and china, papier-mâché or parian bisque heads.

STIMETS, 1864   Cassius P. Stimets of Trenton, N.
J.,and James E. Atwood of New York City patented
an automatic dancing doll in 1864.

STRASBURGER, 1851-   Oscar Strasburger of New York
City established a toy manufacturing, importing
and selling business in 1851. Edward Nuhn was as-
sociated with him at least from 1858 through 1867.
In 1862 Nuhn was living in Europe. By 1871 George
F. Pfeiffer and George Fritz joined Oscar
Strasburger and the firm became known as
Strasburger, Fritz & Pfeiffer. Fritz and
Pfeiffer lived in Europe at that time.
In 1869 they began using the trademark
pictured on the following page which they
registered in 1871. The next year, 1872, the

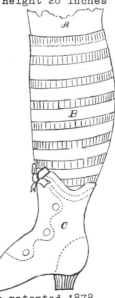

Legs patented 1878
by Mary Steuber

firm was known as Strasburger & Pfeiffer
and supplied toy data for the Christmas issue of HARPER'S BAZAR. This company won a
prize medal at the International Exhibition in Philadelphia in 1876. Their catalog
of around 1876 lists a large number of
dolls; china, bisque, rubber, rag and
worsted as well as doll heads, doll bodies
and doll arms (see below).

Strasburger, Fritz
& Pfeiffer Trademark

The 1879 New York City Directory shows
that George Pfeiffer was living in France
and that George Borgfeldt was employed with
the firm of Strasburger and Pfeiffer. In 1881 George Borgfeldt, Joseph
and Marcel Kahle left Strasburger & Pfeiffer to establish a new company known as Geo. Borgfeldt & Co. In 1913 George J. Pfeiffer was
assistant treasurer of Geo. Borgfeldt & Co. and in 1915 George J.
Pfeiffer was assistant treasurer of the Japan Import and Export
Commission Co. at the same address as Geo. Borgfeldt & Co.

**Excerpts from
Catalog of
STRASBURGER,
PFEIFFER & CO.,
ca. 1876
Courtesy of
Flora Gill Jacobs**

Model Wax Dolls.

Assorted head dresses, light and dark human hair,
steady eyes, eardrops and necklace, wax limbs,
real stockings and nicely painted gaiters,
with tassels; linen embroidered shirt.

No.			
4530/0	13½ in. long, ... per piece,		2.50
" 1	18 " . . . . . "		3.50
" 3	20 " . . . . . "		4.25
" 4	22 " . . . . . "		6.00
" 5	24 " . . . . . "		7.50
" 6	28 " . . . . . "		10 00
" 7	30 " . . . . . "		12.00
" 8	34 " . . . . . "		15.00

French Kid Dolls.

Bisque Moving Head, Natural Hair with Velvet Band,
Kid Jointed Body and Limbs.

J2/0	Size, ... per piece,	2.00
0	"	2.25
1	"	2.75
2	"	3.50
3	"	4.00
4	"	5.00
5	"	6.50
6	"	7.50
7	"	9.00
8	"	10.00
12	"	12.00

Bisque Moving Head, Natural Hair nicely trimmed
with Velvet Bands, Kid Jointed Body, Legs
and Feet, with Bisque Hands.

		Piece.
122 bis		
1	Size, ...	3.75
2	"	4.50
3	"	5.00
4	"	5.50
5	"	6.50

Mechanical Talking Doll,

On Wheels. When in motion speaks, very distinctly,
"Papa" and "Mamma." Fancy Silk Dress,
Bisque Head, Natural Hair and Earrings.

12½ inches long, . . . 1 piece in box,	7.50

Dressed Girl,

Perambulating with Carriage.

Size of Girl, 15 inches high, . . .	
" Carriage, 8¼ inches high, 14 inches long, pce.	2.50

No.	*Dressed Dolls,* with China Heads and China Limbs.			
331/0	9 inches long,	1 dozen in box,		5.50
" 1	10¼ " "	½ " "		7.50
" 2	11¼ " "	½ " "		9.50
336	0R/1 9½ " "	½ " "		4.00
"	4 12 " "	½ " "		7.50
8288	/8308/4 12½ inches long,	½	in box,	7.50
8281	/90/5 13 " "	½	"	9.00

Doll Bodies.

C. S.	*Stuffed with Sawdust, Leather Hands.*		
2/0	6 inches long	½ dozen in package.	1 12
0	7 " "	½ " "	1 25
1	8 " "	½ " "	1 38
2	9 " "	½ " "	1 50
3	10½ " "	½ " "	1 75
4	11½ " "	½ " "	2 00
5	13 " "	½ " "	2 50
6	14 " "	½ " "	3 00
7	16 " "	¼ " "	3 75
8	17½ " "	¼ " "	4 50
9	20 " "	¼ " "	5 50
10	23 " "	¼ " "	6 50
11	24 " "	¼ " "	7 50
12	27 " "	1-6 " "	9 50

	Hair Stuffed, Leather Arms and Closed Fingers.		
0	10 inches long	1 dozen in package.	1 75
1	11 " "	1 " "	2 00
2	11½ " "	1 " "	2 50
3	13 " "	½ " "	3 00
4	15 " "	½ " "	3 50
5	16½ " "	½ " "	4 00
6	18½ " "	½ " "	4 75
7	19½ " "	½ " "	5 50
8	20½ " "	½ " "	6 50
9	23 " "	⅓ " "	7 75
10		⅓ " "	9 00

	Hair Stuffed, Leather Arms, Closed Fingers, High Gaiters.		
0	10½ inches long	1 dozen in package.	2 25
1	11½ " "	1 " "	2 50
2	12½ " "	1 " "	3 00
3	14 " "	½ " "	3 50
4	15¼ " "	½ " "	4 25
5	18 " "	½ " "	5 00
6	19 " "	½ " "	6 25
7	20 " "	⅓ " "	6 75
8	21½ " "	⅓ " "	7 75
9	22¾ " "	⅓ " "	9 00
10		⅓ " "	10 50

	Hair Stuffed, Leather Arms, China Hands, High Gaiters.		
0	10 inches long	1 dozen in package.	3 25
1	11 " "	1 " "	3 50
2	12 " "	1 " "	4 50
3	14 " "	½ " "	5 00
4	15 " "	½ " "	6 00
5	17½ " "	½ " "	7 00
6	19½ " "	½ " "	8 50
7	21 " "	½ " "	10 50
8	22 " "	½ " "	12 00
9	24 " "	⅓ " "	13 50
10		⅓ " "	15 00

Excerpts from Catalog of

STRASBURGER, PFEIFFER & CO.,

ca. 1876

Note that doll bodies are often stamped with a number which corresponds with the numbers shown in these size tables.

Courtesy of Flora Gill Jacobs

STROBEL & WILKEN, 1864-   (see p. 71) (also see Handwerck, pp. 97-99)
Thanks to the excellent booklet RESEARCH ON KÄMMER AND REINHARDT
DOLLS by Patricia Schoonmaker, all of the dolls in the picture shown
below which was taken from PLAYTHINGS, February 1910, p. 4, can be
identified as made by Kämmer and Reinhardt. BABY is mould number
100, MARIE and PETER are 101, CARL is 107, ELISE is 109 and GRETCHEN
and HANS are 114. This leaves only ELSA and WALTER that cannot be
readily identified by number as yet. The heads of these dolls are
marked K⬦X R with the mould number.

4   **PLAYTHINGS**

Character Dolls

Marie

Baby

Hans

Peter

Carl

T A K E N   F R O M   L I F E

T R U E   T O   L I F E

Elise

Elsa

Gretchen

Walter

The Strobel and Wilken Co.

591 Broadway, NEW YORK

Chicago Office
240 ADAMS STREET

T

TERRÈNE, 1863-   Terrène of Paris was listed
as a hairdresser in Paris Directories from
1863 through 1873 and Widow Terrène, toymaker,
was listed in Paris Directories at the same
address, 10 rue de Marché-St. Honoré, from
1881 through 1890. Dolls have been found with
the body marked "J. Terrène, 10 rue de Marché-
St. Honoré". One of these dolls (see picture)
is jointed so that it can walk. It has a wood-
en French fashion type body, metal upper arms
and bisque hands. Terrène won medals at the
Expositions of 1867, 1868, 1872, 1873, and
1874 according to their advertizement.

THÉROUDE, 1842- (see pp. 72-73)   At the Paris
Exposition of 1855 Alexandre Théroude displayed
many types of very pretty mechanical toys.
They were moderately priced which permitted
them to be sold for export and to compete
against foreign products.
    In 1856 Théroud advertized that he was the
inventor of the talking doll (see Maelzel) and
maker of mechanical dolls.

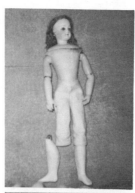
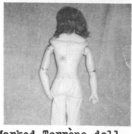

Marked Terrène doll
Courtesy of E.J. Carter

THUILLIER, 1875- (see p. 73)   A. Thuillier
has been found in Paris Directories as early as 1875. Dolls with bisque heads marked
"A. T." have never been definitely identified.
There are at least 3 French doll makers with
the initials "A.T.". Alexandre Théroude (see
pp. 72-73) made mechanical dolls. Adolphe
Thiers of Marseille repaired dolls and A.
Thuillier was the third one. Of these three,
Thuillier seems to be the best choice because of his type of doll and period of operation. In Hart, DIRECTORY OF GERMAN DOLLS,
p. 9, a doll is pictured which has an "A.T."
marked head on a "Heinrich Handwerck" marked
body. (see pp. 97-99) The head contains a
clockwork mechanism to move the eyes from
side to side.

TREDOULAT, 1859   Tredoulat, Sr. and Malvesin,
Sr. of the Paris environs were issued a French
patent in 1859 for durable rubber doll heads
of all sizes and colors.

Doll marked "A 14 T"
Height 29 inches
Courtesy of Roxana Bascom

V

VAUCANSON, 1735-   Jacques de Vaucanson of Paris began to make automatons in 1735. He presented his famous "Flute Player" and "Tambour-
ine Player" in 1738. In 1785 Bischoff, the younger, undertook to
restore the Vaucanson automatons according to Chapuis and Droz,
AUTOMATA, p. 233.

VERDAVAINNE, 1839- (see p. 74)   H. Verdavainne, doll maker, was
listed in Paris Directories from 1839 through 1852 and Alphonso
Verdavainne at a different address was listed from 1847 through 1872.

VERVELLE, 1876   Lucien Alexis Vervelle was granted a French patent
in 1876 for metal doll heads.

VICHY, 1862- (see p. 74)   Henry Vichy of Paris created a bugler automaton about 1900 which used phonographic music. (see Edison pp. 18,
93) This automaton is signed "Henry Vichy, rue Montmorency, Paris",
according to Chapuis and Droz, AUTOMATA, pp. 287-288.

VIDELIER, 1829- (see p. 74)   Videlier was listed in the Paris Directories as a doll maker from 1829 through 1852. In 1861 the Widow
Videlier was listed as a maker of all kinds of dolls, dressed and
undressed. From 1865 through 1882 Brasseur - Videlier are listed
as makers of inexpensive dolls, luxury dolls and jointed dolls,
dressed and undressed dolls and dolls' trousseaux.

VINCENT, 1873   Andre Vincent obtained a French patent in 1873 for
a mechanical "Waltzing Doll" with a papier-mâché body and either a
porcelain or papier-mâché head. The doll pivoted on one foot by
means of a clockwork mechanism.

VOGEL, 1879- (see p. 75)   Fritz Vogel of Sonneberg obtained a French
patent in 1880 for improvements in making doll heads and limbs. In
1930 Max Vogel of Sonneberg was making celluloid doll heads.

W

WALKER, ca. 1855- (see p. 75)   The dating of the Izannah Walker dolls
prior to the 1873 patent date appears to be based on family tradition
supplied by a great niece of Izannah Walker. Johl in YOUR DOLLS AND
MINE reports this family tradition and gives four different dates
for the first Izannah Walker dolls; 1840 (p. 40), 1845 (p. 39), 1848
(p. 37), 1855 (p. 41). Two death dates for Izannah Walker are given:
1886 (p. 39) and 1888 (p. 37). Typographical errors could account
for some of these differences but certainly not all of them. An Izannah Walker doll has been found with "Patented Nov. 4th 1873" written
in longhand inside of the head, but it is not known when it was written.

WEIR, 1866- (see pp. 75-76)   The U. S. patent obtained by Robert
Weir in 1880 was assigned to Samuel Goodman and Daniel Meyers, both
of Philadelphia, Pennsylvania.

WISLIZENUS, 1851- (see p. 76)   A. Wislizenus
registered the trademark OLD GLORY in Germany
in 1902 and stated that it had been used since
1900. Also in 1902 Hamburger & Co. of New York
City registered their trademark OLD GLORY in
the United States. Hamburger & Co. of New York
City was probably the American agent for Wislizenus. Hamburger & Co. registered several
other trademarks in the U. S., including "D.P."
and "H.&C." in 1895, both having been used
since 1893; IMPERIAL in 1898 (see Bawo & Dotter
marks, p. 87); SANTA in 1900 and MARGUERITE in
1902. Hamburger & Co. registered in Germany
"D.P." in 1895; IMPERIAL in 1901; SANTA in 1901;
VIOLA in 1903; MARGUERITE in 1903 and DOLLY
DIMPLE in 1907. Advertizements in PLAYTHINGS
for Hamburger & Co. as late as 1907 listed
Viola, Santa jointed dolls, Imperial kid dolls
and D. P. dressed dolls. The two trademarks
"H. & C." of Hamburger & Co. in 1895 used since
1893, and "H. & Co." of Hinricks & Co. in 1894
used since 1890 have caused some confusion.
  See the Hamburger trademark SANTA which has
"H. Co." on it and the German trademark IMPERIAL

fig. 1

S & H   1249
DEP.
Germany
SANTA.
fig. 2
Wislizenus and
Hamburger
marks found
on dolls

with "H. & Co." on it (also see Bawo & Dotter, p. 87)

Wislizenus registered in Germany the trademarks QUEEN QUALITY in 1910 and in 1919 MEIN GLÜCKSKIND (My Lucky Child) with the initials "A. W." over "W.". These initials have been found on bisque doll heads. "A. W." stamped on a jointed composition body has been noted with a bisque head marked "S.H.". Simon and Halbig heads were used by Hamburger & Co., see SANTA mark fig. 2, p. 120.

German trademark

fig. 1

fig. 2

fig. 3
United States trademarks
Hamburger & Co.

WITTON, 1855   T. F. Witton was listed in the 1855 London Directory as a doll maker.

WOLF, 1870- (see pp. 76-77)   Adolphe Erlebach became a member of the firm of Louis Wolf & Co. in 1888. He was their European buyer until his retirement in 1898. In 1897 Louis Wolf & Co. registered their trademark CINDERELLA BABY in the United States and the very same year, C. M. Bergmann of Waltershausen registered the very same trademark in Germany. Louis Wolf & Co. handled the Bergmann "Celebrated Jointed Dolls" according to a 1904 advertizement. The firm, Louis Wolf & Co., consisted of Thomas E. Stutson, Joseph Schmidt and Julius I. Baer all of Boston, Massachusetts, in 1910 and 1911. When Louis Wolf & Co. of New York registered their trademark CHUBBY in 1915, used since 1914, the firm comprised Thomas E. Stutson, Julius I. Baer and Emil Eschwege.

fig. 1   fig. 2
Louis Wolf & Co. doll marks

Louis Wolf & Co. and
C. M. Bergmann trademark

WOOD, 1868-   Reuben Wood of Syracuse, New York was listed in the 1868-1869 Onondago County Business Directory as manufacturing all kinds of toys and importing French, German and English toys.

Luella Hart in her COMPLETE FRENCH DOLL DIRECTORY provides additional information on the following French doll makers who appeared in
Paris Directories at an earlier date than given in the first edition
of DOLLS, MAKERS AND MARKS:

Aschard, 1839-	Chiquet, 1871-	Fessard, 1848-
Blampoix, 1840-	De Saint Denis, 1842-	Herissey, 1829-
Blondel, 1829-	Desportes, 1876-	Pegard, 1833-
Bonafé, 1876-	Estivalet, 1870-	Rauch, 1862-
Bouloch & Laporte, 1834-	Fauriez, 1862-	Scailliet, 1834-
		Testard, 1829-

COUNTRY OF ORIGIN MARK ON DOLLS

The 1890 Tariff Act, Section 6,"On or after March 1, 1891 all articles of foreign manufacture --- be plainly marked --- as to indicate
country of origin." In the July 1903 issue of PLAYTHINGS magazine,
a New York representative stated that, "Twenty five years ago (1878)
his customers objected to paying a fair price for toys that were not
stamped, 'Made in Germany' or 'Made in France'".

China Doll with Bald Head
Photo by G. Angione

This doll is 26½ inches high, has a red hair wig and china limbs.
Old letters indicate that it belonged to Jennie Jackson who was born
before 1840. Jennie's surname came from the fact that her parents were
slaves of Prsident Andrew Jackson. Jennie Jackson married Mr. DeHart
and became one of the famous Jubilee Singers after the Civil War.
She died about 1910.

INDEX

Names or words in doll marks are listed alphabetically. Other marks such as symbols, initials or numerals are listed in the index under "Marks". Symbols are described for ease in identification. Dolls with the same number on their heads, may or may not be made by the same company and can vary in appearance. Four digit numbers, 1900, 1906, etc. could represent a date but no proof has been found for this assumption. In addition to the names and marks of doll makers the index also aids in identifying trade names of dolls; places where dolls were made; materials used in the fabrication of dolls; types of dolls; important doll books and periodicals; and under "Illustrations" the pictures of dolls shown in this volume and drawings of marks. Modern doll collectors refer to the material of which the head is made but in the 19th century the material could refer to either the head or body. See the foreword for definitions of materials.

Hancock, 113
Hancock mark, 113
HANDBOOK OF OLD AMERICAN TOYS, 100
Handwerck, 71, 97-99, 118, 119
Handwerck marks, 97
Hanlon, 30
Hanover, Prussia, 65
Hans, 60, 71, 118

*Initials in a circle or square are usually read clockwise.

MARKS:
D P, 120, 121
D S, 58
dwarf with ax, 30
eagle, 45, 70, 121
E D, 114
Ɛ, 16, 17
E Germany 9, 103
E 1/2 Germany 9 1/2, 103
ƎK, 99
Eiffel Tower, 42
E I H, 34
E J, 42
elf with ax, 30
ellipse, 1, 11, 14, 15, 17, 29,
    50, 52, 61, 65, 68, 102, 108
E M, 53
F G, 22, 23
F Germany 10, 103
flag unfurled, 70
flames, 45, 61
fleur-de-lis, 11
F R, 11
"F"s crossed, 26, 27
F S & C, 114
G, 26
G a m, 56
G B, 4
Gbr. - K, 45
G F N, v, 21
G Germany 11, 103
G H, 97
girl's head, 17
girl with banner, 104
girl with flag, 70
G J & Sons, 113
globe, 121
G S H, 114
G V, 74
G W, 95, 96
G & H J, 97
G 45520, 2
H, 72, 98, 114, 121
H A, 70
hammers crossed, 64, 114
H B S G, 97
H Co., 121
heart, 64, 86
H G, 97
H Germany 12, 103
H G S, 114
H J R, 91
horse, 86
horseshoe, 33, 99, 107
H S, 71
H & C, 87, 120, 121
H & Co., 76, 120, 121
i, 26, 96
I Germany 13, 103
insect, 96, 102
J, 97, 101
J C, 11
J D K, 111, 43, 44, 103, 104
J Germany 13, 103
J P, 57
J P F, 97
J R, 113
K Germany 14, 103

MARKS:
Kk Germany 14 1/2, 103
K in a bell, 105
K P M, 45, 52
K ✡ R, 71, 72, 118
K & Co., 44, 104
L, 26
L A & S, 2
L B, 26, 46, 69
L C, 48
L Germany 15, 103
L 1/2 Germany 15 1/2, 103
lion, 50
locomotive, 93
lozenges, 56, 111
L W & C, 121
L W & Co., 121
M Germany 16, 103
moon face, 96
mouse, 11
N, 11
N Germany 17, 103
No. 13, 115
Numbers:
  29, 72
  60, 102
  69, 72
  79, 98
  100 K ✡ R, 118
  101 K ✡ R, 118
  107 K ✡ R, 118
  109 K ✡ R, 118
  114 K ✡ R, 118
  152, 103, 104, 121
  164, 104
  169, 114
  171, 104
  180, 104
  186, 104
  187, 104
  189, 104
  190, 104
  195, 104
  211, 43
  215, 44
  216, 77
  247, 42
  250, 33
  253, 108
  256, 108
  260, 44
  262, 44
  275, 33
  301, 42
  310, 108
  319, 44
  323, 107
  329, 4
  341, 107, 108
  351, 108
  370, 107
  372, 108
  390, 77, 107, 108
  401, 77
  719, 67
  769, 114
  890, 53
  971, 108

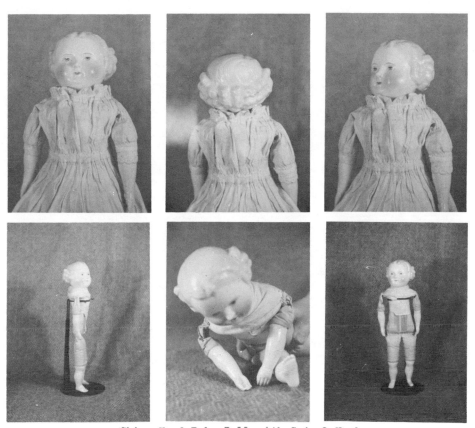

China Head Baby Doll with Swivel Neck

Head turns laterally on wooden ball
Flange head 3 1/2 inches high
Height of doll 13 inches
China limbs, squeak box

This doll was purchased in 1940 by Clara Fawcett from the family of the original owner and came with the following letter:

"It was won at a Sanitary Fair held in Baltimore, Maryland, in 1861. At that fair there was a large wooden shoe filled with dolls of all kinds and in the end sat a little girl representing, 'The old woman who lived in a shoe and had so many children she did not know what to do'. --- This baby doll being one of the left-overs was raffled off and won by my mother. He was already named for General McClellan, whose nick-name was 'Little Mac' and Little Mac he has remained. The clothing is the same in which he was dressed for the Fair and shows the type of clothing worn by babies of the Civil War period."

A drawing of this doll is in Clara Fawcett's book, ON MAKING, MENDING AND DRESSING DOLLS, p. 151, in the chapter on "Some Rare Old Dolls". This doll came into the Coleman collection in 1965.